WOW!
Resumes for
Sales & Marketing
Careers

Other titles in the WOW! Resumes Series include:

Matt DeLuca, *WOW! Resumes for Creative Careers*
Leslie Hamilton, *WOW! Resumes for Financial Careers*
Rachel Lefkowitz, *WOW! Resumes for Administrative Careers*

WOW!
Resumes for
Sales & Marketing
Careers

How to Put Together a
Winning Resume

Chuck Cochran and Donna Peerce

Boston, Massachusetts   Burr Ridge, Illinois
Dubuque, Iowa   Madison, Wisconsin   New York, New York
San Francisco, California   St. Louis, Missouri

Library of Congress Cataloging-in-Publication Data

Cochran, Chuck.
  WOW! Resumes for sales & marketing careers : how to put together a
  winning resume / Chuck Cochran and Donna Peerce.
      p.   cm.
  Includes index.
  ISBN 0-07-012021-8
    1. Résumés (Employment)—Vocational guidance.   2. Marketing—
  Vocational guidance.   3. Selling—   I. Peerce, Donna.
  II. Title.   III. Title: Wow! Resumes for sales & marketing careers
    HF5383.C623   1998
  808′.06665—dc21   98-4969
                                                                          CIP

Author's Note: All names, addresses, and places have been
changed to protect the privacy of individuals. Any similarities
are pure coincidence.

McGraw-Hill

*A Division of The **McGraw·Hill** Companies*

10 11 12 13 14 15 16 17 18 19   BKM BKM   0 9 8 7 6 5

ISBN 0-07-012021-8

*The sponsoring editor for this book was Betsy Brown, the assistant
editor was Kurt Nelson, the editing supervisor was Fred Dahl, and the
production supervisor was Tina Cameron. It was set in Stone Serif by
Inkwell Publishing Services.*

Contents

PART 1

Alphabetical Listing of Resumes

Introduction

Why Is It Important to Read This Book?

WOW! RESUMES FOR SALES & MARKETING CAREERS SHOWS YOU HOW TO:

√ Sell yourself.

√ Create a powerful, attention-grabbing sales tool.

√ Approach your potential employer as you would a prospective client.

√ Use your resume as a sales presentation.

√ Market and promote yourself with your resume.

√ Energize your job descriptions and build powerful sentences with active verbs and adjectives.

√ Showcase your skills and accomplishments.

√ Utilize unique, innovative methods to submit your resume and cover letter.

√ Write resumes for different types of sales and marketing careers.

√ Custom-tailor your resume to specific jobs.

√ Do more than just write a thank-you letter.

People often assume that one generic resume will fit all situations. A person who has been working as a secretary might assume that her or his resume is just fine to use to target a sales position. After all, it landed a position as a secretary, right? Wrong. It is important to read this book to learn how to write a sales and marketing resume, and to discover why this type of resume has to be different from others if you want to get the job!

This is the first book ever dedicated only to sales and marketing professionals that illustrates effective, successful methods for writing a sales and marketing resume that will win you an interview! There are many resume books on the market that look alike and might even advertise, "For Marketing and Sales Professionals," but they don't clearly explain why it's necessary to write a different type of resume for sales and marketing careers. This book does.

Just as a picture is worth a thousand words, so is your resume! If it paints the right picture, then it can land you an interview!

Remember, you're a salesperson with a hot idea to peddle. In this instance, the hot idea is *you!* You are trying to sell yourself to the employer, who is in this case your client. Therefore, you have to view your resume the way you do your sales tools. Use it as if you were preparing a sales presentation. Your resume is one of the most important and powerful tools you'll use in your job search, so make sure it's the best. After all, the resume gets you in the door for that first interview. If you don't have a good resume, your chances of getting that first interview are slim.

We are aware that all resumes sell people, but in this field it is even more important to use all the tools in this book to sell yourself to an employer. Remember, it is your sales presentation.

Everything in life is about sales. The sales and marketing resume is *all* about sales! We can't emphasize this enough. Just look around you. The people who excel in life know how to sell themselves. Whether you're an executive seeking a high-profile sales management position or are looking for a particular position in pharmaceutical sales, industrial sales, or telephone sales, this book will work for you! We will show you how to write a powerful, *"knock their socks off"* sales and marketing resume so you can land that perfect job!

CHUCK COCHRAN
DONNA PEERCE

SALES & MARKETING TIP:

Remember when you write your sales and marketing resume to always stress "benefits," not "features." You won't get hired because you've been a Sales Manager for 10 years (feature), but you will get hired for increasing company profitability by 50% each year for 10 years (benefit).

1

Power-Punchin', Pistol-Packin' Sales Tools

Do You Know How to Sell Yourself?

It sounds simple enough, doesn't it? Tell people about a product and sell it. Introduce yourself to someone and sell yourself. People do it every day, but not all people are successful at it. It's just that many people don't know how to sell a product or themselves in the best way. They don't realize that they have to be *better* at selling than the average person. If you want to be in sales, then you've got to know how to be *better*—how to sell yourself better than your competitors. If you're already in sales, then we assume that you know these principles. Perhaps you've not been as successful as you'd like to be. Maybe you want to advance to a higher level sales and marketing position. In that case, this book will help you brush up on your sales and marketing skills in addition to improving your resume and making it better. Remember, a sales and marketing resume has to be *better* than other resumes.

SALES & MARKETING TIP:

If you believe you are the best for the job, then make the effort to prepare a resume that reflects your confidence.

Seasoned salespeople know that the first few seconds of a sales call are the most important. Anything you can do in those first few seconds to project a total impression of taste, intelligence, and personality will always work to your advantage. Likewise, anything you do in those first few seconds can completely turn off your client (and in this case, your client is your potential employer).

In the same manner, you only have about 5 to 10 seconds to grab someone's attention with your resume. If it's not presented well or written effectively, then it may land in a "stack to read later" or even worse, in a trash can. You can't cut corners. You must pay attention to everything about your resume if you want to land an interview.

An employer who receives your resume for a sales or marketing position in the mail will judge your resume by how well you've presented yourself—by your ability to "sell" yourself. View your prospective employer as your client. You wouldn't take any shortcuts if you were calling on an important client to obtain a multimillion dollar account, would you? You wouldn't meet your client wearing sweatpants (unless you're in the gym), and you wouldn't hand over a brochure about your product that's messy and not written well. You can't take shortcuts with your resume, either. It must be top-notch, first-rate, and by all means, professional.

Sales & Marketing Resumes As Power-Punchin' Sales Tools

Tools make our lives better and help us live more efficient, productive lives. We have tools everywhere, at our fingertips. Gyms and health club facilities are tools to help us become healthier and stronger. Telephones are tools to communicate with each other. Education is a tool that sustains us for the long journey of life. Books are tools that entertain us or show us how to do specific tasks and that can open unknown worlds to us.

SALES & MARKETING TIP:

Your sales and marketing resume is one of your most important sales tools when you are looking for a job!

We need tools to help us when we're looking for a job just as we do in other parts of our lives. Our business contacts become tools to help us network and find out about available jobs; our automobile or public transportation system becomes a tool to help us get to the interview; clothes become tools to make us look better; our personality becomes a tool for interacting pleasingly with others; our dress and appearance are effective tools for creating an impression. In fact, everything we are and have access to can be utilized as positive tools to get that interview and job!

A resume is one of the most important and powerful tools you'll use in your job search process. The resume is still the primary tool for landing a first interview, so without a good resume, your chances of getting that first interview are slim.

SALES & MARKETING TIP:

Your resume is your official sales presentation to your client—the potential employer. Make sure it's spectacular!

Think of your resume as a sales presentation, and think of your potential employer as your client. In fact, your potential employer is a buyer with needs. You want to fulfill those needs with yourself! What is the most effective way to approach a client or potential client? You wouldn't give a potential client a poorly written or unattractive brochure about your product or company. Don't give a potential employer a resume that's not written and presented well.

The following story illustrates how one applicant found a job in sales by allowing us to rewrite her resume so she could use it as a dynamic sales tool to make effective presentations to potential employers.

Alayna Chauvancy

Alayna Chauvancy approached us and asked us to help her write a sales and marketing resume. About 5'4" tall, Alayna was slim with long, dark brown hair and large brown eyes. She was dressed in Levi's and a Harvard sweatshirt and looked like a typical college girl straight from an Ivy League campus. She handed us her old resume, which she said "wasn't working."

We reviewed Alayna's resume and queried her about her background and job search tactics. Alayna had grown up in New York City and had a Bachelor of Science degree in Political Science from Harvard University in Boston, Massachusetts. After graduating from Harvard, she had quickly obtained a position as a sales representative with a magazine company in Atlanta. After three years, she was now ready to find a better job in sales, with an opportunity to earn more money and advance more rapidly. Her heart was set on international sales. But she was discovering that it was much tougher to find a job in sales the second time around than it had been the first time. She was competing with a more diversified pool of candidates and a broader age group.

Alayna had made the mistake of thinking that her degree from Harvard would continue to open doors for her throughout her career. She had been very fortunate to land a sales job almost immediately out of college, and she thought this was a precedent for future jobs. She had assumed that any time she wanted a new job, she would only need to send out her resume to get the job. It would be so easy! Alayna had not realized how competitive the job market was, and that candidates had to be *more outstanding* and do everything *better* if they wanted that next great sales job. In other words, it's not enough to be good and it's not enough to have graduated from a well-known school like Harvard. You have to be *great*! It's not enough to have a good resume; it has to be a *great* resume with aggressive sales power!

Alayna simply didn't know how to sell herself. She had never had to worry about it before, so she hadn't developed any real skills in selling herself. She told us that since her family was from France, she had spent much of her youth in France and spoke fluent French. But she had not highlighted this on her resume, even though she was interested in international sales.

SALES & MARKETING TIP:

Don't depend on your college resume to work for you for the rest of your career. It will need to be revised to be more competitive with seasoned sales and marketing professionals.

Alayna had neglected to revise her resume format from the one she had used right out of college, thinking it was sufficient to get her another interview. People often make this mistake, thinking that their college resume will work for them throughout their careers. But when you enter the world of seasoned sales and marketing professionals, it is imperative that you have a resume that can compete with theirs. Remember, this is your sales tool, and the basis of your sales presentation.

On the following pages we present the resume and cover letter that Alayna had been using, and the revised ones we wrote for her. We designed a brochure style resume for Alayna. (We discuss this style of resume more thoroughly in Chapter 4.) The brochure resume, which consists of a cover sheet and two pages of resume content, serves as the perfect "presentation style" resume and is especially effective for sales and marketing positions. In addition, we developed a cover letter that is more descriptive about Alayna's background and adds to the selling power of the resume.

It is not hard to see the differences between these two resumes and two cover letters. Alayna's resume simply wasn't powerful enough to grab anyone's attention. Alayna had completely overlooked the importance of using her resume as her sales tool—her sales presentation. She didn't understand how important it was to emphasize her international experience. She had definitely cut corners by updating her old college resume, thinking it was sufficient to land her another good job. But she had been wrong.

SALES & MARKETING TIP:

Don't be too brief in your resume. Make sure you give the reader every reason you possibly can to want to interview you.

After we revised her resume and cover letter, Alayna was very successful in marketing herself to potential employers and obtained a high-profile position as a Sales Representative for a cosmetics manufacturing company in France.

You must remember that your resume is your sales tool. Start drilling that into your mind right now! Say it over and over. Write it down if you need extra reinforcement. *You* are a very important product to sell. Work on your attitude, your appearance, your interviewing skills—everything!

Anything you present to a decision maker should aggressively sell you. Your resume and cover letter are the first things you present, so, make sure it's a great presentation. This is only the first step in marketing yourself to an employer, but it is one of the most important steps. Don't treat it lightly, and don't depend on your college resume to open doors for you once you're out in the business world.

Alayna Chauvancy

This is an example of a nonpowerful sales and marketing resume. There are no power statements—no presentation of sales accomplishments. It's boring for a sales resume!

3321 Church Street
New York, New York 20010
(212) 782-4555

OBJECTIVE

A position in sales that will fully utilize my education and experience, and provide an opportunity for career growth.

EDUCATION

B.S.
Major: Political Science
Minor: Business Administration
Harvard University, Boston, MA
Sorority: Chi Omega
Sorority Honors: Pledge Chairman, Vice President, and Social Chairman.

Volunteer
Volunteered for Big Sisters Organization and assisted in fundraising activities.

Graduated Cum Laude.

EXPERIENCE

1994 to Present

Time Warner, Inc.
Atlanta, Georgia
Territory Manager: Sold display positions for Time Warner.

1992 to 1994

The Advertising Group
Boston, Massachusetts
Sales Associate: Sold advertising for this advertising agency on a part-time basis while attending college.

1991 to 1992

Mattel Toys, Inc.
Chicago, Illinois
This was an Intern position that was responsible for assisting product managers and designers.

1989 to 1992

The Gap
Boston, Massachusetts
Sales Associate: Sold clothing to customers part-time while in college.

Alayna Chauvancy

3321 Church Street
New York, New York 20010
(212) 782-4555

This is an example of a poor sales and marketing cover letter. Again, Alayna didn't know how to sell herself, even in the cover letter.

Dear Sir/Madame:

I am interested in a position in sales with your company and have enclosed my resume so you may review my background. I am particularly interested in international sales and would be happy to discuss this with you at your earliest convenience.

Sincerely,

Alayna Chauvancy

Where is the selling power in this cover letter? Where are the statements about accomplishments and international expertise?

This is the Cover Sheet, and is designed much as the cover of a brochure or book, with name, credentials, and address. It serves as an effective sales tool, and can start your sales presentation.

Alayna Chauvancy

A Presentation

of

Professional Sales Credentials

3321 Church Street
New York, New York 20010
(212) 782-4555

Alayna Chauvancy

3321 Church Street
New York, New York 20010
(212) 782-4555

Professional Objective & Profile

A ***Territory Sales Manager,*** *who is an achievement- and goal-oriented business professional with experience building and leading integrated sales and marketing operations for a major company.*

Strong international skills, with fluent written and verbal skills in French. Extensive experience living and working in France and interacting with foreign cultures. Self-directed and self-motivated with strong general sales and account management qualifications in strategic planning and marketing.

*Desire an **International Sales** position that will provide a challenging opportunity to significantly contribute to a company's efficiency, organization, growth, and profitability.*

Summary of Qualifications

- Supervised the sales and distribution of the first *Sports Illustrated Daily* at the 1996 Summer Olympic Games in Atlanta.

- Prepared a marketing analysis to introduce *People Español Magazine* into a chain of 140 bookstores.

- Hands-on experience working in France at *Mademoiselle's Department Store,* an international clothing store for women.

- At Barnes & Noble Bookstore, manage a new venture with *Time, Entertainment Weekly, Sports Illustrated, Fortune* and *People* magazines. Analyze weekly title strategies in all Barnes & Noble Bookstores across the country through direct distribution.

- Manage the sales and forecast market trends of *Fortune* and *Money* magazines in all CompUSA and Egghead Software stores across the country.

- Strong interpersonal skills with ability to effectively communicate and network with all levels of management and personnel. Excellent leader and motivator of others.

Education

Bachelor of Science in Political Science
HARVARD UNIVERSITY
Boston, Massachusetts, 1994
Minor in Business Administration
Graduated Cum Laude

International Sales & Marketing Experience

Sales Associate
MADEMOISELLE'S DEPARTMENT STORE, Paris, France - 1988 to 1989

- *Sales:* Sold and marketed high fashion women's clothing to select clientele in France. Was responsible for all facets of sales including marketing and merchandising.
- *Client Relations:* Established and maintained an exemplary network of international associates as a result of strong French-speaking skills.

National Sales & Marketing Experience

Territory Manager
TIME WARNER, INC., Atlanta, Georgia - January 1994 to Present

- *Sales Management:* Guide and direct overall sales operations for central Tennessee and northern Alabama for *Time Warner Magazines*. Sell profitable display positions for *Time Warner Magazines* in major retail stores. Successfully expanded territory 45% during the first year.
- *Marketing:* Responsible for managing new business development and strategic planning to maximize growth and profitability. Execute marketing plans for individual accounts and personally manage account calls, presentations and negotiations.
- *Client Relations:* Provide superior service to clients through in-depth attention and follow-up to accounts. Effectively respond to clients' requests, inquiries, suggestions, and concerns.
- *Advertising & Promotions:* Assist District Manager and Key Account Manager in conceptualizing, developing and implementing innovative marketing and promotional campaigns in stores. Coordinate specific advertising and promotional activities with retail groups.
- *Personnel, Training & Supervision:* Supervise and lead a team of Store Merchandisers. Delegate work assignments and communicate opportunities in the marketplace.

Advertising Assistant
THE ADVERTISING GROUP, Boston, Massachusetts - 1992 to 1994

- *Advertising:* Assisted in the development and implementation of strategic advertising campaigns for clients. This was a part-time position while in college.
- *Program Development - Research:* Reviewed syndicated research sources for clients and developed a Competitive Spending Analysis Program.
- *Media Relations:* Established and maintained a good working relationship with media personnel including radio, TV and print advertising to negotiate contracts and business planning.

Marketing Assistant
MATTEL TOYS, INC., Chicago, Illinois - 1991 to 1992

- *Marketing & Product Development:* This was an Internship that involved assisting in the development of new doll lines. Assisted Product Managers and Designers with the 1992 Toy Presentations.
- *Research & Analysis:* Conducted research and analyzed market needs, and utilized Lotus Software to create spreadsheets and graphs. Analyzed monthly statistics and developed strategies to more aggressively compete within market.

Sales Associate
THE GAP, Boston, Massachusetts - 1989 to 1992

- *Sales:* Sold merchandise to customers in retail environment.
- *Merchandising & Marketing:* Arranged and designed floor displays to enhance merchandise and increase sales. Implemented company's marketing and advertising campaigns into everyday store operations.

Alayna Chauvancy
3321 Church Street
New York, New York 20010
(212) 782-4555

Thomas Martin
Vice President of Sales
Greenwood Corporation, Inc.
New York, New York

Dear Mr. Martin:

This is definitely a more powerful cover letter and clearly highlights special skills and qualifications.

Are you interested in a highly motivated, goal-oriented **International Sales & Marketing** professional to become an effective leader in your company? I can significantly contribute to your company's team of professionals. For your review, I have enclosed a personal resume which will provide you with details concerning my background and qualifications.

In addition to a Bachelor of Science Degree from Harvard University, I have experience as a *Territory Manager* for T*ime Warner, Inc.* Based in Atlanta, Georgia, I am responsible for managing and marketing the magazine industry throughout the Southeast U.S. This involves managing new business development and strategic planning for retail accounts. I have developed and executed several successful promotions for *Time, InStyle,* and *Sports Illustrated* magazines. In addition to this, I have experience working in Sales for Mademoiselle's, an international clothing store in Paris, France during the summer before I entered Harvard. My family is from France and I have spent most of my summers there, growing up and interacting extensively with foreign cultures. I am fluent in French and can serve as both an interpreter and liaison for your company.

I would like to request a personal interview at your earliest convenience so we can discuss how I can significantly contribute to your team of professionals.

Thank you in advance for your time and consideration. I look forward to speaking with you soon.

Sincerely,

Alayna Chauvancy

Resume Enclosed

2

"Knock Your Socks Off" Resumes

Resumes That Are Packed with Selling Power!

A sales and marketing resume has to be *more* than an ordinary resume. It has to grab someone and literally knock 'em out! Employers want to know that you know how to sell yourself and make a dynamic presentation. Otherwise, why would they want to hire you? If you can't sell yourself in a resume, how can you sell their product or service?

Ask yourself some basic questions. Do you know how to pack your resume with power? Do you know how to take "on the edge" risks by using bold statements and highlighting your accomplishments? Do you know how to use high-impact language to grab someone's attention in 5 to 10 seconds?

When you submit a resume to a potential employer, you must also recognize the employer's needs. Remember, the employer is your client and you must identify your client's needs before you write your resume. Ask yourself these questions:

What to Ask Yourself before You Submit Your Resume

1. Who are you submitting this resume to? The more specific you can be about your target audience, the more successful the resume will be.

2. Why would this client want to read your resume? Highlight special skills and credentials that make you unique or more qualified for this position than anyone else.

3. Will you be sending this resume to more than one person? If so, then you may want to make sure it has a universal appeal for sales and marketing companies.

4. What industry do you want to target? Again, the more specific you can be, the higher your chances of winning the interview and job!

5. Are you committed to only one particular industry? Many people are interested in several industries. Each resume should be specific to the industry you're targeting.

6. Do you want to keep your options open so you can target any kind of company? In this case, you will want a sales and marketing resume with broader, more general appeal that encompasses your overall experience.

7. What do you want to do with your career in the long term? It's important to set goals and look for jobs that will help you achieve your long-term career plans.

8. How much time are you prepared to invest in your job search? You must realize that looking for a job is sometimes harder work than being employed. So, be prepared to invest time and effort into this campaign.

9. Ultimately, what do you want to accomplish with this resume? The resume should help you work toward your goals and achieve your dreams of a career in sales and marketing.

Whether you're going to send your resume to just one person in one industry or to many, this chapter will help you. We'll explore dynamic approaches to writing effective sales resumes that will impress the decision maker who reads your resume. We will provide you with lists of high-impact words to use when describing your skills and accomplishments. We'll also introduce the aesthetics of the resume and its presentation appeal. At the end of the chapter, we'll illustrate several power sales and marketing resumes that pack a real sales punch and win interviews!

There Is a Difference between Sales and Marketing!

The sentence bears repeating: There is a difference between *sales* and *marketing*. Marketing professionals are the creative thinkers who plan and design marketing strategies to help sell and market products or services. Sales professionals actually pound the streets and sell the product. But often, the two are interrelated; some sales jobs require marketing skills, just as some marketing jobs require sales skills. They overlap so much that no matter which job you're targeting, our sales and marketing resumes will work for you. A great marketer knows how to *sell,* just as a great salesperson knows how to *market.*

SALES & MARKETING TIP:

Sales is a business based on relationships. Remember this when you write your resume. Don't pad your resume with false statements, because later you will have to live up to whatever you wrote in your resume. False statements are real relationship busters!

More than marketing, sales is a business based on relationships. You have to know how to build and maintain relationships. Often, your success as a salesperson is based solely on how well you get along with your clients and how well you can identify their needs. Have you ever noticed that most people in sales have dynamic, charismatic personalities? They know how to mingle—how to chitchat with folks on just about any topic—and this is important in sales and marketing careers. They also know how to focus on their clients' needs, and it's their job to fulfill those needs. So when you write a sales and marketing resume, remember that you're in the process of building a relationship with your potential employer even at that very initial moment. Keep this in mind and never put anything false in your resume. You will be expected to live up to everything you put in your resume. If false statements are uncovered, the relationship will sour.

SALES & MARKETING TIP:

The sales and marketing resume is truly a unique one. Contrary to a doctor's CV, which rarely includes anything more than a list of credentials, a sales and marketing resume must paint a picture of your success in great detail to get your point across. This is a very aggressive resume!

Your Resume As a Sales Presentation

We discussed your resume as a sales tool in Chapter 1. A sales tool can be a sales presentation, as well. If you were preparing a brochure to promote a product, you would include certain positive things in the brochure. In this instance, your resume is the brochure—a sales flyer—about your abilities and what you can offer a company.

What Your Sales Brochure (or Resume) Will Accomplish

1. Your resume positions you in front of the employer as you would position a product or service in front of a client.

2. Your resume serves as an advertisement for YOU.

3. Your resume gives the employer the chance to get to know you before you call or meet.

4. Your resume lends credibility to your skills and qualifications (just the way a sales brochure does).

5. Your resume answers the employer's questions about you before you meet.

6. Your resume is an effective tool to show off your merits.

7. Your resume serves as a direct mail piece anytime, anywhere, any place.

8. Your resume SELLS and PROMOTES you!

SALES & MARKETING TIP:

Your resume is your sales brochure, your sales flyer, and you are the product you're promoting and selling.

Stress for Success

You want to be aggressive in your resume and in anything you submit to your potential employer, including the cover letter and salary history. This is no time to be shy or meek about your qualities. In sales, aggressive, assertive qualities count! An employer wants someone who can stand up and say, "Hey, I've got some great talents and qualities that I can bring to this job!" Your resume has to stand up and be assertive. It has to tell the future employer that you can do the job because you've got the skills and talents, and you can do the job *better!*

Just as being aggressive is important in writing a sales and marketing resume, so is the need to allow stress to work for you. If you're clutching your stomach at this point and saying, "Hey, I don't want to be stressed out. How can I be productive if I'm stressed out?" Calm down and read on. There's actually a way to use this stress in a productive way.

SALES & MARKETING TIP:

It's okay to feel stress, but turn the stress energy into positive energy and make it work for you when going for a great job!

In this context, it's okay to experience stress and use it as a positive force in your resume. Stress is energy and you can turn *stress energy* into *positive energy*. A calm, subdued person might not have enough moxie to go after that great sales job! So, let a little stress in—just for success' sake. Use its energy to write a dynamic, powerful resume!

Attention-Grabbing Objectives and Career Profiles

A sales and marketing resume should begin with a bold, attention-grabbing Objective or Career Profile, rather than a mild, one-sentence Objective. Don't write an Objective like this:

Professional Objective: A position in sales.

B-o-r-i-n-g! That Objective would make most of us fall asleep. Be specific. What kind of sales position do you want? Who are you? What are you all about? What qualifications do you possess that will make you better for this job than anyone else? These are the things you want to tell your potential employer right in the beginning—at the top of your resume—in the Objective and Career Profile. This is the first section an employer will read; don't waste this precious moment.

A better way to write an objective would be like this:

PROFESSIONAL OBJECTIVE & CAREER PROFILE

High-caliber **Pharmaceutical Sales Representative** with over 7 years of experience building and leading integrated sales operations for pharmaceutical and medical companies. Consistently successful in building and expanding territories to achieve #1 position in sales growth in the nation. Desire a pharmaceutical sales position that will provide a challenging opportunity to significantly contribute to a company's efficiency, organization, growth, and profitability.

In this *Professional Objective and Career Profile,* the candidate clearly states an interest in a pharmaceutical sales position and highlights the ability to expand and develop sales territories, emphasizing his success in achieving the #1 position in sales growth in the nation. These are concrete power points that a potential employer will be interested in. These statements help to sell you. Remember, an employer wants to know you can achieve results!

SALES & MARKETING TIP:

Try to be creative in your objective. Consider combining your objective into a summary or career profile. The old ". . . to be an Account Executive with opportunity to grow into management. . ." just won't do any more. Capture your reader's attention with your energy and enthusiasm!

You can be daring and different in writing your Objective and Career Profile. You don't necessarily have to follow the norm. There are several unique approaches you can take to grab someone's attention.

Endorsements?

Well, why not? Just as you send reference letters with a resume, you can put a brief endorsement right at the top of your resume. Trust us: It will grab the reader's attention! Use endorsement letters in your Career Profile. This is a different, unconventional, and innovative way to get attention and sell yourself. Use parts of actual letters from previous employers or coworkers at the top of your resume as an eye-catching tool. For example, read how this endorsement works as a summary of one person's qualifications.

JOHN ESCOE
3884 Hiawatha Street
Denver, Colorado 93993
(883) 399-3003

Career Profile

"John Escoe is a very talented sales professional and would be a great asset to any organization. While working for Nabisco, he successfully expanded his sales territory and increased overall annual sales from $200,000 to $1 million in just 2 years. In addition to this, he has a talent for building long-lasting relationships with his clients. In my opinion, a company would be very lucky to have someone like John Escoe on its sales team."

Marvin Schumaker
National Sales Manager for Nabisco

> Notice the unique way this resume begins with an endorsement from a past employer. While this is somewhat unconventional, it is very eye-catching!

You have to agree that an endorsement like this at the top of a resume will draw attention.

Make an Impact!

Don't forget to use high-impact, power words that will assist in selling you in your Objective and Career Summary. Here is a list of powerful adjectives you can use to describe yourself.

Powerful Adjectives to Describe Yourself

acclaimed	high-ranking	positive force in bringing about. . .	self-motivated
accomplished	honored		significant
award-winning	illustrious	proactive leader	solid
consistent	influential	profit-oriented	strong
company's leading. . .	ingenious	prominent	superior
dependable	leading	proven	sustaining
dynamic	loyal	qualified	talented
eminent	motivating	renowned	veteran
esteemed	nation's leading. . .	respected	virtuoso
famous	notable	results-oriented	world-class
gifted	noteworthy	revered	
high-caliber	outstanding	seasoned	

Use positive action verbs in your resume. They are more aggressive and more effective than passive verbs. Review the positive action verbs in this list, then combine them with power adjectives to build power sentences for your cover letter and resume.

Positive Action Verbs

accelerated	controlled	exhibited	kept	processed	served
accomplished	converted	expanded	launched	procured	serviced
achieved	coordinated	expedited	lectured	produced	set-up
acquired	corrected	explained	led	professed	shaped
acted	correlated	experimented	learned	profited	shared
adapted	counseled	expressed	licensed	progressed	showed
addressed	created	extracted	listened	projected	sketched
administered	critiqued	facilitated	located	promoted	simplified
advised	dealt	filed	logged	proofread	sold
analyzed	decided	finalized	maintained	proposed	solved
anticipated	defined	financed	managed	protected	sorted
applied	delegated	fixed	manipulated	proved	spearheaded
appointed	delivered	followed	manufactured	provided	spoke
appraised	demonstrated	formalized	mapped	publicized	stimulated
approved	depended	formed	marketed	purchased	streamlined
arbitrated	designed	formulated	measured	qualified	structured
arranged	detailed	found	mediated	questioned	studied
ascertained	detected	founded	mentored	raised	succeeded
assembled	determined	gathered	modeled	ranked	suggested
assessed	developed	generated	modified	rated	summarized
assisted	devised	governed	monitored	realigned	supervised
assured	diagnosed	graduated	motivated	realized	supplied
attained	directed	guided	named	reasoned	supported
audited	discovered	handled	navigated	received	symbolized
arranged	dispensed	headed	networked	recognized	synthesized
bridged	displayed	helped	nominated	recommended	systematized
briefed	disproved	hired	normalized	reconciled	tabulated
brought	dissected	hypothesized	noted	recorded	talked
budgeted	distributed	identified	obtained	recruited	targeted
built	diverted	illustrated	offered	reduced	taught
calculated	doubled	imagined	officiated	reengineered	tested
catalogued	drafted	implemented	operated	referred	trained
changed	dramatized	improved	ordered	regulated	transcribed
charted	drew	improvised	organized	rehabilitated	transferred
checked	drove	increased	oriented	reinforced	transformed
chose	earned	induced	originated	reinvented	translated
clarified	edited	influenced	overcame	related	treated
closed	educated	informed	oversaw	rendered	transitioned
coached	effected	initiated	painted	reorganized	troubleshot
collected	empowered	innovated	participated	repaired	tutored
commanded	empathized	inspected	perceived	represented	undertook
communicated	enacted	inspired	performed	researched	unified
compared	encouraged	installed	persuaded	resolved	united
compiled	endured	instituted	piloted	responded	updated
completed	enforced	instructed	pinpointed	restored	upgraded
composed	engineered	insured	pioneered	retrieved	used
computed	enlisted	integrated	placed	restructured	utilized
conceived	enhanced	intensified	planned	reviewed	verbalized
conceptualized	ensured	interpreted	played	revised	verified
concluded	entertained	interviewed	praised	risked	warranted
conducted	established	introduced	predicted	satisfied	weighed
confronted	estimated	invented	prepared	scheduled	won
consolidated	evaluated	inventoried	prescribed	secured	worked
constructed	examined	investigated	presented	selected	wrote
continued	exceeded	judged	presided	sensed	
contracted	executed	justified	printed	separated	

Study the sample phrases and sentences below and then practice writing your own in the following section.

"Significantly contribute" is a meaningful phrase that describes you and puts you in the power position of "helping" your potential employer. Remember, it's wise to let employers know what you can do for them, instead of telling them what you want them to do for you!

Sample Phrases:

1. I can <u>significantly contribute</u> to your company's goals with my advanced skills and experience in developing and expanding sales territories.
2. <u>Proactive leader reengineered</u> sales operations . . .
3. <u>Profit-oriented</u> sales and marketing professional <u>built</u> company . . .
4. <u>High-caliber</u> sales and marketing executive <u>spearheaded</u> the development . . .
5. <u>Seasoned</u> marketing professional <u>guided</u> the creation of a . . .
6. <u>Empowered</u> sales professional <u>established</u> all sales quotas . . .

These are high-impact, powerful, and attention-grabbing verbs and adjectives that make the employer take notice!

In the next section, take the power adjectives and verbs that we've listed or ones that you have listed and create your own sentences. Write as many powerful statements about yourself as you can. Let your mind flow freely and have fun with the words. Just brainstorm! Try to incorporate actual figures to document your sales and marketing performance. After you are finished, pick out the very best ones to use in your resume and cover letter.

SALES & MARKETING TIP:

Before you write your resume, think of as many positive things as you can to say about yourself. Write them out on a sheet of paper without regard to structure or organization. Once you have enough phrases, find a resume sample as you read this book that includes experience similar to your sales and marketing career. Next design your own resume, using your phrases in the format of the sample!

Develop Your Own Power Sales & Marketing Phrases

How Many Can You Think Of?

1.

2.

3.

4.

5.

6.

7.

8.

9.

10.

11.

12.

13.

14.

15.

16.

17.

18.

19.

20.

Do You Have Other Documents to Support Your Credentials?

Since you're treating your resume and cover letter as a sales presentation, remember that you can include other documents to support your qualifications. Some of our sales and marketing clients include sales reports that clearly summarize their sales expertise and accomplishments, as well as specific awards and commendation letters from their superiors. Build your portfolio and include these in your sales presentation. These are all assets that can benefit you greatly when submitting your resume to a potential employer. Anything that you can do to make your resume stand apart from others will be effective in getting you that interview!

SALES & MARKETING TIP:

Keep a file of letters of reference, sales awards, commendations, performance reviews, and any other materials that document your sales and marketing success. You can submit these with your resume, or even better, use them as a reason to call back or follow up.

Samples of Power-Packed Resumes

On the following pages are samples of power-packed resumes and cover letters that were successful in landing people important interviews and attractive job offers, and that illustrate the points we've covered in this chapter.

Gabrielle Xavier

Gabrielle, our first example in this chapter, is a high-powered sales and marketing executive in the banking industry. While she had over ten years of experience in sales and leasing of real estate property, her most prominent position was the last four years working as a Marketing Director for a bank. She was on the fast track and was promoted each year. To best highlight her credentials, we wrote an in-depth two-page resume with a cover page (called a brochure resume) in addition to a high-impact cover letter. Notice how we developed the whole resume package into one comprehensive marketing piece. Everything in it is about sales!

> Note the nice, clean cover page to present the resume.

Gabrielle Xavier

A Presentation

of

Professional Credentials

32 12th Street
Queens, New York 10705
(914) 399-0922

Gabrielle Xavier
32 12th Street
Queens, New York 10705
(914) 399-0922

Executive Profile

Empowered **Sales & Marketing Executive** with more than 20 years of experience building and leading integrated Marketing, Sales and Business operations for major corporations. Consistently successful in developing and nurturing client relationships. Talented in initiating and spearheading start-up operations of branch offices, and in positioning finance as a critical business partner, supportive of and responsive to the needs of large and diverse operating units. Talented in leading business opportunities and marketing strategies to maximize growth and profitability, and accomplish mission of integrated operations.

Strong general management qualifications in financial market analysis, planning and all facets of process/productivity/quality improvement. Talented writer who excels in promotions and advertising. Very strong employee relations and team-building skills.

Desire a career opportunity in **leadership and sales & marketing management** that will provide a challenging avenue to significantly contribute to a company's efficiency, growth, and profitability.

Professional Experience
Senior Vice President
Director of Sales & Marketing

FEDERAL SAVINGS BANK, Queens, New York - 1993 to 1996

- *Company Track Record of Success:* Began with this company in 1993 as the *Assistant Vice President and Director of Sales & Marketing.* Advanced to positions of higher levels of responsibility and authority which are highlighted below.
- *Administration & Operations:* As *Senior Vice President* in 1996, was responsible for developing and implementing administrative policies and procedures for bank's operations. Developed and wrote the bank's *Vision/Mission Statement* and implemented objectives and plans into everyday operations. Led a management team which held full responsibility and decision-making authority for establishing policies for Strategic Planning, and Lending & Underwriting procedures.
- *Branch Development:* Assisted in spearheading the design and planning of a new branch office. This involved creating sales & marketing concepts, as well as designs for mortgage origination advertising and branch office rack materials.
- *Sales & Account Management:* Managed new business development, sales, and strategic planning to maximize growth and profitability. Established growth plans for individual accounts and personally managed account calls, presentations, and negotiations.
- *Employee Development:* Utilized and developed the skills and talents of each Officer at the new branch office to maximize efficiency and productivity.
- *Loan Operations:* Reviewed, analyzed and approved Bank Loan Division credits.
- *Director of Marketing:* Managed and directed overall marketing operations for institution. Prepared feasibility studies and investigated markets to determine profitability ratios. Developed and implemented innovative marketing strategies to solicit and maintain business.
- *Team Building:* Effectively built and led an *Origination Team* that significantly increased overall profitability for company.
- *Personnel:* Reengineered personnel administrative operations, which involved rewriting and implementing *Personnel Evaluations* and a *Salary Administration Guide.*

Professional Experience

Vice President & Director of Sales & Marketing, 1995

- **Management:** Managed and supervised all operations and administration of company policies involving delinquencies, foreclosures, bankruptcies and property disposition.
- **Supervision:** Responsible for supervising management staff of problem-oriented properties. Conducted ongoing analyses to evaluate the efficiency and productivity of properties and determined status regarding foreclosures and bankruptcies.
- **Client Relations & Negotiations:** Provided excellent service to clients consisting of outside management companies, court appointed receivers and property owners. Negotiated sales contracts for properties.

Vice President-Mortgage Origination & Director of Marketing, 1994

- **Loan Operations:** Reengineered bank's loan application methods and streamlined operations. Created and implemented spreadsheet formulas to automate all multi-family and mixed use underwriting.
- **Loan & Executive Committee Member:** Worked closely with Compliance Officer and Vice President of Branch Administration to ensure adherence to company's policies and procedures.

Assistant Vice President-Mortgage Originations & Director of Marketing, 1993

- **Broker Relations:** Established and maintained an exemplary network of business associates with mortgage brokers and owners as a result of extensive interaction and strong communication skills.
- **Loan Operations:** Reviewed, analyzed and negotiated loan closings.
- **Employee Relations:** Encouraged and supported a teamlike work environment by creating, writing and producing a company newsletter.
- **Profitability:** Solicited and obtained new mortgage originations which increased profitability.

Documentation Manager-Loan Processor & Director of Marketing

- **Underwriting:** Served as underwriter responsible for reviewing, analyzing and underwriting to conform to bank's lending policies and procedures. Researched, ordered and reviewed *Title Work.*
- **Client Relations:** Interacted extensively with borrowers and their attorneys and provided excellent service by effectively responding to requests, inquiries, suggestions, and/or concerns. Member of Loan Committee.

Assistant Sales Manager
DICK GIDRON CADILLAC, Bronx, New York - 1992 to 1993

- **Company Track Record of Success:** Began in 1992 as a *Biller* and was quickly promoted to *Closer* and then *Assistant Sales Manager.*
- **Sales:** Assisted in managing overall sales operations for automotive dealership.
- **Contracts:** Reviewed, analyzed, prepared and approved Cadillac's contracts with GMAC.
- **Credit Analysis:** Researched and processed Credit Reports.
- **Promotions:** Wrote and developed local promotional campaigns for dealership to increase revenue.

Commercial Property Manager/Investments
Sales & Leasing Administrator & Construction Coordinator
ALFRED WEISSMAN REAL ESTATE INVESTMENTS, Long Island, New York - 1983 to 1992

- **Management:** Managed and directed overall operations for commercial properties which consisted of government office buildings, shopping centers, industrial and office buildings.
- **Sales & Marketing Management:** Created and developed all sales and marketing campaigns to increase business and maximize growth and profitability. Directed sales team to increase sales and leasing, which increased company profitability.
- **Public Relations:** Held high visibility public relations position as the direct liaison to clients, community leaders, national association members and other business affiliates.

Gabrielle Xavier
32 12th Street
Queens, New York 10705
(914) 399-0922

Date

Michael Greenwood
President
First Union Street National Bank
2293 Hampton Street
New York, New York 30033

Her cover letter summarizes and rephrases the most important points of her career that are illustrated in more depth in her resume. The bullet format is a nice touch for readability.

Use bolding for words and phrases you want to stand out!

Dear Mr. Greenwood:

It is my understanding that you are looking for a highly motivated, goal-oriented **Sales & Marketing Executive** to become a leader in your organization. I am confident that, with my experience in Marketing, Sales and Management, I can significantly contribute to your company's efficiency, growth and profitability. I have enclosed a personal resume so you may review my credentials.

My background is comprehensive and includes the following areas of qualifications and expertise:

- Proven track record of success in marketing, management and client relations.
- Excellent skills in reengineering and restructuring marketing operations that have significant impact and yield an increase in profitability for company. Strong strategic and business planning skills.
- Savvy marketing skills with ability to spearhead innovative campaigns to reposition operations to become more competitive and high-profile.
- Financial and analytical expertise in budget development, forecasting and management.
- Adept troubleshooter who can research and identify problems in operations or within employee relations. Very skilled in creative problem-solving techniques.
- Dynamic interpersonal, communication, writing and negotiating skills.
- Proactive leader with effective team-building skills. Empower staff members to think and work independently and in a team environment to accomplish mission of corporate objectives.
- Demonstrated leadership skills with ability to motivate staff to achieve highest objectives.
- Proven ability to define issues, propose solutions, and implement changes.
- Knowledge and experience of computer systems and applications.

I sincerely believe that, with my experience and career aspirations, I would be an asset to your organization. I would like to request a personal interview at your earliest convenience so we can discuss how I can best contribute to your company's goals. I am open to discussing any position that's relevant to my background.

Thank you in advance for your time and consideration. I look forward to speaking with you soon.

Sincerely,

Gabrielle Xavier

Resume Enclosed

Vitus Wong

Often our customers say, ". . . but I don't have much to say on my resume, I've only worked for one company." Of course, we think otherwise. In fact, if you are one of the few who have stable and consistent work experience with one employer, we congratulate you. You are one of the few! Your resume will be just as powerful (and probably more so) as that of someone with five employers over the past ten years!

Vitus Wong had worked for only one employer for 12 years, and he grew in responsibility and job skills throughout his tenure. We wanted to write his resume so the reader could clearly see his various areas of expertise in addition to his marketing skills. Notice that we wrote his resume differently from Gabrielle's (the previous example), based on his unique circumstances.

The brochure resume always starts with a cover
page like this. If you like a two-page resume
better, you can delete this first page.

VITUS WONG

A Presentation

of

Professional Marketing Credentials

392 Stephens Road
Newfield, New Jersey 03002
(609) 903-8923

VITUS WONG
392 Stephens Road
Newfield, New Jersey 03002
(609) 903-8923

Career Profile in Marketing Management

Committed, profit-oriented **Marketing Manager,** with 12 years of experience building and leading integrated marketing operations for major corporation. Consistently successful in conceptualizing, developing, and spearheading innovative marketing and promotional strategies/campaigns that expand market penetration and yield company profitability. Excellent analytical, planning, organizational and negotiation skills. Skilled executive liaison with extensive experience networking with media, vendors, subcontractors and nationwide field offices.

Strong general management qualifications in strategic planning. Talented in developing annual financial objectives and preparing long-range strategic business plans. Solid organizational, management, interpersonal and communications skills with proven track record of making sound decisions.

Desire a career opportunity in marketing management that will provide a challenging avenue to significantly contribute to a company's efficiency, organization, growth, and profitability.

Summary of Qualifications

Track Record of Success:
Background exemplifies a successful track record of career accomplishments which includes 12 years of experience at the *Wall Street Journal.* Consistently advanced throughout career to position of Marketing Manager.

Marketing & Promotions:
Held full decision-making authority for developing and implementing nationwide marketing programs. Skilled in conceptualizing, developing and implementing comprehensive marketing and promotional programs through implementation of various media designed to achieve results. Worked extensively with field offices to coordinate corporate marketing strategies to expand sales and profitability.

Team Building:
Organized and implemented unified approach with field offices toward advertising and promotions. Encouraged and supported a teamlike work environment across the country which increased employee morale, productivity and efficiency. Facilitated numerous meetings and spoke before large and small groups.

Budget Management:
Successfully analyzed multimillion dollar budgets and initiated appropriate strategies to more aggressively control expenditures. Prepared future budgets based on previous year's performance.

Professional Affiliation
American Marketing Association

Advanced Training

> Notice how the first page of the resume specifies various skills he used on the job.

WALL STREET JOURNAL
Dow Jones & Company, Inc., Princeton, New Jersey
Numerous Seminars, Conferences and Classes in Management, Marketing, Forecasting & Analysis, Computer Software, etc.

Professional Management Experience

Marketing Manager
WALL STREET JOURNAL
Dow Jones & Company, Inc.
Princeton, New Jersey - 1985 to May 1997

- *Company Track Record of Success:* Began in 1985 as a *Statistical Analyst* and continuously advanced to positions of higher levels of authority and responsibility due to outstanding job performance. Promoted to *Marketing Assistant* and then to *Marketing Manager.*

- *Marketing Management:* Directed and managed overall administration and operations of marketing operations nationwide. Developed business opportunities and marketing strategies to maximize growth and profitability, expand market penetration, and accomplish mission of integrated operations. Traveled throughout the U.S. to coordinate and implement marketing and promotions campaigns in field offices.

- *Public Speaking:* Liaison between home office and field personnel in the U.S. Spoke in front of large and small groups at field offices and presented information regarding marketing and promotional campaigns generated at the home office. Outlined marketing goals and analyzed long-term strategic planning.

- *Budget Management:* Developed and administered $6 million operating budget for marketing. Analyzed budget variances and initiated appropriate strategies to more aggressively control expenditures. Prepared future years' budgets based on previous expenditures and changes in organizational structures.

- *Forecasting & Analysis:* Responsible for researching, forecasting and analyzing radio and T.V. markets to determine profitability ratios.

- *Market Research:* Coordinated market research activities, tracked and maintained database and competitor information, and assisted with product/service development and marketing strategies.

- *Direct Mail:* Planned strategic direct mail campaigns targeted to nationwide consumer markets. Worked with advertising staff and freelancers to write, develop and produce direct mail literature.

- *Promotions & Advertising:* Conceptualized, developed and implemented innovative promotional and advertising programs/campaigns through implementation of various media designed to achieve desired results. Planned and developed P.O.S. (point-of-sale) materials for retail businesses. Significantly increased business and company profitability.

- *Vendors & Subcontractors:* Worked with outside vendors, subcontractors, and freelance writers to produce promotional and advertising materials including media kits, rate cards, brochures, print advertising, and broadcast commercials. Monitored job performance to ensure accuracy and adherence to specifications.

- *Media Buying:* Interacted closely with major advertising agencies to research, analyze and buy advertising time on radio and television.

- *Media Relations:* Established and maintained an excellent network of business associates with media personnel as a result of extensive interaction and strong communication skills.

- *Personnel & Supervision:* Interviewed and hired Marketing Assistant. Delegated work responsibilities, supervised and evaluated job performance.

VITUS WONG
392 Stephens Road
Newfield, New Jersey 03002
(609) 903-8923

Date

Judith Shaverdian
Executive Director of Marketing
The New York Times
21st Avenue
New York, New York 99303

> Vitus had a friend and colleague at this company. Notice that the contact is the first thing mentioned in the letter. As a way to get the reader's attention, this is a very good idea!

Dear Ms. Shaverdian:

Joe Allen, a friend and employee at the *New York Times,* suggested that I submit a resume for the position of Marketing Manager. I am a highly successful **Marketing Manager,** and am very confident that, with my extensive experience and talents, I can significantly contribute to the *New York Times'* team of marketing professionals. I have enclosed a personal resume so you may review my credentials.

My qualifications and areas of expertise include the following:

- Ability to conceptualize, develop and initiate comprehensive nationwide marketing campaigns for the *Wall Street Journal* to expand market penetration and increase sales.
- Effective team-building skills. Strong motivator and leader with ability to empower associates to work together as a team to achieve maximum results.
- Talented public speaker with experience traveling nationwide to corporate field offices to organize and coordinate innovative marketing strategies. Spoke in front of large and small groups to provide information regarding marketing strategies.
- Extensive business networking expertise. Continuously built and maintained an exemplary network of business associates as a result of interaction between media, subcontractors, suppliers and businesses.
- Financial and analytical expertise in budget development, forecasting and management.
- Demonstrated leadership, communication and negotiation skills.
- Proven ability to define issues, propose solutions, and implement changes.
- Knowledge and experience in computer systems and applications including Excel, Lotus, Word and Mainframe for data.

I sincerely believe that, with my experience and career aspirations, I would be an asset to your organization. I would like to request a personal interview at your earliest convenience so we can discuss how I can contribute to the *New York Times'* long-term goals.

Thank you in advance for your time and consideration. I look forward to speaking with you soon.

Sincerely,

Vitus Wong

Resume Enclosed

Hannah Svenson

Hannah Svenson was a Harvard graduate and an extremely competent and marketable sales professional. She had so much information, we actually wrote and designed a three-page version of her resume. While we don't necessarily recommend this, in certain situations it can be the best thing. To make it less overwhelming we prepared a brochure resume that is an 11 × 17-inch sheet folded in half. This allows one 8½ × 11-inch side for the cover page and three additional 8½ × 11-inch sides for her resume information.

Because the brochure opens up like a book, the reader is still holding a one-page document and doesn't have to flip through several pages. This is a perfect format for someone with extensive skills or credentials.

HANNAH SVENSON

A Presentation

of

Professional Credentials

74 Dogwood Drive
Minneapolis, Minnesota 08023
(202) 889-8263

HANNAH SVENSON
74 Dogwood Drive
Minneapolis, Minnesota 08023
(202) 889-8263

As the reader opens the brochure, this page is on the left hand side. (We show you how to lay out this resume in Chapter 4.)

Executive Profile

Multi-talented, high-caliber **Executive Vice President of Sales & Marketing,** with 25 years of experience building and leading integrated sales & marketing operations for domestic and international corporations and financial companies. Have held highly visible, leadership positions, and have earned a reputation for continually making a positive bottom-line difference while fostering excellent employee relations and maintaining a high profile in business. Extensive international travel throughout Europe, South & Central America, and Canada.

Consistently successful in reengineering overall operations to minimize and maintain costs and increase profitability. Talented in developing and leading business opportunities and marketing strategies to maximize growth and increase revenue. Experienced in forming start-up operations, and in positioning finance as a critical business partner, supportive of and responsive to the needs of large and diverse operating units.

Strong general management qualifications in business operations, financial market analysis, planning and all facets of manufacturing improvement. Outstanding analytical, planning, organization, and negotiation skills with expertise developed in solid capital formation, mergers, acquisitions, and divestitures. Excellent employee training, development and leadership skills. International executive liaison with experience interacting with foreign business leaders and officials throughout the world. Attended numerous seminars by Stephen R. Covey and conscientiously implement the *"Seven Habits of Highly Effective People"* into everyday life and work.

Desire a career opportunity in **leadership and management** that will provide a challenging opportunity to significantly contribute to a company's organization, growth, and profitability.

Advanced Education & Executive Training

Master of Business Administration
HARVARD UNIVERSITY, Boston, Massachusetts, 1980
GPA: 3.75/4.0

Bachelor of Science in Political Science
FAIRFIELD UNIVERSITY, Fairfield, Connecticut, 1973

Community Affairs & Affiliations

Kempo Karate (Kung Fu) - Black Belt
Volunteer Instructor at School and Member of Leadership Team
Participate in fundraisers for *"Kick Drugs Out of America."*
Organizer & Manager of United Way National Campaign
Manage all facets of United Way Campaign, which involves in-depth interaction with community businesses and organizations.

Executive Experience

Executive Vice President
MINNESOTA ELECTRONICS COMPANY
Minneapolis, Minnesota - 1995 to Present

- **Sales, Marketing & Operations Management:** Recruited to direct an aggressive reorganization and profit/performance improvement program of company, which is a distributor of wire, cable, and electronic goods. Hold full financial and operating responsibility for the corporation and all division business, sales, and marketing affairs.
- **Company Reorganization:** Launched a companywide reengineering and market repositioning to meet company expectations for revenue growth and profit improvement.
- **Departmental Development:** Streamlined operations and helped develop and implement a Product Development Department. Formulated policies and procedures to develop innovative sales, marketing, and business plans to expand revenue and increase profitability.
- **Sales, Business Development & Profitability:** Manage new business development and strategic planning to maximize growth and profitability. Develop and expand markets with O.E.M. manufacturers throughout the world. Establish growth plans for individual accounts and manage account calls, presentations and negotiations. Assisted in growing company sales from $4.5 million to $7 million.
- **Client Relations:** Continuously establish and maintain an exemplary network of business associates throughout the world as a result of extensive interaction and strong communication skills.
- **Budget Management:** Review, analyze, manage and administer budget for operating expenditures. Prepare future years' budgets based on previous expenditures and changes in organizational structures.

Executive Vice President & Chief Financial Officer
MINNEAPOLIS & ST. PAUL RECYCLING, INC.
Minneapolis, Minnesota - 1993 to 1995

- **Executive Management:** Responsible for developing this startup bulky waste recycling company, which was unique in that it recycled construction and demolition debris. Responsible for all sales, marketing and business operations.
- **Client & Community Relations:** Worked extensively with state officials, community leaders, businesses and organizations to solicit and obtain support for this recycling company. Established and maintained an excellent network of business associates due to strong communication skills.
- **Budget & Finance Management:** Managed and analyzed budget for operating expenditures. Reviewed monthly and year/quarter-end reports and analyzed budget variances. Initiated appropriate strategies to more aggressively control expenditures and changes in organizational structures.

Executive Vice President
NORTHERN CAPITAL GROUP, INC.
Minneapolis, Minnesota - 1986 to 1993

- **Manager:** Developed and managed overall operations of this investment banking firm, which raised capital for other people. Successfully raised over $25 million in capital from public and private sources for clients' start-up operations, and raised $11 million for Minneapolis & St. Paul Recycling, Inc.

Executive Experience

- **Executive Liaison:** Liaison between financial markets and customers in need of financial capital. Negotiated financial contracts between customers and financial markets. Analyzed and assessed customers' business plans and determined eligibility for capital investments.
- **Marketing & Advertising:** Planned, developed and implemented innovative marketing strategies to expand and develop business.
- **Finance Management:** Managed financial, accounting, budgetary, business and strategic planning.

Vice President & Founder
GLOBAL ENTERPRISES
San Francisco, California - 1984 to 1986

- **Founder & Management:** Managed and directed overall sales and marketing operations, as well as administration of financial operations and management programs. Guided U.S. companies in marketing and selling their software products overseas. This involved developing innovative marketing strategies to promote products.
- **International & Domestic Client Relations:** Established and maintained an excellent network of business associates nationally and internationally as a result of extensive interaction and outstanding communication skills.
- **Account Management:** Managed new sales and business development and strategic planning to maximize growth and profitability. Established growth plans for accounts and personally managed account calls, presentations and negotiations.
- **Research & Market Analysis:** Researched, analyzed, and identified potential markets and proposed new products to these markets based on technology trends.

Director of International Sales & Marketing
VIDEO GAMES WORLDWIDE
Palo Alto, California - 1981 to 1984

- **Marketing, Management & Business Development:** Managed and directed international sales, marketing and business operations which involved the development and expansion of the international market. Established long-term strategic business goals to maximize growth and profitability and developed subsidiaries and distributorships around the world.
- **Finance Management:** Held full responsibility for developing and administering all financial affairs including investment solicitations, investor relations, budget development, capital expenditure authorization, financial analysis/reporting and contract negotiations. Created and implemented global financial models and operational systems increasing profits by 20%.
- **International Affairs:** Developed an extensive knowledge of foreign corporate systems, banking, and global reporting practices. Established an exemplary network of business associates internationally.
- **Management & Supervision:** Supervised and managed a staff of 40 personnel members, plus all the international controllers around the world. Delegated responsibilities and monitored overall job performances to ensure accuracy and adherence to policies.
- **Company Acquisitions:** Initiated company acquisitions, set up 4 subsidiaries within 6 months, and established over a dozen distributorships which increased international sales from $3 million to $500 million within one year.
- **Investments & Auditing:** Identified and reclaimed $3.5 million of $5 million international investment previously considered worthless. Implemented internal audit reviews uncovering $40 million in domestic division inconsistencies.
- Held other positions at Computer Corporation, Maybelline, and General Electric Credit Corporation prior to the ones highlighted in resume.

HANNAH SVENSON
74 Dogwood Drive
Minneapolis, Minnesota 08023
(202) 889-8263

Date

David Pappalia
President & Owner
Times Market, Inc.
79 Oaklane Drive
Minneapolis, MN 39933

> Do let the company know how you heard of a position, and be specific about the job you're interested in.

Dear Mr. Pappalia:

After talking with your sales manager last week, I discovered that you are looking for a highly motivated, goal-oriented **Executive Vice President of Sales & Marketing** with global experiences to become a leader in your organization. I am confident that, with my experience and education, I can significantly contribute to Times Market, Inc.'s growth and profitability. I have enclosed a portfolio so you may review my credentials in detail.

As you will note, I am a seasoned professional with more than 25 years of domestic and international experience building and leading operations for major corporations and industries. My areas of expertise and qualifications include the following:

- Proven track record of success in sales and marketing management, negotiations, corporate policy development, corporate investments and acquisitions, and financial analysis.
- Talented in restructuring and reengineering national and international sales and marketing operations and financial programs that yield reduced company costs and increased profitability.
- Strong "owner's" mentality developed from working in a family business while in high school and college. Utilize a *"What if I owned the business?"* approach to cost control and to making a positive bottom-line difference.
- Throughout career have successfully managed and administered multimillion dollar budgets and initiated appropriate strategies through contract negotiations and marketing strategies to aggressively control expenditures.
- Proactive leader with effective team-building skills. Empower associates to think and work independently and in a team environment, which increases employee efficiency and productivity.
- Proven ability to define issues, propose solutions, and implement cost-effective as well as profitable changes.

I sincerely believe that, with my experience and career aspirations, I would be an asset to your organization. I would appreciate an opportunity to meet with you to discuss your upcoming plans and long-term goals. I have some excellent ideas about how my leadership and management abilities could be instrumental in achieving success for your company.

Thank you in advance for your time and consideration. I will be following up with a phone call to arrange a personal meeting.

Sincerely,

Hannah Svenson

Portfolio Enclosed

Klaus von Schuland

Klaus von Schuland was an outstanding professional with a proven track record of sales accomplishments who asked for a two-page resume. He had many awards that exemplified his sales and marketing expertise in the medical industry, and we determined that these should appear on the first page of his resume for the greatest impact. Notice how his consistent experience in the same industry really shines and lends even more credibility to his already strong credentials. Companies do like candidates who have great track records and at least three years with their most recent employers.

Klaus von Schuland
99 Airport Road
Louisville, Kentucky 40023
(502) 030-0032

Career Profile in Sales

Dynamic, profit- and results-oriented **Medical Sales Specialist** with more than 7 years of experience building and leading integrated sales and marketing operations for major medical corporations. Proven track record of success in leading and building business opportunities and marketing strategies to maximize growth and profitability. Especially talented in reengineering and repositioning sales operations to increase market share and revenue. Excellent analytical, planning, organization and negotiation skills. Executive liaison with physicians, medical centers and hospitals with ability to develop and nurture strong client relationships.

Desire a challenging opportunity in **leadership and sales management** to significantly contribute to a company's efficiency, organization, growth, and profitability.

Summary of Sales Awards

- *President's Club, Med Company, Inc. Sales Award, 1996*
- *Sales Leader, Med Company, Inc. Sales Award, 1996*
- *Representative of the Quarter, Med Company, Inc. Sales Awards, 1996, 1995*
- *Cardiovascular Alliance Teamwork Award, Med Company, Inc. Sales Award, 1996*
- *Regional Gold Awards, Med Company, Inc. Sales Awards, 1996, 1995*
- *Circle of Merit Awards, Astra-Merck Pharmaceuticals, 1993, 1992*
- *Innovation Panel Awards, Astra-Merck Pharmaceuticals, 1992, 1991*
- *Business Team of the Year, Med Company, Inc. Sales Award, 1990*

Medical Sales Experience

Angioplasty Sales Specialist
MED COMPANY, INC.
Louisville, Kentucky (Home Office in Des Moines, Iowa) - 1993 to Present

- <u>Sales:</u> Recruited to Med Company, Inc. to direct an aggressive reorganization of sales operations and initiate high-volume sales in the highest dollar-potential market in the country. Responsible for expanding business and selling medical devices to hospitals throughout Nashville, Tennessee and Atlanta, Georgia.
- <u>Profitability & Sales Accomplishments:</u> After successfully reengineering sales operations, increased revenue from **$225,000 year to $1.7 million annually** in just 2½ years. This was the fastest revenue growth in the nation. Achieved **#1 in sales** in the U.S. in 1996. Sold the largest single order - $213,300 - in Med Company, Inc.'s Interventional Vascular history. Recipient of the 2 highest Med Company, Inc.'s Sales Awards - the **President's Club and Sales Leaders,** 1996.
- <u>Account Management & Business Development:</u> Responsible for managing new business development and strategic planning to maximize growth and profitability. Establish growth plans for individual accounts and personally manage account calls, presentations and contract negotiations.
- <u>Client Relations/Service:</u> Continuously establish, nurture and maintain client relationships as a result of extensive interaction and strong communication skills.

Continued

- **Contract Systems Development:** Designed and implemented 3 major innovative contracts for physicians that became models for Med Company Inc.'s contracting department. Led the southwest region in innovative contract signings and negotiated and won 4 major accounts in 3 years.
- **Physician Education Training:** Responsible for planning, coordinating and attending physician education meetings nationally and internationally. Educate physicians on coronary angioplasty/stenting procedures as related to Med Company, Inc.'s equipment.
- **Columbia/HCA Steering Committee:** Communications liaison between company and the Columbia/HCA Steering Committee. Provide information to the committee regarding new medical products, practices and procedures.
- **Diversity Council:** Appointed to serve as *Representative of the U.S. Cardiovascular Sales Force* on the *Med Company, Inc. Diversity Council.*
- **Marketing:** Conceptualized and designed innovative marketing and sales materials for utilization by other sales representatives.
- **Employee Supervision:** Supervise and manage Clinical Specialist. Delegate responsibilities and monitor overall job performances to ensure accuracy and adherence to company policies.

Medical Sales Representative
PFIZER PHARMACEUTICALS
Youngsville, New Jersey - 1991 to 1993

- **Sales:** Responsible for selling pharmaceuticals to physicians and hospitals. Led sales cycle from initial client consultation through presentations, price negotiations and closings. Solicited and obtained new clientele, as well as maintained existing accounts.
- **Business Development:** Hired to reposition and grow market share in New Jersey. Developed business opportunities and marketing strategies within the southeast district. Expanded market penetration and provided direction for long-range business focus to meet industry changes.
- **Profitability & Sales Accomplishments:** Won **Circle of Merit Awards,** 1992-1993 and Innovation Panel Awards, 1991-1992. Reengineered sales operations and improved market share from the lowest ranking of 9th to 2nd. Expanded market penetration of **Lozine by 295%** during a period of budgetary downsizing.
- **Systems Development:** Created, developed, and incorporated a new system to record sales call information, which efficiently increased district productivity.
- **Research & Marketing:** Coordinated market research activities and surveys. Developed and implemented innovative marketing strategies to penetrate market and expand sales.

Cardiovascular Sales Specialist
AZURE PHARMACEUTICALS
Philadelphia, Pennsylvania - 1990 to 1991

- **Sales, Profitability & Accomplishments:** Responsible for selling pharmaceuticals to physicians and hospitals. Built market share from 14% to 28% for LOZOL in one year, which was the highest market share in the nation. Achieved **#2 market share in the nation for ANSAID,** in the *highly* competitive market of non-steroidals. Won **Business Team of the Year Award** in 1990.

Education
Bachelor of Arts in Communication Arts - GPA: 3.8/4.0
Major: Public Relations - Minor: Biology
THE UNIVERSITY OF KENTUCKY, Lexington, Kentucky, 1985

Klaus von Schuland
99 Airport Road
Louisville, Kentucky 40023
(502) 030-0032

Date

Kenneth Freeland
Executive Director of Sales
Pennington Pharmaceuticals
9920 Bostonian Road
Cincinnati, Ohio 49933

> It's important to address your cover letter to a specific person—the decision maker who will be reading your resume!

Dear Mr. Freeland:

It is my understanding that you are searching for a results- and profit-oriented **Medical Sales Specialist** to manage and direct the Ohio and Kentucky territory. With my track record of success in increasing sales and profitability, I am confident that I can become a vital leader in your company. I have enclosed a professional portfolio so you may review my credentials.

In addition to a *Bachelor of Arts in Communication Arts* with a minor in Biology, I also possess more than 7 years of experience. My areas of expertise and qualifications include the following:

- Numerous sales awards throughout career as a result of outstanding performance and a strong commitment to success.
- Special talents in reengineering and repositioning sales operations to increase market share and revenue.
- Ability to manage new business development to maximize growth and profitability.
- Hands-on experience in training physicians in angioplasty procedures as related to special Med Company, Inc. equipment.
- Effective team-building skills with supervisory and management experience.
- Proven ability to define issues, propose solutions, and implement changes.

I sincerely believe that, with my experience and career aspirations, I would be an asset to Pennington Pharmaceuticals. I plan to telephone you in a few days to arrange a personal meeting so we can discuss ways that I can contribute to Pennington's goals.

Thank you in advance for your time and consideration. I look forward to speaking with you soon.

Sincerely,

Klaus von Schuland

Resume Enclosed

3

Don't Fall into the Pits!

Major Do's & Don'ts for Your Sales & Marketing Resume

Too often, people have preconceived ideas about what they should or should not include in a resume. There are numerous resume books on the market that say "Do this, do that . . . follow this rule, follow that rule." We don't believe there are any real rules when it comes to writing resumes. However, there are some common-sense concepts that you should understand when you write your resume, and those are what we will illustrate in this chapter.

SALES & MARKETING TIP:

This exercise has helped others: If you are ever in doubt as to how to prepare your resume, ask yourself,"Who is the intended reader and what is needed for this job? What will the reader want to see?" Then, write your resume as if you were answering those questions.

Common Pitfalls

1. Don't limit your resume to one page if it prevents you from writing about a comprehensive career background.

2. Don't write in vague, broad statements.

3. Don't write lengthy descriptions of your job with no breaks, like a boring monologue that leaves you gasping for air. Keep a nice rhythm in your writing. Read your resume out loud to feel this rhythm. Just as a song has a

rhythm to it, so does prose. Reading your resume aloud will help you to identify any sentences that are too long or too short. (You may have to do this several times to actually feel the rhythm.)

4. Don't put salary requirements (or past salary) in your resume. If employers want a salary history or your requirements, they will ask. Don't assume anything.

5. Don't use flashy graphics, photos, or designs on the resume. (Even though this is your sales presentation, you must remember that your client is a potential employer, so save designs and graphics for other documents.)

6. Don't use bright resume paper such as yellow, red, or orange.

7. Don't fold your resume when submitting it to an employer. Mail it flat in a 9 × 12-inch envelope whenever possible.

No-Rules Resumes

Most of our clients need not only resume assistance but also career assistance, coaching, and guidance throughout the job search process. They are often full of confusion and questions about the right things to do out there in the job market. Many resume books on the market offer conflicting advice, and job seekers are in more of a quandary than ever about what to do or not do. We base all of our opinions, advice, and career directions on actual experience. We have learned throughout the years what actually works. Here are some of the most common questions we hear from our resume clients and our answers.

Question: Is it true you should always limit your resume to one page?

Answer: The answer is simply no! It is a myth that you should always limit your resume to one page. Most professionals won't do themselves justice with one page. Employers are realistic. They know that if you're a professional, there's no way that you can condense your entire work history and education to one page of text. You'll end up leaving out some very important information about yourself.

Question: Is it important to have a cover letter?

Answer: Yes! Never, ever send a resume without a cover letter. You wouldn't drop by a potential client's office without introducing yourself, would you? In the same way, a cover letter introduces you to your potential client (employer).

Question: Won't I be bragging if I write about my accomplishments and sales increases?

Answer: No! You must create a sense of excitement in the reader about who you are! Entice the reader. Make this potential employer want you! You can't be humble at this point. You have to be proud of your accomplishments. You're in sales, right? Salespeople are not humble or meek about their products; they can't afford to be. The same goes for your resume. You can't afford to be shy. Be aggressive in all aspects of your resume and cover letter—your entire portfolio.

Question: Should I use abbreviations in my resume, like MSA for metropolitan surrounding area?

Answer: We recommend that you write out the term the first time it is used in your resume and cover letter. If it is used a second time, then it's okay to abbreviate it. Not all companies use the same acronyms to describe something, so don't make them wonder what the abbreviations stand for.

Question: Should I put my current salary and my salary expectations in my resume?

Answer: Never! If an employer does ask for a Salary History, then it's vital that you submit one, or you won't even be considered. But a Salary History is a document separate from your resume. (See Chapter 5 for the winning way to present a Salary History.) A company likes to know that you'll follow directions. They also don't want to waste your time if your Salary History isn't in line with what they're offering. For example, if you're earning $300,000 a year and the job being offered is going to pay only $40,000, then it would be a waste of time for both you and the employer to schedule an interview.

Question: Can I be different in preparing a sales and marketing resume—use wild, bold-colored paper or add pictures of myself?

Answer: Only if you're in a very creative field. In sales and marketing, you must be more conservative in your approach. Even though your resume is your sales presentation, you still need to remember to use good taste when preparing it. Any graphics or designs can be used on sales documents that are included in your portfolio, but as for the resume itself, use only neutral colors such as gray, beige, or white. A potential employer might view an orange resume as representative of someone who's desperately trying to get attention, and you don't want to appear desperate.

Important Info on a Sales & Marketing Resume

1. Do highlight accomplishments and honors.

2. Do highlight any advanced training or special seminars you've attended, such as the Stephen Covey Seminar, Zig Ziglar, Dale Carnegie, etc.

3. Emphasize your track record of success by illustrating how you increased sales or expanded territories. Use actual sales numbers and data to increase your credibility.

4. Do mention major accounts you solicited and obtained, companies that have international and national reputations such as General Mills, Westinghouse, General Electric, Coca Cola, etc.

5. Do write a personal statement or mission. Let the employer know a little about you!

6. Do bullet information to draw the eye to specific points.

7. Do send your business card with your resume if you have one. Make it as easy as possible for the employer to remember you.

8. Do send a cover letter with your resume!

9. Always send a (separate) Salary History if the employer requests one. If you fail to do this, you won't even be considered for the position.

10. Always send a thank-you letter after an interview. (We'll discuss this in more detail in Chapter 5.)

Resumes That Were Rescued from the Pits!

On the following pages are four Before and After resumes. The Before versions are actual resumes from our clients that were written and designed very poorly and had been extremely ineffective in getting interviews. We rewrote them using all the principles we've been discussing in this book. Compare the Before and After versions to see how we added power and the ability to *sell*.

Graham Taylor

The first resume belongs to Graham Taylor. When he came into our office, he looked quite glum and discouraged. About 6'2", with dark hair cropped short on top, Graham couldn't understand why he wasn't getting interviews. He had a good background in sports marketing and thought that his work history was strong enough to get him an interview with any sports company. One glance at his resume and we understood why he wasn't getting interviews. Read on to see how we rewrote his resume so he could get interviews and land the job that was perfect for him!

Graham Taylor
2993 Palms Beach
Orlando, Florida 99333

Director of Marketing for Motorsports
National Communications, Inc.
Orlando, Florida
Responsible for 6 motorsports teams in the U.S. This includes marketing and advertising. Handle all personnel issues and scheduling.

General Marketing Manager
International Sports Museum, Los Angeles, California
Responsible for marketing for this nonprofit organization.

Marketing Specialist and Tournament Producer
Worldwide Sports Management
Daytona Beach, Florida
Managed marketing for golf tournaments.

Marketing Specialist
Traveling Sportsman, Inc., Trenton, New Jersey
Marketing specialist for company.

Marketing Specialist
SPORTS TEAMS OF AMERICA, Miami, Florida

EDUCATION: B.S. in Marketing, Florida State University, Miami, Florida

REFERENCES: Available upon request.

PERSONAL: Loves all kinds of sports, auto racing, swimming, fishing, and skiing. Married with 2 children.

This Before version was literally screaming for help! Graham didn't stand a chance of getting a good interview with this resume. There's no phone number on the resume. Nothing is highlighted or bolded, and there's no Objective or Career Profile. This resume has no sales power at all!

This is not enough of a job description to really explain what Graham did. Also, he doesn't list any dates in the resume. An employer will want to know for how long and when you were at these companies!

Personal issues need not be included in a resume unless they specifically pertain to a job you're targeting.

GRAHAM TAYLOR

A Presentation

of

Executive Credentials in Marketing

**2993 Palms Beach
Orlando, Florida 99333
(293) 399-0029**

GRAHAM TAYLOR

2993 Palms Beach
Orlando, Florida 99333
(293) 399-0029

Executive Profile

High-caliber **Sports Marketing Executive** with more than 15 years of experience building, leading and directing integrated sports/marketing events and activities for national companies. In-depth background in directing sales, marketing, corporate fundraising and sponsorship programs for major Fortune 500 corporations. Experienced in conceptualizing, creating and implementing innovative promotional and marketing events for golf tournaments and motorsports.

Held high-visibility public relations positions as the direct liaison to clients, community leaders, national association members and other businesses. Skilled executive and public relations liaison with experience in developing and maintaining an exemplary network of business associates as a result of strong communication skills. Strong general management qualifications in organizational and strategic planning and all facets of process/productivity/quality improvement. Effective team-building skills with excellent background in personnel training, development and leadership.

Desire a **leadership and management position in sports marketing** that will provide a challenging opportunity to significantly contribute to a company's efficiency, organization, growth, and profitability.

Executive Experience

Director of Marketing for Motorsports
National Communications, Inc.
Orlando, Florida - 1995 to Present

- **Marketing Management:** Manage and direct overall marketing operations and administration of 6 national motorsports teams which include *Marlboro Cup Racing, Sports Drag Racing and Hydroplane Racing Association.*
- **Marketing, Advertising & Promotion:** Conceptualize, create and produce innovative marketing and advertising strategies to promote the programs listed above with various Fortune 500 corporations. On an ongoing basis, develop and direct comprehensive promotions and media campaigns targeted for a specific customer base.
- **Publicity & Promotions:** Serve as *Public Spokesperson & Executive Liaison* between company and 6 national motorsports teams. Act as *Authorized Spokesman* for the release of information to the public and to the news media concerning special activities and events. Coordinate and organize publicity events and promotional strategies to promote teams and revenue.
- **Program Development:** Assisted in spearheading a $71 million national program called *The Sports America Phone Card Sweepstakes* and *International Phone Card Sweepstakes.*
- **Client Relations:** Consistently establish and maintain an exemplary network of business associates with Fortune 500 companies as a result of extensive interaction and strong communication skills.
- **Scheduling & Itineraries:** Responsible for scheduling and coordinating all hospitality for racing-related events for major clients of Marketing Enterprises for Sports.
- **Budget Management:** Prepare, administer and control budgets for marketing, promotions, and advertising.

Executive Experience

General Marketing Manager

International Sports Museum, Los Angeles, California - 1992 to 1995

- **Marketing Management:** Managed overall marketing operations and administration of this not-for-profit facility that displays, preserves, and showcases the history of sports cars. Responsible for formulating and implementing company policies and procedures into everyday operations.
- **Community & Public Affairs:** Worked extensively with community leaders, officials and businesses to coordinate public events and promotional activities. Developed a strong network of business associates throughout the U.S. as a result of working with Board Members who lived in various parts of the U.S.
- **Marketing & Advertising:** Conceptualized, developed and implemented marketing and advertising programs that included sponsorship programs for Fortune 500 corporations.
- **Account Management:** Responsible for managing new business development and strategic planning to maximize growth. Established growth plans for individual accounts and personally managed account calls, presentations, and negotiations.
- **Clientele:** Major clientele included the GM Master Card, MCI Telecommunications, Chevrolet Motor Division, and more.
- **Fundraising:** Solicited and obtained over $700,000 in sponsorship which included cash, trades, and donations.
- **Special Promotional Events:** Planned and organized the launch *Sports Across America Phone Card Sweepstakes,* which was the largest payout sweepstakes in the U.S. with over $71 million in cash and prizes for 1997.
- **Licensing & Contract Negotiations:** Responsible for negotiating contracts and obtaining licensing for sponsors with Chevrolet Motors Division/General Motors Corporation. Also, coordinated all licensing and merchandising programs for a 2,200 sq. ft. upscale gift shop.
- **Event Planning & Development:** Planned and organized the *Inaugural American Heritage Festival with Motorcycle Motor Company and GM Motors, the Telecommunications Pre-Paid Phone Card Program, Sports Cars for Kids Christmas,* and more.

Marketing Specialist & Producer

Traveling Sportsman, Inc., Trenton, New Jersey - 1987 to 1992

- **Marketing:** Conceptualized, developed and implemented marketing programs to promote golf tournaments.
- **Producer:** Responsible for producing professional golf tournaments for *The Senior PGA* and *The Senior Series.*
- **Media Production:** In charge of developing, organizing and coordinating media production which included print, radio & television.
- **Fundraising:** Spearheaded the solicitation and obtaining of $350,000 from local sponsors for each event. Coordinated the Pro-Am events and numerous evening gala affairs.
- **Volunteers:** Organized and scheduled 2,000 volunteers for the golf tournaments.

Marketing Specialist

Sports Teams of America, Miami, Florida - 1980 to 1987

- **Marketing Management:** Managed overall marketing operations for the sponsorship and promotional programs of nationally known sports-related projects including *The GMC Truck Traveling Sportsman, The Outdoor Trail, The Outdoorsman, Treasures of the Sea, The Heartland Jam, The Heartland Thunderfest,* and the *Inboard Division of the American Power Boat Association.* Also, managed promotional activities for USAir at *The Players Championship of The PGA Tour.*

Education

Bachelor of Science in Marketing
Florida State University, Miami, Florida, 1979

GRAHAM TAYLOR
2993 Palms Beach
Orlando, Florida 99333
(293) 399-0029

Date

Jonathon Njoku
Director of International Marketing
International Motorsports, Inc.
2003 Stephens Court
New York, New York 03092

Always mention where you have heard of the job opening—if there is one.

Dear Mr. Njoku:

I recently read an article in the *Wall Street Journal* about International Motorsports, Inc., and it was mentioned that you plan to increase your marketing efforts in the following year. With a strong background in sports marketing and the desire to work for a reputable company such as International Motorsports, Inc., I am submitting my resume for your review. I am confident that I can be a leading member of your company.

In addition to a *Bachelor of Science in Marketing* from the University of Florida, I also possess the following qualifications and expertise:

- Proven track record of success in **Sports Marketing** with more than 15 years of experience building and leading sports marketing events and activities for national companies.
- Comprehensive experience directing corporate fundraising and sponsorship programs for major Fortune 500 companies.
- "Hands-on" experience in marketing all types of sports events including golf tournaments and motorsports.
- Public relations executive with past experience in high-visibility positions as the direct liaison to clients, community leaders and national sports association members.
- Demonstrated background in establishing and maintaining a strong network of business associates through extensive national marketing campaigns and strong communication skills.
- Effective team-building skills with excellent background in personnel training, development, and leadership.

I sincerely believe I will be an asset to your organization and plan to call you within a few days to arrange a personal meeting. Meanwhile, if you have any additional questions, please feel free to contact me at my home telephone number or address.

Thank you in advance for your time and consideration. I look forward to speaking with you soon.

Sincerely,

Bulleting information about your accomplishments is very effective. The bullets draw the eye to special points you highlight in your letter.

Graham Taylor

Portfolio Enclosed

Karen Parker

Karen Parker telephoned us from Saskatchewan, Canada. She explained her work experience and complained that she was having no luck finding a job. After she faxed us her resume, we understood why. Karen had not adequately described her experience on her resume. Without a solid career history, there was no way she could be competitive with other candidates. Karen hadn't effectively communicated her skills even on a fundamental level, so she was unable to get interviews.

After an in-depth interview on the telephone, we were able to glean valuable information that was significant in Karen's background. After she received the resume we wrote for her, she called to say, "Wow! I'm blown away by how great I look on paper! I just underestimated my experience."

Immediately after Karen began distributing her new resume, the interviews and job offers began to come her way.

Karen Parker

**P. O. Box 9938
Pilot Butte
Saskatchewan, Canada SOG 320
(299) 983-0929** _____

Objective: A position in Sales & Marketing that will fully utilize my experience.

Sales Manager National Accounts
CANADIAN BOOT COMPANY
Saskatchewan, Canada - 1996 to Present

Sales & Marketing Manager
MOUNTAINEER BOOTS
Portland, Oregon - 1994 to 1996

President of Sales & Marketing
CANADIAN FOOTWEAR - 1992 to 1994

Vice President of Sales Operations
TRACKERS FOOTWEAR, Canada - 1990 to 1992

Vice President of Sales & Marketing
ALL CHILDRENS' DIVISIONS, A Trackers Footwear Company - 1987 to 1990

Director of Sales & Marketing
NIKE, INC., Beaverton, Oregon - 1983 to 1987

Corporate Vice President
Sales, Marketing & Product Development
MICHAELS & COMPANY - 1978 to 1985

Karen Parker

P. O. Box 9938
Pilot Butte
Saskatchewan, Canada SOG 320
(299) 983-0929

To Whom it May Concern:

Font and style of letter are not very appealing. Letter is not balanced. Never address a letter To Whom It May Concern. This is very cold and impersonal!

I am interested in obtaining a position in sales and marketing. I have enclosed my resume for your review. I have an extensive background, as you will see in my resume.

I would like to arrange a meeting with you at your earliest convenience. Thank you in advance for your tiem and consideration.

Sincerely,

Karen Parker

Never leave misspelled words in your letter or resume. Proof everything several times!

Karen's cover letter contains no "oomph"—no real sales power. It is nothing more than a brief note and would not hold anyone's attention for more than a few seconds.

KAREN PARKER

A Presentation

of

Executive Marketing Credentials

P. O. Box 9938
Pilot Butte
Saskatchewan, Canada SOG 320
(299) 983-0929

Karen Parker

P. O. Box 9938
Pilot Butte
Saskatchewan, Canada SOG 320
(299) 983-0929

Executive Profile

I am a high-caliber **Executive Sales & Marketing Director,** with more than 20 years of experience building and leading integrated sales and marketing operations for high-profile nationwide retail companies. I place a strong focus on team-building and employee relations, for without a unified force, businesses cannot excel. One of my greatest contributions to a company is my positive team approach toward staff members which leads to unified efforts and ultimate success. A proactive leader and motivator, I serve as a mentor for my staff and take great pride in developing their skills and talents to their maximum potential so they can achieve optimum results. I create a team-oriented environment and introduce a participative decision-making style which results in high employee morale and company profitability.

My background exemplifies a successful track record of career accomplishments which include executive positions as **President, Vice President of Sales & Marketing,** and **Corporate Vice President** for leading retail industries. I am talented in reengineering and restructuring companies to position them in higher profile markets to increase sales and profitability. In addition, I have built and nurtured client/business relationships throughout my career and have established an exemplary network of business associates in the retail industry. Experienced in all facets of process/productivity/quality improvement, I am skilled in developing, introducing, and expanding new product lines into a competitive marketplace. With in-depth experience in conceptualizing and developing business opportunities and marketing strategies, I can maximize growth and profitability for integrated operations. I am an executive liaison with comprehensive analytical, planning, organizational and negotiation skills.

I won't make the mistakes of early career ventures. I am confident in my perceptions, abilities and wisdom to make sound decisions based on experience and a track record of success. My knowledge of business, people, and the retail industry surpasses that of most business executives. I am unique in the fact that I care. I serve as a role model for peers and associates and possess the highest level of professionalism and work ethics. I offer my skills in an effort to lead and guide your company to success.

Education

Bachelor of Science in Marketing & Advertising
CANADIAN ACADEMY, Saskatchewan, Canada

Executive Marketing & Sales Experience

Sales Manager National Accounts
CANADIAN BOOT COMPANY
Saskatchewan, Canada - 1996 to Present

- *Sales Management:* Manage and direct overall national sales operations for lines of footwear. Responsible for strategic planning of all integrated sales and marketing.

Executive Marketing & Sales Experience

- *Team Building - Employee Relations:* After taking over sales operations, created a team-oriented structure and introduced participative decision-making style, which has resulted in a successful sales and operations management team.

Sales & Marketing Manager
MOUNTAINEER BOOTS
Portland, Oregon - 1994 to 1996

- *Company Track Record of Success:* Served in 2 executive positions including, **President** and **Vice President of Sales Operations** for different divisions of Mountaineer Boots.
- *Company Reengineering:* Recruited to direct an aggressive reorganization and profit/performance improvement sales program for Mountaineer Boots to make it marketable to other companies. Provided direction for long-range business focus to meet industry changes and requirements.
- *Manufacturing:* Managed overall operations and administration of one factory. Oversaw the scheduling, production and distribution of footwear.

President of Sales & Marketing
CANADIAN FOOTWEAR, Quebec, Canada - 1992 to 1994

- *Management:* Launched a fine dress and casual shoe program to sell to major retailers and upscale independent stores. Led companywide reengineering and market positioning program to achieve revenue growth and profit improvement. Restructured all key departments which included personnel staffing and development. Held full financial and operating responsibility for division.
- *Sales & Profitability:* Achieved significant profitability as a result of designing and implementing new sales programs, which increased overall profitability for company.
- *Account Management:* Established growth plans for individual accounts and personally managed account calls, presentations, and negotiations.
- *Budget Management:* Managed, analyzed and projected budget for operating expenditures. Analyzed budget variances and initiated appropriate guidelines to more aggressively control expenditures.

Vice President of Sales Operations
TRACKERS FOOTWEAR, Quebec, Canada - 1990 to 1992

- *Sales Management:* Directed and managed overall sales operations for this company. Expanded the distribution base to department stores and fine independents nationwide, while also controlling markdowns. Developed innovative marketing strategies to increase sales.
- *Product Introduction:* Planned and directed the introduction of Trackers Footwear in stores throughout Canada and the U.S. Successfully positioned brand as one of the leading products in the marketplace through high-impact marketing, advertising and promotional strategies.
- *Profitability:* Increased sales revenue by **$5.5 million** and margins by 8.5%

Vice President of Sales & Marketing
ALL CHILDRENS' DIVISIONS, A Trackers Footwear Company - 1987 to 1990

- *Management:* Brought in to build up distribution to include major department stores and fine independents. Held full P&L responsibility for all children's divisions of Trackers Footwear, including *Toddler Schools, Schools Brands* and *Street Smart Athletics.*

More Detailed Information Available Upon Request

> Do point out how you increased profitability!

> You don't have to list <u>all</u> <u>jobs</u>; you can mention that more information is available upon request.

Karen Parker
P. O. Box 9938
Pilot Butte
Saskatchewan, Canada SOG 320
(299) 983-0929

Date

Jacqueline DuMaurier
Executive President of Sales & Marketing
French-American Boot Company
3772 Forest Way
Quebec, Canada SOG 200

> Letter is addressed to a specific person, and mentions a mutual friend and employer, which will grab the employer's attention.

Dear Ms. DuMaurier:

A mutual friend and employer of French-American Boot Company, Mr. Pierre Denzine, suggested that I submit a resume for the position of **Director of Sales & Marketing** for the U.S. & Toronto Division. As he suggested, I am enclosing my resume so you may review my background and credentials.

As you will note in my resume, I am not a beginner, but rather a seasoned professional with more than 20 years of experience building and leading integrated sales and marketing operations for high-profile nationwide U.S. and Canadian companies. My areas of expertise and qualifications include the following:

- Successful track record of success as *President, Vice President of Sales & Marketing* and *Corporate Vice President* for leading retail industries.
- Special talents in reengineering companies to position them in higher profile markets to increase sales and profitability.
- Skilled in building and nurturing client/business relationships. Continuously establish and maintain an exemplary network of business associates in the retail industry.
- Proactive leader and motivator with a positive approach toward team-building.
- Utilize a participative decision-making style which results in increased employee morale and productivity.
- Serve as role model for peers and associates in the retail industry.

This is only a small overview of my strengths and abilities. I will call you within a few days to arrange a meeting to discuss how I can significantly contribute to your company's goals.

Sincerely,

Karen Parker

Portfolio Enclosed

> It's vital to use a strong closing in your sales and marketing cover letter. Be aggressive in making the decision to call and set up an appointment!

Skyla Preston

Skyla Preston was a dynamic Marketing Executive for an entertainment company in Los Angeles. However, she didn't have strong writing skills and had no idea how to express herself in a resume.

While Skyla made a concerted effort to put her resume and cover letter together, she fell short of an impressive marketing piece that could compete for the most lucrative sales and marketing jobs. Based on her strong credentials and experience, we wrote a two-page power sales resume and a cover letter that literally rolled over her competition, landing her in first place for many job offers!

Skyla Preston
401 Alcoa Street
Studio City, California 93882
299-998-9733

**EDUCATION: B.S. in Marketing & Entertainment
University of California, Los Angeles, California**

PROFESSIONAL EXPERIENCE;

Marketing Specialist, Southern California Entertainment Agency
Los Angeles, California - 1994 to Present
Handled all marketing and organizing of new marketing campaigns. Wrote advertising for marketing materials. Worked with music employees and coordinated copyrights and licensing. Also had to work at trade shows and music events.

Marketing Representative, MTV, California Division, 1989 to 1994
Handled all marketing of campaigns for MTV. Had to write marketing materials.

Marketing Director, Whirlwind Productions
San Francisco, California - 1987 to 1989
Booked concerts for production company and responsible for all marketing operations. Wrote all marketing materials as needed.

PERSONAL;

5'9", Blonde hair, Blue eyes. Weight: 120 lbs. Background in modeling. Loves aerobics and inline skating. Single and available to travel.

Skyla Preston

401 Alcoa Street
Studio City, California 93882
299-998-9733

Dear Sir/Madam:

I am seeking a position in Marketing that will fully utilize my background and experience. I am very talented and have extensive experience in the **Marketing & Entertainment Industry.** I have enclosed a resume for your convenience.

My background includes six years of comprehensive experience in marketing and promotions and I have excellent writing and editing skills with experience writing news releases, press kits, brochures, feature stories, and direct mail.

I would like to set up an interview as soon as possible.
Thank you in advance for your time and consideration. I look forward to speaking with you soon.

Sincerely,

Skyla Preston

Skyla Preston

401 Alcoa Street
Studio City, California 93882
299-998-9733

Professional Objective & Profile

I am a highly talented **Marketing & Entertainment Industry** professional with 6 years of experience building and leading integrated marketing operations for entertainment agencies and production companies. Consistently successful in reviewing copyrights and negotiating contracts with entertainment artists and companies. Skilled in developing and spearheading innovative marketing programs that increase overall company profitability. Possess strong writing skills with experience writing and editing news releases, press kits, brochures, direct mail and feature articles.

I would like to obtain a **marketing position in the music industry** that will fully utilize my strengths and talents in marketing and entertainment, and where I can significantly contribute to the company's efficiency, organization, growth, and profitability.

Education

Bachelor of Science in Marketing & Entertainment

UNIVERSITY OF CALIFORNIA, Los Angeles, California, 1987

Summary of Qualifications

Business, Artist & Entertainment Relations:

More than 10 years of experience building and maintaining an exemplary network of business relationships with artists, entertainment and production companies, and executive entertainment staff members. Ability to effectively communicate with all types of individuals in both small and large corporate business environments.

Marketing & Promotions:

Successful background in developing and implementing strong marketing campaigns to promote artists and entertainment events. Have worked extensively with management companies and booking/talent agencies to coordinate promotions.

Marketing Experience in the Music Industry

Marketing Specialist

Southern California Entertainment Agency

Los Angeles, California - 1994 to Present

- *Company Reorganization - Marketing Management:* After taking over marketing operations, turned the company into a significant leader in the marketplace. Was responsible for totally restructuring and reengineering marketing methods to more efficiently streamline operations and increase profitability for company.
- *Creative Writing & Editing:* Wrote and edited all promotional, advertising and publicity materials for agency and for more than 40 entertainment artists. This included press kits, brochures, news releases, feature stories, and direct mail.

Jobs are clearly described and written in a style that's easy to read.

Skyla Preston
Page 2

Continued

- *Layout & Design:* Responsible for designing layouts for written materials and coordinating print production.
- *Contract Evaluations:* Evaluated, analyzed, reviewed and negotiated contracts between artists and music venues and promoters.
- *Record Label Production & Artist Development:* Coordinated copyrights and licensing of the songs, etc. Responsible for developing and promoting the careers of artists in the entertainment industry. As a result of designing and implementing strategic promotions and publicity campaigns, and successfully producing a top quality album for a traditional jazz band, this band was nominated to perform in the *California Jazz Festival.* This involved extensive interaction with recording studio, musicians, artists, and managers. Coordinated album credits and release information.
- *Public Relations:* Communications liaison between the public and California Entertainment Agency. Provided information to the public regarding entertainers and special events. Served as agency liaison between agency artists and the *California Jazz Festival,* and the *West Festival,* which involved extensive interaction between community businesses and organizations.
- *Direct Mail - Computer Operations:* Developed, coordinated and maintained a comprehensive mailing list to promote jazz festivals and music concerts nationally and locally. Set up, updated and maintained direct mail lists on computer system.
- *Budget Management:* Analyzed and administered operating funds allocated for marketing and publicity. Analyzed budget variances and initiated appropriate strategies to more aggressively control expenditures.
- *Trade Shows & Special Events:* Arranged and designed booths and facilitated trade shows and special events to promote agency and entertainment artists.

Marketing Representative
MTV, California Division, Los Angeles, California - 1989 to 1994
- *Public Relations & Promotions:* Directed overall promotions and marketing operations for MTV events at the University of California. Liaison between MTV Marketing Department in New York and the University of California. Instrumental in coordinating promotional campaigns to promote MTV.
- *Media Relations:* Coordinated all promotional, publicity, and marketing materials which consisted of news releases, brochures, and feature stories.

Marketing Director
Whirlwind Productions, San Francisco, California - 1987 to 1989
- *Marketing for Entertainment Productions:* Directed all marketing operations for music concerts. Organized and booked concerts and special events for the University of California, which involved scheduling all facets of production, lighting and stage crews, equipment, and entertainment personnel. Worked extensively with artists, celebrities, executive entertainment staff members, and entertainment production companies. Reviewed and negotiated contracts and copyrights with entertainment artists and companies.
- *Writing & Editing:* Wrote and edited promotional and advertising materials which consisted of news releases, brochures, flyers, and feature stories.
- *Marketing Management:* Chairperson, responsible for directing overall operations, marketing, and administration of this university in-house production company.
- *Entertainment Sponsors:* Solicited and obtained corporate sponsors for music events. Called on community businesses, organizations and agencies, and personally managed account calls, presentations and negotiations.
- *Budget Management:* Managed and administered a $200,000 annual operating budget.

Skyla Preston
401 Alcoa Street
Studio City, California 93882
(299) 998-9733

Date

Bob Templeton
Director of Marketing
West Coast Marketing Company
9737 Surfside Drive
Portland, Oregon 08833

> Always address your letter to someone specific if at all possible.

Dear Mr. Templeton:

It is my understanding that you are you looking for a highly motivated, goal-oriented **Marketing & Entertainment Industry** professional to become a leader in your organization. An employer of West Coast Marketing Company and a mutual friend, Frank Johnson, recommended that I submit a resume for the position of *Director of Marketing,* Oregon operations. I am confident that, with my background in marketing and promotions, I can significantly contribute to your team of professionals. I have enclosed a personal resume so you may review my credentials.

My areas of expertise and qualifications include the following:

- Six years of comprehensive experience in marketing and promotions encompassing positions as *Marketing Director, Marketing Specialist,* and *Marketing Representative.*
- Excellent writing and editing skills with experience writing news releases, press kits, brochures, feature stories, and direct mail.
- Demonstrated leadership, communication and negotiation skills.
- Proven ability to define issues, propose solutions and implement changes.
- Knowledge of, and experience in, computer systems and applications.
- Strong interpersonal skills with ability to establish and maintain an exemplary network of business associates.

I sincerely believe that, with my experience and career goals, I would be an asset to your organization. I will follow up with a phone call in a few days to request a personal interview. I will be looking forward to discussing how I can significantly contribute to your team of professionals.

Thank you in advance for your time and consideration. I look forward to speaking with you soon.

Sincerely,

Skyla Preston

Resume Enclosed

Gregory Stevens

Gregory Stevens was looking for a high-powered sales position. He had grown as much as he possibly could in his position of Sales Manager for a company that sold Arbitration & Resolution Systems. But, like our other clients, he simply wasn't having any luck getting an interview. He couldn't understand it. Leaning back in a chair, he sighed, "I know you're supposed to keep your resume to one page, so I didn't write very much on it. I didn't want to go to two pages." We looked at his skimpy resume and told him, "That's not true. If you're a professional with a few years of experience, chances are you'll need a two-page resume. It's an old-fashioned idea that you should keep it to one page."

Gregory's was a common mistake. While some individuals can be too wordy, we often find that just the opposite is true—some don't include enough relevant details about their jobs to adequately explain what they've done! As you may have noticed, each of the "Before" examples in this chapter made that error.

To be true to your abilities, you must explore your talents and strengths in depth, and present them in enough detail so the reader will fully understand the scope of your experience. Make sure you include *more* than enough information about yourself and each job you held when you write the first draft of your resume. You can always edit and delete information when you write your final draft. And, of course, proof your resume and cover letter thoroughly several times to make sure there are no errors!

SALES & MARKETING TIP:

Write the first draft of your resume so that you have more information than you need. When writing your final draft, it is better to delete extraneous information you don't need than to finish your resume and realize you didn't write enough.

Gregory Stevens
9800 Taylor Street
Philadelphia, Pennsylvania 39928
(383) 399-2169

OBJECTIVE

Desire a Sales position that will provide an opportunity for career advancement and professional development.

EDUCATION

B.S. - Major: Business Administration
                    PENNSYLVANIA UNIVERSITY

WORK HISTORY

1993 to 1997

Sales Manager, Regional Consultant, Arbitration & Resolution Systems, Inc., Philadelphia, PA. Sold services to individuals and called on judges. Supervised and trained employees.

1992 to 1993

Assistant Manager, Exercise Plus Lockers, Inc., Philadelphia, PA. Helped Manager in all duties.

1988 to 1991

Property Manager, Suburban Properties, Inc., Philadelphia, PA. Managed properties for company. Showed and leased apartments. Handled budget, used computer, and handled legal issues.

PERSONAL

Involved in physical fitness. Works out 5 times a week. Single and age 30. Very willing to travel.

REFERENCES

Furnished upon request.

Gregory Stevens
9800 Taylor Street
Philadelphia, Pennsylvania 39928
(383) 399-2169

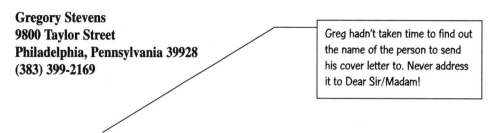

Greg hadn't taken time to find out the name of the person to send his cover letter to. Never address it to Dear Sir/Madam!

Dear Sir/Madam:

I would like to obtain a position in Sales with your company. I have enclosed a resume which outlines my education and experience.

I am single and available to travel as needed. I am looking for a salary of $45,000 with commission.

Thank you for your time.

Sincerely,

Gregory Stevens

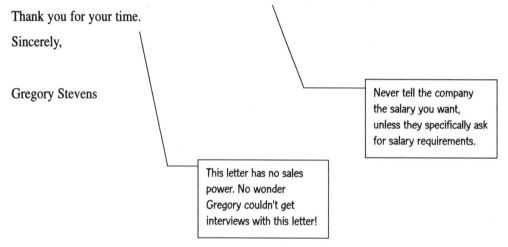

Never tell the company the salary you want, unless they specifically ask for salary requirements.

This letter has no sales power. No wonder Gregory couldn't get interviews with this letter!

GREGORY STEVENS

9800 Taylor Street
Philadelphia, Pennsylvania 39928
(383) 399-2169

> Our version has a much more powerful Objective & Profile, which will interest the reader. It has selling power!

PROFESSIONAL OBJECTIVE & PROFILE

Multi-talented **Sales** professional, with more than 9 years of experience building and leading integrated sales and management operations for major corporations. Strong background in sales, marketing, management, customer service and client relations. Skilled in developing annual financial objectives and preparing long-range strategic business plans. Talented in leading and developing business opportunities and marketing strategies to maximize growth and profitability, and accomplish mission of company.

Desire a **Sales & Marketing** position that will provide a challenging opportunity to significantly contribute to a company's efficiency, organization, growth, and profitability.

EDUCATION

Bachelor of Science in Business Administration
PENNSYLVANIA UNIVERSITY, Philadelphia, Pennsylvania

MOTIVATIONAL TRAINING

Zig Ziglar, Dale Carnegie

> It is a positive to highlight any advanced training or motivational seminars.

PROFESSIONAL EXPERIENCE

Sales Manager
Regional Consultant
ARBITRATION & RESOLUTION SYSTEMS, INC.
Philadelphia, Pennsylvania, - January 1993 to June 1997

- **Sales & Account Management:** Responsible for directing and managing overall sales administration and operations of company. Solicited and obtained new clientele, as well as managed existed accounts. Called on bar associations, executive management staff, and insurance companies as well as former and retired judges to sell and implement *Arbitration & Resolution Systems.*
- **Business Development:** Responsible for managing new business development and strategic planning to maximize growth and profitability. Established growth plans for individual accounts and personally managed account calls, presentations, and negotiations. Presented *Arbitration & Resolution Programs* at Bar Association meetings throughout Pennsylvania.
- **Profitability:** Expanded sales growth of Arbitration & Resolution services in a 5-state region and successfully doubled sales each consecutive year which increased overall profitability for company.
- **Client Relations & Service:** Established and maintained an exemplary network of business associates as a result of extensive interaction and strong communication skills. Followed up on all sales calls to provide attention to detail and superior service.
- **Contract Negotiations:** Negotiated contracts with former and retired judges to promote services exclusively.
- **Employee Training & Supervision:** Responsible for managing, training, and supervising 4 employees. Delegated work responsibilities and monitored overall job performances to ensure adherence to standards, policies and procedures.

GREGORY STEVENS

> Job descriptions are clearly described and easy to read.

PROFESSIONAL EXPERIENCE

Assistant Manager
EXERCISE PLUS LOCKER, INC.
Philadelphia, Pennsylvania - January 1992 to January 1993

- **Management:** Assisted in managing and directing overall operations of retail operations.
- **Sales & Profitability:** In charge of selling merchandise to customers in retail environment and successfully increased sales and profitability for company.
- **Merchandising & Marketing:** Arranged and designed attractive floor and window displays to enhance merchandise and increase sales. Implemented corporate's innovative marketing and advertising strategies into everyday store operations to increase sales.
- **Customer Service:** Provided excellent service to customers by assisting them with merchandise selection and by effectively responding to requests, inquiries, suggestions, and/or concerns.
- **Employee Management:** Interviewed, hired, trained and supervised 2 employees. Assigned job responsibilities and supervised job performances to ensure accuracy and adherence to company policies and procedures.
- **Inventory & Purchasing:** Monitored inventory levels of merchandise and purchased as needed.

Property Manager
SUBURBAN PROPERTIES, INC.
Philadelphia, Pennsylvania - May 1988 to November 1991

- **Management:** Managed 400 residential rental properties in Philadelphia, which involved all facets of operations, employee management, budget, vendor and subcontractor relations, and marketing.
- **Marketing & Advertising:** Responsible for marketing apartment units to prospective tenants. Showed apartments and coordinated leases. Utilized effective marketing strategies to promote rentals and increase occupancy levels.
- **Customer Service:** Provided excellent service to tenants by quickly and efficiently responding to requests, inquiries, suggestions, and/or concerns.
- **Budget Management:** Analyzed and managed a budget for operating expenditures and property projects. Responsible for financial performance analysis and business planning development and functions. Analyzed budget variances and initiated appropriate guidelines to more aggressively control expenditures and increase productivity. Established budget guidelines and operated within budgets. Responsible for all rental collections and bank transactions.
- **Computer Operations:** Installed computer software and was able to more efficiently update and maintain data regarding tenants and finance.
- **Vendor & Subcontractor Relations:** Responsible for negotiating contracts with vendors and suppliers and for hiring subcontractors to perform maintenance and repair services on properties.
- **Legal Procedures:** In charge of performing skip traces and facilitating eviction procedures.

References Available Upon Request

GREGORY STEVENS

9800 Taylor Street
Philadelphia, Pennsylvania 39928
(383) 399-2169

Date

Laura Grant
Director of Sales & Marketing
Socks & Shoes Footwear Company
2083 Aryan Way
Philadelphia, Pennsylvania 39928

> Special qualifications are bulleted so the reader can quickly scan Gregory's accomplishments. This letter is much more powerful than the one Gregory had written for himself (and much more successful in getting him interviews!).

Dear Ms. Grant:

According to your advertisement in last Sunday's edition of *The Pennsylvanian Newspaper,* you are looking for a highly motivated, goal-oriented sales professional at Socks & Shoes Footwear Company. I sincerely believe that I can become a top-notch producer and leader in your company. As requested, I have enclosed a personal resume which will provide you with details concerning my credentials.

My areas of qualification and expertise include the following:

- Dynamic, results- and profit-oriented sales professional with ability to expand business, increase sales, maximize growth, and achieve profitability.
- Solid organizational, management, interpersonal and communications skills with a proven track record of making sound decisions.
- Ability to effectively establish and maintain a strong network of business relationships as a result of extensive experience communicating with executive management staffs, former and retired judges, and bar associations.
- Management and supervisory experience with ability to lead and guide associates to achieve their maximum potential.
- Style that exhibits maturity, leadership, high energy, teamwork, and the ability to relate to a wide variety of people.
- Proven ability to define issues, propose solutions and implement changes.
- Demonstrated communication and negotiation skills.
- Knowledge of, and experience in, computer systems and applications.

I sincerely believe that, with my experience and career aspirations, I would be an asset to your organization. I will be calling within the next few days to arrange a personal interview to discuss how I can best contribute to your company's goals.

Thank you in advance for your time and consideration. I look forward to speaking with you soon.

Sincerely,

Gregory Stevens

Resume Enclosed

4

First Impressions Last Forever

"Hello, I'd Like You to Meet . . ."

You know what it's like when you meet someone for the first time. For example, a friend introduces you to someone you've never met before. "John," your friend says, "I'd like you to meet Ariel. She's the manager of the southeast division of a very successful industrial company." Ariel extends her hand and you offer yours, firmly shaking her hand, noticing that her grip is not too tight nor too flimsy, but *just right.* In a brief moment, you observe that she's about 5'9", slender but not too skinny, she has nice skin, and a pleasing smile, and dresses conservatively, wearing a dark blazer with dark pants. Immediately, you like her. No more than two minutes have passed, but already, both you and she have formed some kind of opinion about each other.

In most situations, we subconsciously form an opinion about someone we just met within a few moments. Unfortunately (or fortunately, whichever the case may be) the old cliché is true—*You don't get a second chance to make a first impression.* Generally, that first impression lasts a lifetime. This isn't always fair, it's just the way it is. First impressions count in everything and everywhere, including resumes. It is commonly agreed among career experts that you have only about 10 seconds to grab someone's attention with your resume. It is vital that you make those 10 seconds count!

SALES & MARKETING TIP:

You don't get a second chance to make a first impression. Make sure yours is a great one!

Good Looks Count

We hear every day that "Looks aren't everything," but in the case of a resume, that's not true. With so little time to grab an employer's attention, looks are a crucial part of *everything.* Of course, once you have the employer's attention, your writing has to be impeccable if you want to hold their attention.

A key feature of the successful sales and marketing resume is not only how it is written, but also how it is presented. Your sales and marketing resume is your sales tool, so it's important that it's presented as a sales presentation. We will discuss several styles of resumes that have proven to be successful time and time again.

In addition to the style of resume, it is also important to pay attention to the way you deliver your resume. In sales and marketing, you can be bold with your deliveries and try different, innovative approaches to getting your resume before the employer. Let the reader be cautioned, however: Use these techniques at your own risk. We have heard amazing success stories, but we have also heard otherwise.

SALES & MARKETING TIP:

You are taking on-the-edge risks when you use creative strategies to reach the decision maker. Find out who the decision maker is and what he or she likes, and do whatever you think he or she would respond to best. Use your imagination!

Our clients have told us some interesting stories about trying to get interviews. Hiring managers have related amusing stories too. For example, one man told us how after having lunch with the sales manager of a major newspaper, he had a good laugh when he received a resume in a colorful pop-up book form. He said it would have been great if the candidate was applying for a design position or a children's book writer's position, but for an executive sales job, it was inappropriate. (The hiring manager believed this candidate belonged in a much more creative environment.)

When in doubt, be conservative. If you do decide to take on-the-edge risks, make sure you do your homework and are confident that the recipient will appreciate a more daring approach. Whatever you do that's extraordinary, make sure it relates to the employer's (the hiring manager's, sales director's, etc.) personality and interests so that you achieve maximum positive impact!

Some Innovative, On-the-Edge Risks and Approaches to Get Noticed

1. Send your resume by balloon-o-gram! What employer wouldn't enjoy the novelty and creativity involved in having a resume delivered by a balloon? One of our clients told us that she had her resume delivered to a potential employer this way and when they interviewed her, they told her it was one of the most creative methods used to get their attention that they had ever seen. They hired her on the spot!

2. Federal Express your resume to the key contact at the company. Nothing makes an employer feel as special as having someone Fed-Ex a resume specifically to him or her. The employer knows you're serious about the job and that you won't take any risk of not getting your resume into the *right* hands. You've already made a head start in building a relationship with this employer.

3. Send your resume as a singing telegram. (Use the singing as a way to introduce you, like a cover letter. Don't have the talent sing your whole resume. That could be annoying.) Again, this is a clever, attention-grabbing way to make the employer notice and *remember* you!

4. Send your resume with lunch. Call and find out what your potential employer likes to eat for lunch and have it delivered—with your resume! One client said that he called the President of a company to find out what the Director of Sales liked to eat for lunch. The President said sushi. The candidate arranged to have a table reserved for the Director of Sales at a popular sushi bar, and had his resume waiting on the table. Needless to say, this Director of Sales was very impressed and immediately called him to ask him for an interview.

5. Send your resume as a video! This is a new, unique approach to submitting a resume, and may be used more

in the future as companies become more high-tech and busy. It actually requires a high level of marketing savvy and good public speaking skills on your part. (But if you're in sales, then you probably have great public speaking skills, right?) You can locate a production house to set up the taping of a video resume by checking your local library, career counselor, or phone book for the name of one in your area. On the video you simply tell the potential employer about your accomplishments and abilities. You've all seen videos that sell products, right? It's one of the most effective methods used by network marketing companies today. They distribute videos that highlight their products to potential sales representatives and customers and effectively sell their products. You will be using a video to sell yourself as the product.

6. E-mail your resume! There are still bugs to work out in this system, so we recommend sending a hard copy of your resume in addition to the e-mail version. If you do decide to send it via e-mail, call the company first to find out what type of software they use.

7. Send your resume on a disk. Call the company to find out what type of computers and software they use. Make sure your disk is compatible with theirs. We still recommend sending a hard copy of your resume, even if you do send the disk. An employer can't carry your resume (on disk) with him or her.

8. Send a basket of flowers with your resume attached.

9. Send a box of candy or a box of homemade chocolate chip cookies with your resume attached (if you've discovered the decision maker loves sweets)!

10. Actually call the company and do some research. Find out what your potential employer has a particular fondness for, and use that to attach your resume. It could be a variety of things, including a golf putter, tickets to a sports event or the theater, gourmet coffee, etc.

Different Styles of Resumes

Generally, there are three different styles of resumes: one-page, two- to three-page, and brochure. Many people think that they must limit their resumes to one page, but that's not true. In today's busy, hectic world, employers want to see more about you on a resume than before. They don't have time to call you in for an interview if they don't think you possess the qualifications they're seeking. Sometimes, a one-page resume simply isn't long enough to fully describe your special talents and skills. Employers are realistic and know that if you've accomplished much at all in your life, you need a two-page resume.

If you are using a one-page resume to send to multiple employers, always add on the bottom that a more comprehensive portfolio is available upon request. If employers are interested, they may call you for this more extensive portfolio. That's when it's important to have a brochure on hand.

In the following section, we'll describe the different styles of resume and the pros and cons of each.

Important Facts for Compiling Your Sales & Marketing Resume

1. Always put your phone number and address on the resume. You'd be surprised at how many people forget to include their phone numbers. Make it as easy as possible for an employer to contact you. If you have an e-mail address, fax, cellular phone, and/or pager, include these too!

2. Do write an Objective and Career Profile at the top of your resume. This is important, for it's the first thing an employer will read, and it relates in a brief 5 seconds the most important things about you and why you should be called for an interview. It is definitely okay to use the first person when writing the Objective and Career Profile. However, for the rest of the resume, write in third person. Use first person only when writing an Objective.

3. Use only one or two fonts when writing the resume. Using multiple fonts will distract from your message, and you may lose your potential employer's interest. Generally, the fonts that are easiest to read are New Times Roman, Hiroshige, Arial, or fonts used in printing books and periodicals.

4. Use a 10 or 11 point font size for general text, and a 13 or 14 point size for headings and special sections. Anything smaller is hard to read and may actually get your resume tossed in the trash can!

5. Be consistent in all the **bolding** of titles and in *italicizing* special points in the resume.

6. Make sure there is plenty of white space in your resume. A resume that has no margins looks cluttered and wordy. Make sure the margins are wide enough to make a nice, appealing design.

7. Use the entire page. Don't submit 1½ pages or 2½ pages. Keep your resume balanced, no matter what style you decide to use.

8. Don't use photos or graphics unless they're appropriate. If you are including forms or graphics about sales accomplishments, then you may want to design interesting graphs to illustrate sales. However, put these on a separate sheet to include in your portfolio; don't put them on the resume itself.

9. Use a high-grade resume paper in a conservative color: light gray, light blue, beige, or cream. White tends to be rather dull and not very effective when you're trying to grab someone's attention.

10. Center or align text to make your resume balanced and pleasing to the eye!

A Brochure Sales Presentation Resume

One of the most effective long version resumes you can use in a sales and marketing career is the brochure resume. It is basically a two-page resume that is copied onto 11 × 17-inch paper and folded into 8½ × 11-inch so it opens up like a booklet. It is your sales presentation; just as you would use a brochure to sell a product, this brochure is used to sell you! It really is a powerful visual presentation and an excellent sales tool. We have illustrated how you can make your own.

Making the Brochure Resume

On three 8½ × 11-inch sheets, print out your cover page and two-page resume. Take an 11 × 17-inch sheet of nice resume paper and run it through the copier so only the cover page is copied on one half. Then turn the 11 × 17-inch sheet over and run it through the copier again so the two pages of the resume are copied onto the two inside sides of the 11 × 17-inch sheet. Plan on experimenting a few times until you get it to copy just as you want.

Making the Brochure Resume

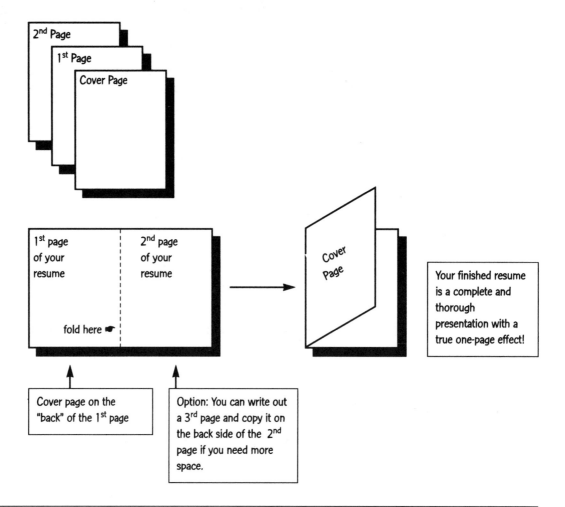

Pros and Cons of Different Resume Lengths

One-Page Resume

PROS

- Easy to read and handle
- Cost-effective to mail in large quantities
- Excellent for a brief summary of credentials
- Good for young professionals with limited experience

CONS

- Not detailed enough
- May seem or be incomplete

Two-Page Resume

PROS
- Thorough and detailed
- Plenty of room to expand on relevant experience

CONS
- Cumbersome to handle two sheets
- More difficult to mail

Brochure Resume

PROS
- Thorough and detailed
- Plenty of room to expand on relevant experience
- Option to go to a third page
- Convenience and ease of a one-page resume

CONS
- More costly
- More cumbersome and expensive to prepare and mail

The Internet—Electronic Resumes

The Internet and the Information Age will definitely revolutionize the way some employers find candidates in the future, but it will never eliminate the need for an attractively designed and well-written visual sales presentation! You will always need your sales brochure for those initial face-to-face interviews and to sell yourself effectively.

Even in sales and marketing, you may be asked to submit a resume for scanning into a large employer database. Some large employers keep all their incoming resumes on a large database by scanning each resume they receive into their system. The only difference between a scannable resume and your presentation resume is that the scanned resume is printed in a basic Times Roman or Courier font without the use of any bolding, underlines, or italics. If you know that a company scans resumes, send them a scannable resume, and then send a nice presentation copy to the key contact person—the person doing the actual hiring. In this instance, it would probably be the Director, Vice President, or President of Sales and Marketing. Always research the company to find out this person's name before you send your resume. It's much more effective to send it to the person who is actually the decision maker. So send a resume that can be scanned into a database for the Human Resources Department, but submit a presentation resume to the actual decision maker.

In addition to a scannable version, you may have an occasion to send an electronic version of your resume with your e-mail on the Internet. This is an inexpensive way to submit a resume, but not always the most effective. If you choose to attach your resume to an e-mail, you must remember that you have no control over what readers actually see once they receive the resume. They may not use the same computer system or fonts as you, and your resume may lose some of the text enhancements and spacing. To avoid this headache, send your resume in a file that is in a universal text format, or write your resume as an original e-mail instead of attaching it to an e-mail message.

We have by no means even scratched the surface of job searching electronically and on the Internet, and we do recommend more in-depth study of this form of job seeking. From a sales and marketing standpoint, your resume will be written with the same principles covered throughout this book whether you are submitting it by mail or by e-mail.

Since resume scanning technology is widely used in larger companies, we've provided an illustration of how this kind of resume differs in format. Once a resume is scanned into a system, it is found and identified by key words that are included in the resume. If a company needs a new Marketing Manager, they search their database for all the resumes that have the phrase *Marketing Manager* in them. The computer prints out all the resumes that could be considered for this position.

This method saves the company great expense in paper filing systems and staff time. The resume displayed here has been converted for scanning by simply removing all the bolding, underlines, and italics that would confuse the computer. Generally speaking, scanners like white paper, black ink, one type size (10 to 12 point), and one type style (Times Roman or Courier) with no text enhancements.

VITUS WONG
392 Stephens Road
Newfield, New Jersey 03002
(609) 903-8923

Career Profile in Marketing Management

Committed, profit-oriented Marketing Manager, with 12 years of experience building and leading integrated marketing operations for major corporation. Consistently successful in conceptualizing, developing, and spearheading innovative marketing and promotional strategies/campaigns that expand market penetration and yield company profitability. Excellent analytical, planning, organizational and negotiation skills. Skilled executive liaison with extensive experience networking with media, vendors, subcontractors and nationwide field offices.

Strong general management qualifications in strategic planning. Talented in developing annual financial objectives and preparing long-range strategic business plans. Solid organizational, management, interpersonal and communications skills with proven track record of making sound decisions.

Desire a career opportunity in marketing management that will provide a challenging avenue to significantly contribute to a company's efficiency, organization, growth, and profitability.

Summary of Qualifications
Track Record of Success:
Background exemplifies a successful track record of career accomplishments which includes 12 years of experience at the Wall Street Journal. Consistently advanced throughout career to position of Marketing Manager.

Marketing & Promotions:
Held full decision-making authority for developing and implementing nationwide marketing programs. Skilled in conceptualizing, developing and implementing comprehensive marketing and promotional programs through implementation of various media designed to achieve results. Worked extensively with field offices to coordinate corporate marketing strategies to expand sales and profitability.

Team Building:
Organized and implemented unified approach with field offices toward advertising and promotions. Encouraged and supported a teamlike work environment across the country which increased employee morale, productivity and efficiency. Facilitated numerous meetings and spoke before large and small groups.

Budget Management:
Successfully analyzed multimillion dollar budgets and initiated appropriate strategies to more aggressively control expenditures. Prepared future budgets based on previous year's performance.

Professional Affiliation
American Marketing Association

Advanced Training
WALL STREET JOURNAL
Dow Jones & Company, Inc., Princeton, New Jersey
Numerous Seminars, Conferences and Classes in Management, Marketing, Forecasting & Analysis, Computer Software, etc.

Marketing Manager
WALL STREET JOURNAL
Dow Jones & Company, Inc.
Princeton, New Jersey - 1985 to May 1997

Refer back to Chapter 2 to see how Vitus' resume looked before conversion to a scannable resume.

Company Track Record of Success: Began in 1985 as a Statistical Analyst and continuously advanced to positions of higher levels of authority and responsibility due to outstanding job performance. Promoted to Marketing Assistant and then to Marketing Manager.

Marketing Management: Directed and managed overall administration and operations of marketing operations nationwide. Developed business opportunities and marketing strategies to maximize growth and profitability, expand market penetration, and accomplish mission of integrated operations. Traveled throughout the U.S. to coordinate and implement marketing and promotions campaigns in field offices.

Public Speaking: Liaison between home office and field personnel in the U.S. Spoke in front of large and small groups at field offices and presented information regarding marketing and promotional campaigns generated at the home office. Outlined marketing goals and analyzed long-term strategic planning.

Budget Management: Developed and administered $6 million operating budget for marketing. Analyzed budget variances and initiated appropriate strategies to more aggressively control expenditures. Prepared future years' budgets based on previous expenditures and changes in organizational structures.

Forecasting & Analysis: Responsible for researching, forecasting and analyzing radio and T.V. markets to determine profitability ratios.

Market Research: Coordinated market research activities, tracked and maintained database and competitor information, and assisted with product/service development and marketing strategies.

Direct Mail: Planned strategic direct mail campaigns targeted to nationwide consumer markets. Worked with advertising staff and freelancers to write, develop and produce direct mail literature.

Promotions & Advertising: Conceptualized, developed and implemented innovative promotional and advertising programs/campaigns through implementation of various media designed to achieve desired results. Planned and developed P.O.S. (point-of-sale) materials for retail businesses. Significantly increased business and company profitability.

Vendors & Subcontractors: Worked with outside vendors, subcontractors, and freelance writers to produce promotional and advertising materials including media kits, rate cards, brochures, print advertising, and broadcast commercials. Monitored job performance to ensure accuracy and adherence to specifications.

Media Buying: Interacted closely with major advertising agencies to research, analyze and buy advertising time on radio and television.

Media Relations: Established and maintained an excellent network of business associates with media personnel as a result of extensive interaction and strong communication skills.

Personnel & Supervision: Interviewed and hired Marketing Assistant. Delegated work responsibilities, supervised and evaluated job performance. Trained Marketing Assistant in all areas of marketing and promotions.

Now that we have discussed the different styles of resumes, it's time to look at the power cover letter and other materials you need in your job search, including the Salary History, Follow-Up Letter, and Thank-You Letter. These are all instrumental in selling you. In Chapter 5, we discuss these letters and explain why they're important sales tools.

5

Right Down to the Letter!

Killer Sales & Marketing Letters

Almost everyone knows that it's essential to send a cover letter with every resume. The cover letter introduces you to your client, your potential employer. It is one of your most important sales tools. In fact, it is even more important than the resume itself, according to 60% of managers surveyed by Accountemps, an international temporary staffing service based in Menlo Park, California. In today's tough job market, an employer may not even read your resume if your letter is weak. In the sales and marketing field, it's even more crucial to have an empowered, aggressive sales letter.

What to Include in Your Sales & Marketing Letter

1. Always include your phone number and address in the cover letter. We are always surprised when people neglect to do this. Never forget this common-sense rule: Make it as easy as possible for the employer to contact you!

2. Include an e-mail address or pager number if you have one. Again, this makes it easier for the employer to contact you.

3. Never address a letter *To Whom It May Concern* or *Dear Sir or Madam!* How cold and impersonal! Always call the company to find out the name of the person who will read your letter. (The exception is when the company clearly states "No calls.") An employer notices if you've

taken the time to do a little research and find out who the decision maker is.

4. Be specific about the job you're interested in. A major company may have several openings and have no idea which one you're targeting.

5. Write an interesting, attention-grabbing opening in the letter. Don't begin with the usual, *boring,* "This letter is in response to the advertisement . . ." Do you want to put employers to sleep before they even get to the resume? Do some research to find out what's going on in the company and use this information as an interesting opener, such as "I just read in the *Wall Street Journal* that your company had a record year in sales. When I saw your ad for a District Sales Manager, I knew at once that I could contribute to your dynamic sales team!"

6. Use bullets to draw the reader's eye to your qualifications. Sometimes, key points are buried in a letter and hard to find. Bullets eliminate that problem.

7. If an employer asks for salary requirements, it's best to write at the bottom of your letter, "Salary Negotiable." You don't want to overprice or underprice yourself. However, if you won't negotiate salary, then ask people in the industry to estimate what the employer is offering, and then be specific about your requirements. Don't use too broad a range in required salary; keep it between $5,000 and $10,000.

8. End your letter on an action-oriented, proactive note such as, "I will call you within a week to schedule an appointment." Remember—in sales, you must be aggressive!

When composing the cover letter, remember that it's a sales letter! Letting the company know that you know a little about them will make them feel special. Always research the company and let them know that you are aware of their expansions, problems, interests, or priorities. This makes a hiring manager feel that you are truly interested in the company and not just a job.

Explain your qualifications and skills that meet the company's needs or requirements. Be enthusiastic and aggressive about the company. If you have a good idea that would be beneficial in some way to the company, by all means mention it!

> **SALES & MARKETING TIP:**
>
> Your Sales and Marketing Cover Letter may actually be more important than the Resume itself. It serves as a powerful sales tool and must entice the reader to want to read your resume!

Explain any unique talents or accomplishments that set you apart from all the others who send in their resumes. For example, if the position is in international sales in France and you speak fluent French, state that in both your resume and the cover letter.

Incorporate a positive attitude in the cover letter. Project warmth and friendliness. Remember, this letter is going to be read by an actual person; don't treat that person like a robot.

Always emphasize what you can do for them, not what they can do for you!

Take the initiative in setting up an appointment. Clearly ask for an interview, and then announce that you'll call the office to arrange a meeting.

Keep your letter to one page. A two- or three-page letter is simply not appropriate. That's why you have a resume!

Always keep in mind that you are marketing yourself to a potential client (employer). If the cover letter does not create a sense of excitement and entice the reader, then it's probably a waste of your time to have written it, as well as a waste of time for the reader to read it! This potential client (employer) has probably read a zillion cover letters and resumes before yours. The reader is probably tired of the same old introductions, *"This letter is in response to your recent advertisement. . . ."* Be fresh and exciting! Be aggressive and assertive! Show this potential client (employer) that you are different and that you know how to *sell!* Be specific in telling employers how they will benefit if they hire you. This is imperative. List your top achievements in the cover letter. Just as you would tell a potential client the benefits of a product you're selling, you want to emphasize the benefits of hiring *you. You* are the product in this case!

We have included Sales and Marketing Cover Letters with several of the resumes in other chapters. Review them to see how they follow the guidelines we have outlined here. On the following pages are four more killer Sales and Marketing Cover Letters that illustrate our points and can be used as specific guides for writing your own cover letter.

MARIA SEPULVEDA
232 Orion Court
Chicago, Illinois 27222
(514) 223-9987

Date

John Templeton
Director of International Sales
International Headquarters
Thompson's Medical & Pharmaceutical Global Corporation
272 Dougal Street
New York, New York

> The letter is correctly addressed to a specific individual, who is the key decision maker for this job.

Dear Mr. Templeton:

It is my understanding that you are looking for a multilingual **International Marketing Executive** to become a leader of your South American sales operations. I recently read in the *Wall Street Journal* that Thompson's Medical & Pharmaceutical Global Corporation exceeded all sales projections last year by 67%, and has become a leader in the medical and pharmaceutical industry. I am confident that I can significantly contribute to your team of sales professionals and have enclosed a personal resume for your review.

In addition to a Master's of International Business Degree from the University of Arizona, I also have more than 20 years of experience encompassing positions in management, sales, and marketing. My qualifications and areas of expertise include the following:

- Experienced in spearheading the development, expansion, and growth of an international marketing department for Svenson's Worldwide Medical Corporation throughout the world, and have increased sales 78% globally.
- Multilingual with fluent reading and speaking skills in Spanish, French, English, and German.
- Grew up in Ecuador and traveled extensively throughout South America.
- Strong interpersonal skills with ability to effectively communicate with diverse cultures all over the world.
- Proven track record in strategic planning, business analysis and development, and all facets of sales and marketing.
- Proactive leader who empowers employees to achieve their maximum potential.

I sincerely believe that, with my experience and career aspirations, I could be an asset to your organization. I will follow up this letter and resume with a phone call, so we can arrange to meet. I would like to discuss with you plans for developing your business into the South American market. I believe I can offer valuable insights about the culture and economic structure.

Thank you for your time. I will speak with you soon.

Sincerely,

> Special Qualifications are bulleted to draw the eye to this important information.

Maria Sepulveda

Resume Enclosed
Salary Negotiable

> She didn't underprice or overprice herself with salary requirements.

ISSIM NWANKWO
198 Adams Drive
Houston, Texas 44982
(676) 204-3030

Date

Russell Holiday
Vice President of Sales & Marketing
American Airlines
24995 Cactus Street
Dallas, Texas 40053

> Do be specific about any sales accomplishments you've achieved. This is not the time to be shy!

Dear Mr. Holiday:

I am a profit-oriented **Sales Manager,** who would like to become a leader at American Airlines. I recently read an ad in the *Houston Newspaper* that advertised a Sales Management position at American Airlines. My background clearly exemplifies a track record of success and I am confident that I can be successful in developing sales for American Airlines. I have enclosed a personal resume so you may review my qualifications.

In addition to a *Bachelor of Science in Business Administration* from Texas University in Houston, I also have more than 19 years of professional experience. My qualifications and areas of expertise include the following:

- Managed and directed overall sales operations for a $100 million district for Delta Airlines. Exceeded all sales goals and increased local sales more than $20 million, which significantly increased company profitability.
- Held full decision-making authority for a region which exceeded $1.6 billion annually.
- Totally reengineered sales & marketing operations which involved hiring and training national sales staff.
- Developed an innovative marketing plan that maximized growth and profitability by expanding market penetration.
- Financial and analytical expertise in budget development, forecasting, and management.
- Effective team-building skills with ability to empower associates to achieve their maximum potential.
- Multilingual with fluent reading and speaking skills in English, French, and Spanish.

I am confident that I will be an asset to your organization, and would like to contact you to set up an appointment following receipt of this letter and resume. I have outlined some strategic sales and marketing plans, which I think will be beneficial to American Airlines, and look forward to discussing these with you.

Thank you in advance for your time and consideration.

Sincerely,

> Notice this proactive approach to setting up an interview!

Issim Nwankwo

Resume Enclosed

Brigette Adams
454 Larksmore Drive
Seattle, Washington, 44200
(880) 343-9399
brig.adams@aol.com

Date

Ellen Shriver
Executive President of Marketing
HERTZ Corporation
20003 Daniel Street
Seattle, Washington 30003

> Do mention how you know of an opening, and if an employee recommended you, be sure to mention that person's name!

Dear Ms. Shriver:

Steven Ward, a friend of mine and a Sales Representative at Hertz Corporation, suggested that I submit a resume to you for the position of **Marketing Director.** I am excited about this position because I have kept abreast of Hertz's innovative marketing strategies to expand business within the next 5 years. I am confident that, with my 10 years of experience as *Director of Marketing* at Avis Corporation, I could be an integral member of your team and could significantly contribute to Hertz's efforts.

I hold a *Bachelor of Science in Business Administration & Marketing* from Washington State University, and have had tremendous success in my sales and marketing endeavors. My qualifications and areas of expertise include the following:

- Broke all company sales records at Avis as a result of dynamic client relations skills and strong networking abilities.
- Increased sales by 77% within one year by developing innovative marketing strategies to expand sales territory.
- Restructured sales and marketing operations that yielded significant company profitability the first year as Director of Marketing.
- Talented in developing business opportunities and marketing strategies to expand market penetration, maximize growth and profitability and accomplish mission of company.
- Demonstrated leadership skills with ability to motivate and inspire employees to work together as a team to produce top results.
- Solid organizational, interpersonal and communications skills with a proven track record of making sound decisions.
- Proven success in all areas of marketing, management, and client relations.

I am confident that, with my experience and skills, I would be an asset to Hertz Corporation. I will telephone you within the next week to arrange a time for an interview so we can discuss how I can best contribute to your goals.

Thank you in advance for your time and consideration. I look forward to our meeting.

Sincerely,

Brigette Adams

Resume Enclosed

Petro Xoinis
43003 Barbera Street
San Francisco, California 00300
(403) 293-2993

Date

Janelle Hudson
Director of Sales & Marketing
Coast Communications Service, Inc.
2202 Hillsboro Street
Los Angeles, California 73893

A strong, powerful, and unique first sentence will certainly get the employer's attention! This sentence is a dynamic sales tool in itself and displays a daring, on-the-edge risk in writing a sales letter.

Dear Ms. Hudson:

My *"What if I owned the business?"* approach to cost control and profitability makes me a valuable asset in any company. I would now like to use this approach as your next **Sales & Marketing Manager,** the position advertised in the *San Francisco Newspaper* last Sunday. I am confident that, with my extensive sales and marketing management experience, I could significantly contribute to your company's goals.

My areas of qualification and expertise include the following:

- More than 15 years of experience managing and directing sales and marketing operations for the San Francisco Communications Company.
- Expanded operations to include northern California, Oregon and Washington, and tripled over-all sales revenue, which resulted in profitability increase of more than $3 million.
- Continuously make a positive bottom-line difference while fostering excellent employee relations and maintaining a high profile in the industry and business community.
- Personal commitment to quality and excellence.
- Strong skills in initiating business start-up operations, analyzing market potential and expanding territories.

I will telephone you next week so we can arrange a personal meeting to discuss how I can contribute to your company's goals and profitability. I am excited about this opportunity and look forward to our meeting.

Sincerely,

Petro Xoinis

Resume Enclosed

Always be assertive about taking the next step.

The Salary History

One rule in the resume world is that you never submit a Salary History unless the employer asks for it. If the employer does request a Salary History, then it is imperative that you send it in order to be considered for the job.

You can use the Salary History to your advantage. Since you want to be aggressive in all the materials you submit to a potential employer, remember to use each piece as a sales tool. Emphasize one significant accomplishment in your Salary History. Make everything count that the employer reads. Instead of simply listing annual salaries for each job, include one accomplishment that you achieved at each company. That refocuses readers on your special skills and talents and is very effective in making them remember you! On the following page is a sample of a Salary History that includes accomplishments.

Petro Xoinis
43003 Barbera Street
San Francisco, California 00300
(403) 293-2993

Salary History

Sales & Marketing Manager
SAN FRANCISCO COMMUNICATIONS COMPANY
San Francisco, California - 1982 to 1997
Accomplishment
Expanded operations to include northern California, Oregon and Washington, and tripled overall sales revenue, which resulted in profitability increase of more than $3 million.
$75,000 Annual Salary
Plus Company Car, Bonuses, Profit-Sharing
and Employee Benefits

Sales Representative
DIGITAL COMMUNICATIONS COMPANY
San Francisco, California - 1979 to 1982
Accomplishment
Expanded sales territory and increased overall sales by
75% the first year, which resulted in an increase of more than $125,000 in profits.
$62,000 Annual Salary
Plus Employee Benefits & Bonuses

> The last two or three jobs are all you need to list on the Salary History. It is not important to list jobs that you had earlier in your career unless they are significant.

The Follow-Up Letter

Some of you may wonder what a follow-up letter is. It's actually a second cover letter. For example, suppose an employer went on vacation at the same time you sent your cover letter and resume. Perhaps the secretary took the letter and resume and filed them somewhere. Perhaps they were lost. When the employer returns from vacation, your resume and cover letter are nowhere to be found. So, it's important that you send a follow-up letter and resume . . . just in case! Remember these guidelines:

Guidelines for a Follow-Up Letter

1. If you've sent someone a resume and cover letter and haven't heard anything for ten days or so, then it's a great idea to send a follow-up letter. The person you sent the letter and resume to could have been out sick, traveling on business, or on vacation; or maybe your documents were simply misplaced!

2. Most people never think about sending a follow-up letter, so you immediately stand out from the competition when you send one.

3. In the follow-up letter, simply reiterate your qualifications and skills, and again suggest a meeting. It's a second chance to sell yourself, so take the opportunity and do it!

On the following page is a sample follow-up letter for our friend Vitus, who has been featured throughout this book.

VITUS WONG
392 Stephens Road
Newfield, New Jersey 03002
(609) 903-8923

Date

Judith Shaverdian
Executive Director of Marketing
The New York Times
21st Avenue
New York, New York 99303

In the follow-up letter, it is a good idea to reemphasize your qualifications and accomplishments, in case your initial letter was lost or misplaced.

Dear Ms. Shaverdian:

Approximately two weeks ago, I submitted a resume for your review. Having received no reply, I am enclosing a second resume in case my previous correspondence was lost or misplaced. I would like to reiterate that I am a highly skilled, goal-oriented **Marketing Manager** and would like to become a leader in your organization.

My qualifications and areas of expertise include the following:

- Ability to conceptualize, develop and initiate comprehensive nationwide marketing campaigns for *The Wall Street Journal* to expand market penetration and increase sales.
- Effective team-building skills. Strong motivator and leader with ability to empower associates to work together as a team to achieve maximum results.
- Talented public speaker with experience traveling nationwide to corporate field offices to organize and coordinate innovative marketing strategies. Spoke in front of large and small groups to provide information regarding marketing strategies.
- Extensive business networking expertise. Continuously built and maintained an exemplary network of business associates as a result of interaction between media, subcontractors, suppliers and businesses.
- Financial and analytical expertise in budget development, forecasting and management.
- Demonstrated leadership, communication and negotiation skills.
- Proven ability to define issues, propose solutions, and implement changes.
- Knowledge and experience in computer systems and applications including Excel, Lotus, Word and Mainframe for Data.

I sincerely believe that, with my experience and career aspirations, I would be an asset to your organization. I would like to request a personal interview at your earliest convenience to discuss how I can contribute to your company's goals.

Thank you in advance for your time and consideration. I look forward to speaking with you soon.

Sincerely,

Vitus Wong

Resume Enclosed

When a Thank-You Letter Isn't Enough

Most candidates know that it's important to send a Thank-You letter after the interview, but you should do *more* than just send a Thank-You letter. You should also telephone the person you had an interview with. Since everyone else is sending just a note after an interview, calling will help you stand out from the competition.

Imagine an employer receiving a note that says, "Thank you for meeting with me, Mr. Stansfield. I sincerely believe I possess the qualifications you're seeking for this position, and I hope to hear from you soon." The employer then stacks this Thank-You note with the others that have been arriving all week.

It has become very common to send Thank-You notes after an interview. Job seekers have become more sophisticated in their job search strategies, but this particular strategy has become so common that it no longer makes much of an impact. The employer who interviewed you *expects* to receive a Thank-You note and may regard it as very commonplace. As a prospective employee, you gain no advantage for your effort. Therefore, especially in sales and marketing, it's vitally important for you to do more than the other candidates are doing.

First, let's discuss how to write a proper Thank-You note. Then we'll discuss what more you can do to make that employer remember you!

Writing a Proper Thank-You Note

1. Write your Thank-You letter within 48 hours of your interview.

2. In the opening paragraph of your Thank-You letter, express your appreciation for the interview and let the employer know that you enjoyed meeting him or her and discussing employment opportunities.

3. In the second paragraph, reinforce your understanding of the job's requirements and how you can fulfill the company's needs. Highlight your special qualifications and reemphasize your strengths.

4. In a third paragraph, you might suggest ways that you could contribute to the company's goals. This shows that you've given it some thought and are truly interested in the position.

5. In closing, mention that you're available to discuss your ideas and strategies at a further meeting. Mention that you will follow up with a phone call to ensure that he or she received this note. Do everything possible to keep the door open for another meeting.

VITUS WONG
392 Stephens Road
Newfield, New Jersey 03002
(609) 903-8923

> In your Thank-You letter, mention anything special about your qualifications that make you more perfect for this job than someone else!

Date

Judith Shaverdian
Executive Director of Marketing
The New York Times
21st Avenue
New York, New York 99303

Dear Ms. Shaverdian:

This letter is to thank you for our recent interview concerning a Marketing Management position at the *New York Times*. It was a pleasure meeting you and discussing employment opportunities.

As I mentioned to you in our meeting, I am an experienced Marketing Manager and take pride in my track record of success throughout my career. I work well with all types of individuals and it is this teamwork approach toward my employees that has made me successful. I am confident that I could successfully expand sales by utilizing innovative marketing approaches.

Again, thank you for our meeting. If you have any additional questions concerning my qualifications, please do not hesitate to contact me. I'll be looking forward to hearing from you again soon.

Sincerely,

Vitus Wong

Petro Xoinis
43003 Barbera Street
San Francisco, California 00300
(403) 293-2993

Date

Janelle Hudson
Director of Sales & Marketing
Coast Communications Service, Inc.
2202 Hillsboro Street
Los Angeles, California 73893

> This Thank-You letter reemphasizes qualities that would be beneficial to the company.

Dear Ms. Hudson:

I appreciate the time you gave me yesterday afternoon. I thoroughly enjoyed meeting you and discussing employment opportunities. I felt our meeting was both enjoyable and informative.

After thinking about your Sales & Marketing Management position and the goals set for it by headquarters, I'm confident that I would be able to meet and exceed those numbers. As we discussed, I've had extensive experience in building and expanding sales territories for San Francisco Communications Company and I tripled overall sales, which resulted in a profitability increase of more than $3 million. My record has been stellar, with numerous awards and bonuses for outstanding increases in revenues and new accounts.

I consider your Sales & Marketing Management position to be consistent with my plans for growth. Additionally, your company is a leader in the industry, with an outstanding reputation for rewarding top producers, and I believe this job would be an excellent career move for me.

Again, thanks for the meeting, and I will telephone you soon to ensure receipt of this note.

Sincerely,

Petro Xoinis

The Important Telephone Call

It's now time for the telephone call, which plays an integral role in getting you that *second* interview, and the job! Without a considerate phone call, your Thank-You letter will more than likely be forgotten. Before calling your potential employer, do some research about the company, which will give you an advantage in the phone conversation. Then, five to seven days after mailing your Thank-You letter, telephone the person you interviewed with, to "make sure my note was received."

SALES & MARKETING TIP:

Take an aggressive, assertive approach after you've had one interview. Send a Thank-You letter, and then follow up with a phone call. This is a great way to win a second interview!

Of course, once you telephone the interviewer, he or she will tell you that your note was received. This is another opportunity for you to talk to the employer and make an impression. Remember, your competition is probably still at home, sitting by the phone and hoping to hear from the employer. You've taken an aggressive, assertive approach and contacted the employer yourself. You now have the opportunity to deepen your relationship and move ahead of other applicants by engaging the employer in an interesting, stimulating conversation.

This is the time to discuss anything concerning the position that might still be unclear to you. It also gives the employer the opportunity to ask you any questions that he or she has thought about. It's good to ask an insightful question about the job, the sales and marketing department, or the company itself. If you've heard anything significant about the company through your preliminary research—any plans for developing business or marketing strategies—discuss these with the employer at this time.

Introduce a topic that piques the employer's interest and opens the door for you to have a meaningful conversation that will be remembered. If you noticed golf clubs in his or her office and you're a golf lover, bring this up! Finding that mutual interest will form a bond between the two of you. Take one step further and suggest that you and the employer arrange a second meeting to discuss additional strategies for the new position or another topic that you're both interested in. Or, if you want to discuss a mutual interest, such as golf, invite the employer out for lunch. You're a salesperson; be aggressive and sell yourself! If you're successful in arranging a second interview, you'll gain an enormous advantage over other applicants.

You can't always count on getting a second interview, but by making follow-up phone calls, you'll strengthen your relationship with the person doing the hiring and will be more likely to become the leading contender. Let the other applicants sit hopefully by the telephone while you're aggressively building a relationship with the person who can hire you.

6

And the Final Contestants Are . . .

We Proudly Introduce Our Sales & Marketing Contestants

Pursuing a sales and marketing position is just like being a contestant in a game show. You are a contestant competing for the grand prize—the job. In this final chapter, we look at a wide variety of sales and marketing professionals and define five different types of sales and marketing positions: Closers, Relationship Builders, Hungry for Success, Team Builders, and Creative Think Tanks. While all sales and marketing professionals have similar responsibilities, some skills are more prevalent in certain types of positions. Which type is the best fit with your skills and experience?

CLOSERS: Just Sign on the Bottom Line, Please!

Most sales professionals are Closers. They are big-time, hard-nosed sales professionals who close big deals and bring in the checks for their employers. Without them, the company won't make any money. Without them, no one gets a paycheck. They are vital to a company or organization. It doesn't matter how well you can mingle with others or talk the lingo. If you can't close the deal, then you're not a very effective sales professional. These professionals thrive on competition and are often paid extremely well for their performance. Usually they receive a salary plus a commission. The higher the commission, the more motivated the sales professional. Resumes for these sales professionals illustrate the productivity and ability of the candidate to negotiate successful deals for the company. Closers include most **Account Executives** and **Sales Representatives** because most of them have to close deals. These Closers could sell anything—copiers, life insurance, automobiles, pharmaceuticals, airplanes, whatever! Whatever they're selling, they will get the bottom line signed.

RELATIONSHIP BUILDERS: How About a Game of Golf?

All salespeople build relationships, especially **Sales Managers**, **Directors** and **Account Executives.** Even associates in retail sales and automobile sales build relationships. Any time you're dealing with the public in any form, you're in the process of building a relationship. What sets Relationship Builders apart is that they will continue to call on and do repeat business with the same accounts. Closers may have very minimal repeat business and may continually have to prospect for new business. No matter what kind of sales you're in, your ability to build, nurture, and maintain a relationship (either short- or long-term) will probably determine whether you'll achieve success or not.

Many of the most profitable sales deals are negotiated on the golf course or in a dining room. Deals are negotiated in gyms, in dance halls, on weekend trips to exotic resorts—there is no limit to where profitable sales deals can be closed. Many companies find that 80% of their business is generated from 20% of their existing customer base. The best sales professionals recognize this situation and are skilled Relationship Builders. Their job is to nurture and develop client relationships. Their resumes illustrate growing market share or increased repeat business as a result of on-going communication and contact with their customers.

HUNGRY FOR SUCCESS: Just Give Me a Bite!

These are the entry-level salespeople who want to start a career in sales or want to transition from a different career into a sales and marketing career. They just need a chance to prove themselves and are Hungry for Success. People are drawn to sales for many reasons, but the most common reasons are money and independence. **Recent college graduates** or professionals who are **switching careers** to sales need resumes that bring out special points of their career histories such as communication, problem solving, customer service, and sales support skills that tie in closely with their goals in sales and marketing. Of course, to be truly successful in sales, you need to be Hungry for Success, so every sales professional has this characteristic. It's just that entry-level salespeople have to be **very** hungry and aggressive to get that first sales job!

TEAM-BUILDERS: We Build Business through People!

These are management people who build sales teams. They are the **Sales Directors, District Managers, Area Managers, Presidents,** and **Vice Presidents** of companies. They hold high-profile positions and lead their sales and marketing teams to generate profitability for their companies. They are positive thinkers, team builders, and motivators. They must lead and inspire seasoned sales and marketing professionals. They must develop, nurture, and oversee the training of new sales representatives and maintain a strong support base for the company's clientele.

CREATIVE MARKETING THINK TANKS: Professionals Who Plan Big Marketing Projects

Marketing professionals are the Creative Think Tanks of their companies. They can be **Presidents, Vice Presidents,** or **Directors of Marketing,** or they can be part of the **marketing team.** They know how to dream, plan, develop, and create programs to support sales. They are different from sales professionals although they may be part of the sales team too. They often support sales efforts and are very instrumental in helping a company achieve profits and expand sales territories.

THE SALES VOICE: How Do You Sound?

In **Telemarketing Sales,** it is important that you have a good speaking voice. In fact, since you don't have eye contact with the person you're trying to sell a product to, your voice is your only sales tool. It's important that you have a pleasing, positive attitude. A person on the telephone will quickly decide whether to talk to you or not, based on a variety of factors. The tone and sound of your voice can mean everything. (If you're in telemarketing or inside sales, record your voice and then play it back. How do you sound?) Telemarketers succeed by becoming Closers who are Hungry for Success.

COME ON IN: When the Customer Comes to You!

In **Retail Sales** and **Inside Sales**, the customer comes to you. The company generally advertises aggressively to generate inquiry calls or walk-ins. When customers call or come in, they talk to an Inside Sales Representative. From this point, the sales representative becomes a Closer and Relationship Builder.

Part II

Part II includes all of our sales and marketing contestants (as we call them in this book). Each individual is like a contestant on a game show, vying for the prize—a job. They have all had to use their resumes as *sales presentations*—effective *sales tools* to *sell* themselves. They have all had to be aggressive and assertive in their job search strategies, remembering to follow up with phone calls and thank-you notes. They have learned how to be better than their competitors and how to illustrate this in their sales and marketing resumes.

On each of the resumes in Part II we have indicated whether the professionals are *Closers, Relationship Builders, Hungry for Success* (entry-level sales), *Team Builders,* or *Creative Think Tanks*. Often, these categories overlap. *Team Builders* are often *Creative Think Tanks,* and *Relationship Builders* are *Closers* and *Hungry for Success* professionals. The one thing all of these resumes have in common is the powerful ability to sell the candidate!

Part II
Resume Samples

1. Advertising Account Executive
2. Advertising Account Executive/Recruitment & Entertainment
3. Advertising—Corporate Sales
4. Area Sales Manager (Food Sales)
5. Assistant Marketing Manager (International Sales & Marketing/Plastics Industry)
6. Automobile Sales Manager
7. Catering Sales Manager
8. Direct Sales & Marketing
9. Direct Sales Management
10. Director of Sales and Education (Beauty & Cosmetics Industry)
11. District Sales Manager (Direct Sales)
12. District Sales Manager (Financial & Insurance Products/Automobile Industry)
13. Engineering Account Executive
14. Entertainment Marketing
15. Entry-Level Marketing
16. Executive Marketing & Sales
17. Executive Marketing Director
18. Executive Sales & Marketing Director
19. Executive Sales Manager
20. Executive Sales & Marketing Manager

21. Finance and Banking Related Sales
22. Industrial Sales
23. Inside/Outside Industrial Sales Professional
24. International Marketing Executive (Finance Specialist)
25. International Marketing Manager
26. International Sales (Asia/Pacific Rim)
27. International Sales (Latin)
28. Investments & Trading Financial Sales & Marketing
29. Investments & Trading Sales & Marketing
30. Medical Sales
31. Medical Sales
32. National Account Sales Manager
33. Periodical Sales & Marketing Manager
34. Pharmaceutical Sales
35. Pharmaceutical Sales & Marketing
36. Printing & Graphics Sales Representative
37. Property Management Sales
38. Regional Forms Sales Representative
39. Retail Department Manager
40. Retail Sales Associate
41. Retail Sales Manager
42. Retail Sales Specialist
43. Sales Executive (Automotive Industry)
44. Sales Manager (Transportation Industry)
45. Sales & Marketing Executive (Plastics)
46. Sales & Marketing (Printing Industry)
47. Sales & Marketing Professional
48. Sales Professional (Music & Entertainment Industry)
49. Sales Representative (Medical & Pharmaceutical)
50. Sales Representative (Real Estate—Vacation Condominiums)
51. Sales Representative (Retail Foods)
52. Sales Representative & Sales Support
53. Sales/Service Manager (Information Management Systems)

Closer, Relationship Builder

JANE FORTHWRIGHT

A Presentation

of

Professional Credentials

Confidentiality Requested, Please

7654 Roosevelt Ave.
Charleston, West Virginia 25304
(304) 229-0009

JANE FORTHWRIGHT

7654 Roosevelt Ave.
Charleston, West Virginia 25304
(304) 229-0009

Professional Objective & Profile

An Account Executive who is an achievement- and goal-oriented business professional with more than 6 years of experience building and leading integrated sales and marketing operations for major companies. Strong general sales and account management qualifications in strategic planning and advertising.

Desire a business arrangement that will provide a challenging opportunity to significantly contribute to a company's efficiency, organization, growth, and profitability.

Education

Bachelor of Science in Psychology
Bachelor of Arts in Political Science
OHIO WESLEYAN UNIVERSITY, Delaware, Ohio, 1989

Summary of Qualifications

- *Track Record of Success:*
  Background exemplifies a successful track record of career accomplishments with 6 years of professional experience encompassing positions as Account Executive and Management Trainee.

- *Advertising & Marketing:*
  Successful in conceptualizing, developing and executing effective, creative marketing and advertising campaigns for clients. Skilled in working with all facets of the media including radio, T.V. and print advertising.

- *Business Analysis & Development:*
  Research and develop business opportunities and marketing strategies that will maximize growth and profitability for company.

- *Account Management:*
  Interact extensively with clients and manage business development, budget, and negotiations. Ability to develop and build client relationships.

- *Client Relations:*
  Extremely talented in establishing and maintaining superb client relations as a result of effective communication skills. Proven track record of making sound decisions in all areas of client relations.

Do highlight any special promotional work such as media production and media placement.

Professional Experience

Account Executive
THE CHARDONNAY GROUP - ADVERTISING AGENCY

Charleston, West Virginia - 1993 to Present

Account Management: Responsible for managing new business development and strategic planning to maximize growth and profitability. Establish growth plans for individual accounts and personally manage account calls, presentations, and negotiations.

Budget Management: Manage clients' marketing budgets with full P&L responsibility for accounts.

Advertising & Promotion: Conceptualize, create, develop and implement innovative marketing and promotional campaigns for clients. Develop, direct and monitor comprehensive communications and advertising programs through implementation of various media designed to achieve designed results.

Media Production: In charge of developing, organizing and coordinating media production for advertising which includes radio, T.V. and print. Direct and supervise broadcast productions to ensure adherence to clients' specifications and requests.

Media Placement: Work closely with media personnel to place media, and continuously establish and maintain business relationships with media personnel.

Marketing Research: Conduct demographic and marketing research to target potential clients.

Leadership: Provide leadership for accounts to meet goals and performance objectives.

Account Executive
DIAL COMMUNICATION CORPORATION

Charleston, West Virginia - 1992 to 1993

Sales & Marketing: Responsible for direct sales and marketing of computer software and communications equipment throughout a multi-state territory. Solicited and obtained new clientele, and maintained existing clients.

Departmental Development: Developed an Emergency Management Division with concentration on government contracts.

Client Relations & Service: Provided excellent service to clients through follow-up and attention to accounts.

Management Trainee
TGI FRIDAY'S RESTAURANT

Charleston, West Virginia - 1990 to 1992

Began as a Server and Bartender at TGI Friday's, and was promoted to Management Trainee. Gained valuable experience in customer service, the food & beverage industry, and in business operations and administration.

References Available Upon Request

PLEASE DO NOT CONTACT PRESENT EMPLOYER

If you're in a very sensitive, high-profile position, it's okay to put "Do Not Contact Present Employer" on your resume.

JANE FORTHWRIGHT

7654 Roosevelt Ave.
Charleston, West Virginia 25304
(304) 229-0009

Date

Anthony Camarota
Director of Advertising
Stevens Advertising Group
2883 National Street
Charleston, West Virginia 25304

> Be sure to send your letter to a specific decision maker. (We have included some cover letters in this section that do not have an address or title. They can be personalized as needed.)

Dear Mr. Camarota:

It is my understanding that you're interested in a highly motivated, goal-oriented *Public Relations & Advertising Professional* to become a leader in your organization. I believe that I can significantly contribute to your company's efficiency, growth and overall profitability. For your review, I have enclosed a personal resume which will provide you with pertinent details concerning my background and qualifications.

As you will note, I am not a beginner, but rather a seasoned professional with 6 years of career experience, encompassing positions and responsibilities in the following areas:

- Account Management
- Advertising, Marketing & Promotions
- Public Relations
- Client Relations
- Media Production
- Budget Management
- Sales

My success throughout my career is largely due to my ability to prioritize responsibilities and to effectively interact with a broad range of clientele. Currently an *Account Executive* for *The Chardonnay Group,* I am responsible for managing all areas of major accounts, which includes new business development and planning. I am in charge of conceptualizing, creating and developing strategic marketing and promotional campaigns for clients and prepare and administer control budgets for operating expenditures. I sincerely believe that, with my experience and career goals, I would be an asset to your organization.

I would like to arrange a personal interview with you at your earliest convenience to discuss how I can significantly contribute to your team of professionals. Please feel free to contact me at my home telephone number or address if you have any additional questions.

Thank you in advance for your time and consideration. I look forward to speaking with you soon.

Sincerely,

Jane Forthwright

Professional Portfolio Enclosed

> This is definitely a type of sales position that requires a Relationship Builder. In any kind of entertainment business, building relationships is even *more* crucial to success!

Teresa Wohlberg

Professional Credentials in Advertising

6767 Kingsbury Road
Nashville, Tennessee 37222
(615) 979-0909

Teresa Wohlberg

6767 Kingsbury Road
Nashville, Tennessee 37222
(615) 979-0909

Professional Objective & Profile

Highlight specific areas of expertise you have developed. This is the first thing an employer will read.

A dynamic, achievement-oriented business professional is seeking a position that will fully utilize experience and education in *Public Relations, Marketing, Entertainment,* and *Promotions.*

Self-directed and self-motivated. A strong leader with ability to guide and direct associates to achieve their maximum potential. Desire a career avenue that will provide a challenging opportunity to significantly contribute to a company's efficiency, organization, growth and profitability.

Education

Master of Science in Corporate Communications
EVANWOOD COLLEGE
St. Charles, Missouri, 1996

Bachelor of Science in Electronic Media
MISSOURI STATE UNIVERSITY
Springfield, Missouri, 1993

Do highlight any type of entertainment and public relations experience that you have. It illustrates your ability to be outgoing, community-oriented, and personable, and shows you can be successful in building client relationships.

Academic Affiliations

Sigma Sigma Sigma National Sorority
Membership Director & Public Relations Committee Head

Summary of Qualifications

* ***Promotions & Advertising:***
In-depth background in writing and producing promotional materials including newsletters, flyers, and news releases, to promote and advertise academic programs.

* ***Entertainment Experience:***
As a *St. Louis Rams Cheerleader* from 1995-1996, gained valuable experience in all facets of coordinating special sports and cheerleading entertainment events for the public.

* ***Public Relations & Public Speaking:***
Skilled in public relations and public speaking. Experienced Public Speaker who facilitated booths at College Fairs and provided information to the public regarding University and curriculum. Skilled in networking with community businesses and organizations, and in developing and establishing excellent business relationships.

Professional Experience

Account Executive
GLOBAL CINEMA NETWORK
Nashville, Tennessee - 1996 to Present

Sales: Responsible for selling advertising to businesses for movie theaters. Solicit and obtain new accounts, as well as maintain existing ones.

Market Research - Territory Development: Research target market areas and develop and establish new clientele base for company.

Client Services: Provide excellent service to clients by following up on sales calls, and by responding to specific requests, inquiries, and/or concerns to ensure excellent implementation and follow-through on business.

Business Networking: Continuously establish and maintain an excellent network of business associates through extensive contact and interaction with community businesses and organizations.

Assistant Director of Admissions
Coordinator of Recruitment Publications
MARYVILLE UNIVERSITY
St. Louis, Missouri - 1995 to 1996

Recruitment & Admissions: Responsible for assisting in overall administration and operations of Recruitment & Admissions.

Marketing: Successfully increased number of enrolled students on a continuing basis as a result of developing and implementing strong marketing and promotional campaigns.

Public Information: Liaison between students and department. Provided information to students and families regarding scholarships and financial assistance.

Promotions: Wrote and produced innovative, creative promotional materials including news releases, newsletters and flyers to promote school and for recruitment of new students.

Student Relations: Established and maintained an excellent rapport with students by providing them with assistance in all areas of Admissions.

Special Events & Public Speaking: Coordinated and set up booths to recruit students at College Fairs throughout the state. Spoke regularly in front of large and small groups and provided information regarding the University and its curriculum.

Assistant Director of Admissions
Financial Aid Counselor
LINDENWOOD COLLEGE
St. Charles, Missouri - 1993 to 1995

Responsibilities were basically the same as those described above and included all areas of Public Relations, Promotions, and Student Relations.

Teresa Wohlberg
6767 Kingsbury Road
Nashville, Tennessee 37222
(615) 979-0909

Date

If there's no way to find out who will be reading your letter, then you may have to simply address the Employment Director.

Dear Employment Director:

I am a highly motivated, achievement-oriented business professional who is seeking a position in your organization. My background includes experience in *Public Relations, Marketing, Entertainment* and *Promotions,* and I believe that I can significantly contribute to your company's efficiency, organization, profitability and overall growth. For your review, I have enclosed a professional resume which will provide you with pertinent details concerning my background and qualifications.

In addition to a *Master of Science in Corporate Communications* from Evanwood College in St. Charles, Missouri, I also have 3 years of professional experience encompassing positions as *Assistant Director of Admissions & Coordinator of Recruitment Publications, Financial Aid Counselor,* and *Account Executive.* My success is largely due to my ability to prioritize responsibilities and manage multiple projects simultaneously. In addition, I developed excellent skills in *Public Relations & Public Speaking* while serving as a *St. Louis Rams Cheerleader* in 1995. Confident and self-motivated, I am a strong leader and take pride in my organizational and management abilities. I sincerely believe that, with my experience, education and career goals, I would be an asset to your organization.

I would like to request a personal interview at your earliest convenience so we can discuss ways that I can significantly contribute to your team of professionals. Please feel free to contact me at my home telephone number or address if you have any additional questions concerning my qualifications.

Thank you in advance for your time and consideration. I look forward to speaking with you soon.

Sincerely,

The second paragraph is written as a mini resume. Since the cover letter may be even *more* important than the resume itself, be sure to highlight your <u>best</u> accomplishments here!

Teresa Wohlberg

Resume Enclosed

This person is a Closer and Relationship Builder. Most salespeople are also Hungry for Success. In Advertising Corporate Sales, a salesperson incorporates just about all of the sales characteristics.

Rachel Terrel
8945 Sneed Avenue
Nashville, Tennessee 37299
(615) 367-9090

Professional Objective & Profile

Seeking a sales position that will provide a challenging opportunity to significantly contribute to a company's organization, efficiency, growth, and profitability by increasing new account base and by providing superior service to existing clients.

Goal-oriented with strong organizational skills. Enthusiastic and energetic. Ability to manage new business development and strategic planning to maximize growth and profitability. Skilled in establishing growth plans for individual accounts and personally managing account calls, presentations, and negotiations.

Summary of Qualifications & Accomplishments

By categorizing your *Areas of Qualifications,* you make it easy for an employer to scan your resume quickly and know within a few seconds what you can do.

Sales Awards & Honors:
1995 Sales Manager of the Year.
Booked single largest day group in the history of the Park.
1995 Distinguished Sales & Marketing Award.

Always highlight any Sales Awards or Honors. Don't be shy about bragging about yourself!

Client Relations:
Easily establishes excellent rapport with clients and makes effective sales presentations to all levels of decision-makers including top corporate executives and administrators.

Sales & Marketing:
Skilled in cold-calling, generating leads, cultivating accounts, and developing new as well as repeat clients. Talented in developing, directing, and monitoring comprehensive communications through implementation of various media designed to achieve desired results and a favorable corporate image.

Employee Relations & Leadership:
Strong leader and motivator of others. Encourage and support a teamlike work environment, which increases employee efficiency and productivity. Ability to motivate and guide associates to achieve their maximum potential.

Education

<u>*Bachelor of Science*</u>
Major: Mass Communications with Emphasis in Advertising
MIDDLE TENNESSEE STATE UNIVERSITY
Murfreesboro, Tennessee, 1990
Financed 100% of college expenses.
Dean's List, 1989, 1990
Member of American Advertising Federation
Ad Club Member

Corporate Sales Account Executive
OPRYLAND USA
GAYLORD ENTERTAINMENT COMPANY
Nashville, Tennessee - 1992 to Present

> Definitely specify how much you increased sales and revenue. You're communicating success!

- *Sales:* Responsible for selling Opryland attractions, including *Opryland Theme Park, General Jackson Showboat, The Grand Ole Opry,* and *Ryman Auditorium* to corporate businesses. Solicit and obtain new business, as well as maintain existing accounts through attention and follow-up to all sales.
- *Profitability:* Consistently achieve and surpass sales quotas which results in an increase in overall profitability for company. Increased total sales by more than 90% over the previous year. For example, doubled admissions and increased revenue from *$1,046,584* in 1994 to *$2,129,930* in 1995.
- *Client Relations & Services:* Provide superior service to clients through attentive follow-up and by effectively responding to requests, inquiries, suggestions, and/or concerns. Continuously interact with community businesses, organizations, and agencies to develop and maintain an exemplary network of business associates.
- *Marketing Research:* Prepare feasibility studies, research and investigate corporate businesses to determine profitability ratios.

Sales Manager
JACK THOMPSON & ASSOCIATES
Nashville, Tennessee - 1991 to 1992

- *Management:* Managed sales operations for local and national travel publications targeted specifically toward the group travel market. Built business through networking and successfully negotiating contracts.
- *Sales:* Increased total sales 15% and new business by 20%.
- *Research & Marketing:* Researched target market areas, and responsible for strategic planning and development of integrated sales, marketing and business development strategies targeted to potential clients.
- *Client Relations:* Held full responsibility for the development and nurturance of client relationships. Provided excellent service by assisting them with advertising, and by effectively responding to requests, inquiries, suggestions, and/or concerns.
- *Production - Layout & Design:* Responsible for production of advertising materials which included layout, design and proofing of copy.

Advertising Sales Representative
COMMUNICATIONS, INC.
Brentwood, Tennessee - 1990 to 1991

- *Sales:* Managed advertising sales operations for the Chamber of Commerce publications. Solicited and obtained new clients as well as maintaining existing accounts.
- *Business Development:* Developed business opportunities and marketing strategies and plans to maximize growth and profitability in order to expand market penetration.
- *Client Relations & Services:* Consistently established and maintained an exemplary network of business associates as a result of in-depth contact and interaction. Provided excellent service to accounts by following up on all sales and promotions.
- *Advertising & Promotions:* Conceptualized, created, developed and implemented innovative marketing and promotional strategies for clients.

References Available Upon Request

This type of sales job includes the characteristics of Closers, Relationship Builders, Hungry for Success, and Team Builders.

HARRY BORGEN
2766 Lone Oak Road
St. Louis, Missouri 88776
(887) 887-8787

Professional Objective & Career Profile

High-Caliber Sales Manager with over 21 years of experience in sales and sales management. Consistently successful in leading sales teams to achieve #1 position in the District and in the nation.

Strong general management qualifications in strategic planning, business development and growth, promotions, and process/productivity/quality improvement in sales operations. Excellent experience in personnel training, development, supervision and leadership. Skilled executive liaison.

Desire a management position in sales that will provide a challenging opportunity to significantly contribute to a company's efficiency, organization, growth, and profitability.

Summary of Qualifications

Track Record of Success:
Background exemplifies a successful track record of career accomplishments which encompass more than 21 years of experience in sales and sales management. Quickly advanced from position of *Sales Representative* at Keebler to *Area Sales Manager,* and assumed responsibilities of *District Sales Manager* in his absence.

Sales Accomplishments:

> *Nominated Area Sales Manager, 1990.*
> *Nominated for Outstanding Performer, 1989.*
> *Ranked in the top 5% 1991-1993 in the Southeast Region.*
> *Placed #1 in 2 separate National Sales Contests for volume growth.*
> *Ranked #1 in the District in the Nation.*
> *Maintained an overall budget accomplishment of 98.6% during 8 years as an Area Sales Manager.*

Emphasize all your Sales Achievements and Honors. This illustrates that you are definitely success- and profit-oriented. You get things done!

Business Growth & Development:
In-depth background in managing business development and strategic business planning. Personally responsible for expanding territory and increasing business for Keebler. Established growth plans for major account, Wal-Mart, and increased business more than 60% in one year.

Food Industry:
Besides having an extensive background in *Sales Management* for Keebler, also possess extensive experience in the Food Industry including 13 years of experience as a *Supervisor & Head Grocery Clerk* for Kroger Food Stores. Was in charge of all inventory, purchasing, pricing, and supervision of staff.

Client Relations & Customer Service:
Committed to providing superior service to clients and customers by providing attention to accounts, and by effectively responding to requests, inquiries, suggestions, and/or concerns.

Employee Relations:
Encourage and support a teamlike work environment, which increases employee morale, efficiency and productivity.

Computer Operations:
Experienced using computers including handheld computers, *Norand* and *AT&T.*

Professional Sales Management Experience

Area Sales Manager
KEEBLER COMPANY
St. Louis, Missouri - 1987 to 1996

> If possible, do quantify your achievements by stating <u>how much</u> you increased sales!

- *Company Track Record of Success:* Began with Keebler in 1987 as a *Sales Representative* and in 5 months was promoted to *Sales Supervisor* covering West Tennessee, North Mississippi and Arkansas. In just 10 months, was promoted to *Area Sales Manager.* A brief overview of responsibilities is highlighted below.

- *Sales Management:* Guided and directed a $3 million sales territory for West Tennessee, North Mississippi, Northeast Arkansas, Southeast Missouri and Southwest Kentucky. Successfully took over additional responsibilities of the District Manager in his absence, while still managing own territory, and achieved an increase of 47% in sales for company.

- *Profitability:* Consistently led branch sales teams to achieve *#1 in sales,* which increased overall profitability for company. Recipient of numerous Sales Awards for outstanding job performances.

- *Business Development & Growth - Account Management:* Managed business development and strategic planning to maximize growth and profitability. Established growth plans for major account, Wal-Mart, and grew the business more than 60% the first year. Personally managed account calls, presentations, and negotiations.

- *Client Services & Relations:* Provided excellent service to accounts through attentive follow-up to clients. Established and maintained an excellent network of business associates as a result of strong communication skills and superior service.

- *Personnel, Training & Development:* Interviewed, hired, trained and supervised sales associates in all areas of sales and customer service.

- *Budget Analysis & Management:* Analyzed budget variances and initiated appropriate strategies to more aggressively control expenditures.

- *Marketing:* Worked closely as a team with National & Regional Marketing Staffs to design strategic sales, marketing and budget objectives. Created and developed innovative marketing strategies to increase sales and overall profitability.

- *Promotions & Advertising:* Spearheaded the promotions and introduction of new products in the marketplace, and developed aggressive, successful promotional and marketing campaigns. Negotiated promotional contracts to increase category growth.

Sales Representative
ABC CHEMICAL COMPANY
St. Louis, Missouri - 1996 to Present

- Responsibilities are basically the same as those described above, and include all areas of sales, marketing & advertising, customer service, and client relations.

HARRY BORGEN
2766 Lone Oak Road
St. Louis, Missouri 88776
(887) 887-8787

It's always best to keep your cover letter to one page. Remember, it's an integral part of your *dynamic* marketing tools!

Date

Dear Director of Personnel:

Are you looking for a highly motivated, goal-oriented Sales Manager to become a leader in your organization? I am interested in a sales position with your company, and believe that I can significantly contribute to your company's efficiency, profitability, and overall growth. For your review, I have enclosed a professional resume which will provide you with pertinent details concerning my background and qualifications.

As you will note, I am not a beginner, but rather a well-seasoned professional with more than 21 years of experience in sales, management, supervision, client relations, and the food industry. My success is largely due to my ability to prioritize multiple responsibilities and to effectively lead sales teams to expand and grow territories which yield company savings and profitability. I have been successful throughout my career due to my strong interpersonal and leadership skills. I sincerely believe that, with my experience and career goals, I would be an asset to your organization.

I would like to request a personal interview at your earliest convenience so we can discuss ways that I can significantly contribute to your team of professionals. Please feel free to contact me at my home telephone number or address if you have any additional questions.

Thank you in advance for your time and consideration. I look forward to speaking with you soon.

Sincerely,

Harry Borgen

Resume Enclosed

Judy Peerless
7765 40th Ave South
Miami, Florida 55335
(665) 553-5533

> This job incorporates all the categorized sales functions, including Closers, Relationship Builders, Hungry for Success, and Team Builders.

Professional Objective & Profile

High-caliber, empowered *Assistant Manager in Marketing* with more than 4 years of experience building and leading integrated sales and marketing operations for Mitsui & Company (U.S.A.), Inc. and more than 10 years of experience in business administration.

Seeking a position that will provide a challenging opportunity to significantly contribute to a company's efficiency, organization, growth, and profitability. Consistently successful in positioning finance as a critical business partner, supportive of and responsive to the needs of large and diverse operating units.

Strong general management qualifications in sales, strategic planning, project and inventory management, budget analysis, and contract negotiations. Strong leader and motivator of others who has excellent cross-functional team skills.

Education

Bachelor of Business Administration - Finance
FLORIDA ATLANTIC UNIVERSITY
Boca Raton, Florida, 1991

UCLA Study Abroad
SOTHEBY'S LONDON, London, England, 1990
Assessing Works of Art

Real Estate License
GOLD COAST SCHOOL OF REAL ESTATE
Boca Raton, Florida, 1986

Summary of Qualifications

Track Record of Success:
Background exemplifies a successful track record of career accomplishments which encompass positions as *Assistant Manager, Marketing, Assistant to Controller* and *Realtor.* Quickly advanced throughout career to positions of higher levels of responsibility and authority due to outstanding job performance.

Management:
Fast-track promotion through a series of increasingly responsible positions while at Mitsui & Company (U.S.A.), Inc., managing and directing large-scale marketing and sales operations. Conduct ongoing analyses to analyze and evaluate the efficiency, quality, and productivity of diverse marketing operations. Establish and maintain short- and long-range goals.

International & Domestic Sales & Procurement:
In-depth background in Sales, Marketing and Procurement in the U.S., Japan and Mexico. Responsible for managing the entire sales cycle from client identification and account development through presentations, contract and price negotiations, and final sales closings.

Computer Operations:
Proficient in *WordPerfect, Lotus, Dbase, STX12 EDI.*

Each job function is carefully categorized so the reader can quickly summarize the entire scope of her responsibilities.

Judy Peerless
Page 2

Assistant Manager, Marketing
MATSUI & COMPANY (U.S.A.), INC.
Miami, Florida - 1992 to Present

- *Company Track Record of Success:* Began with company as a *Trading Assistant.* In 1993 was promoted to *Sales Assistant,* and then in 1994 advanced to *Assistant Manager, Marketing.* Report directly to the Vice President and General Manager.
- *Management:* Responsible for directing and managing the Plastics & Chemicals Department which achieves approximately *$12 million in sales* annually. Products include Plastics, Raw Resins & Finished Goods, Rubber, Machinery and Tooling.
- *Sales, Marketing & Procurement:* In charge of purchasing, selling and marketing plastics and chemicals to major corporations throughout the U.S. and abroad, with a special emphasis in plastics and rubber. Responsible for new business development and strategic planning to maximize growth and profitability. Establish growth plans for individual accounts and personally manage account calls, presentations, and supplier negotiations. Negotiate, control and maintain approximately $10 million annually in materials.
- *Account Management - Contract Negotiations:* Hold direct responsibility for the development/nurturance of client relationships, core prospect marketing, all accounting/financial affairs, competitive contract negotiations, bidding/quotes, and management of entire project.
- *Client Relations:* Provide superior service to clients through follow-up on all sales and close attention to accounts. Effectively respond to clients' requests, inquiries, suggestions, and/or concerns.
- *Profitability:* Negotiated cost down measures which resulted in a 17% savings, and increased sales from *$8.8 million to $12.0 million annually (a 38% increase in 2 years),* which increased overall profitability for company.
- *Budget Management:* Review monthly and year/quarter-end reports and analyze budget variances. Initiate appropriate strategies to more aggressively control expenditures. Prepare future years' budgets based on previous expenditures and changes in organizational structures. Design budget forecasting and analysis plans.
- *Material Requirements Planning:* Responsible for all material planning and acquisition, including localization of materials.
- *Inventory Control:* Monitor inventory of products and efficiently utilize in order to minimize and maintain inventory costs.

Assistant to Controller
SILVER COAST CONSTRUCTION
Hollywood, Florida - 1989 to 1991

- *Accounting:* Responsible for all accounts payable, accounts receivable and payroll.
- *Collections:* In charge of collecting past due accounts. Contacted customers and negotiated payment schedules.
- *Reports:* Reviewed and prepared monthly and year/quarter-end reports.
- *Computer Operations:* Utilized WordPerfect, Lotus and a customized program to enter data regarding customers and their accounts.

Realtor
J.J. SCHIRRMAN & ASSOCIATES
Ft. Lauderdale, Florida - 1986 to 1989

- *Sales & Marketing:* Sold residential and commercial real estate.

It isn't necessary to elaborate extensively on past jobs (unless they're relevant to the one you want). Your current job is the most important and the one to write the most about!

BEN KEILER
6776 Sedberry Avenue
Gailbraith, New York
(212) 254-0666

> As in all Sales Management positions, this job requires that you be a Closer, Relationship Builder, Hungry for Success, and a Team Builder.

Professional Objective & Profile

High-Caliber **General Sales Manager** with more than 6 years of experience building and leading integrated sales, finance and insurance operations in the automotive industry. Strong general management qualifications in strategic planning, organizational reengineering, budget management, and process/productivity/quality improvement. Consistently successful in positioning finance as a critical business partner, supportive of and responsive to the needs of large and diverse operating units. Talented in leading and developing business opportunities and marketing strategies to maximize growth and profitability.

Desire a management position that will provide a challenging opportunity to significantly contribute to a company's efficiency, organization, growth, and profitability.

Education

Bachelor of Science in Business Administration (Pursuant)
NEW YORK STATE COLLEGE
New York, New York - *GPA: 3.5/4.0*

Professional Accomplishments

Salesperson of the Month (numerous times)
Completed Bronze Level Training in 1995 & 1996, Chrysler Corporation

Military

UNITED STATES ARMY, 1988 to 1996
2 Years Active Duty, 4 Years Reserves, 2 Years Inactive Reserves

> Listing Military Experience is an asset because it shows that you've been trained in disciplinary tactics, and this is appealing to any employer.

Professional Management Experience

> This signifies your ability to interact well with customers and ensure customer satisfaction, which is vital in any sales job.

General Sales Manager
Finance & Insurance Manager
HARPETH CHRYSLER-PLYMOUTH-JEEP-EAGLE
New York, New York - 1994 to April 1997

- *Company Track Record of Success:* Began as the *Finance & Insurance Manager* and was promoted to *Sales Manager* and then to *General Sales Manager.*
- *Management:* Managed and directed overall administration and operations of automobile dealership which achieved an average 189 sales per month (110 new cars). Reengineered management methods which streamlined operations and increased sales. Conducted ongoing analyses to evaluate the efficiency, quality and productivity of operations.
- *Profitability:* Rated as the **#1 Leasing Dealer** in the southeast territory and **#1 in Sales** in Nashville, which significantly increased overall profitability for company.
- *Customer Service:* After taking over management position, increased the SSI (sales satisfaction index), from the 80's to 92%.
- *Personnel & Supervision:* Interviewed, hired, trained and supervised staff members. Managed 2 new car managers, 2 finance managers and a used car manager. Delegated work responsibilities and monitored overall job performances to ensure accuracy and adherence to specifications, rules, and regulations.

> Notice how strong, active verbs are used throughout resume to emphasize _ACTION!_

Professional Management Experience

- **_Budget Management:_** Managed, analyzed, and administered a multimillion dollar budget for operating expenditures. Responsible for financial performance analysis and business planning and development functions. Analyzed budget variances and initiated appropriate guidelines to more aggressively control expenditures and increase profitability. Established budget guidelines to operate more efficiently.
- **_Employee Relations:_** Developed and implemented employee relations programs to increase morale, productivity and efficiency. Encouraged and supported a teamlike work environment.
- **_Advertising, Promotions & Marketing:_** Organized, coordinated and implemented company's advertising and marketing strategies into everyday operations. Set up and arranged special activities and events to promote company and its services. Managed and administered a $45,000 monthly advertising budget.
- **_Media Relations:_** Worked extensively with media personnel to coordinate advertising for print and radio. Develop, direct and monitor comprehensive communications and advertising programs through implementation of various media designed to achieve desired results.
- **_Fundraising:_** Organized and coordinated fundraising activities to promote Chrysler.

Finance & Insurance Manager
JONES CHRYSLER-PLYMOUTH-ISUZU, New York, New York - 1992 to 1994

- **_Company Track Record of Success:_** Began as a Sales Associate and advanced to position of Finance & Insurance Manager.
- **_Management:_** Full responsibility for managing and directing all financial and insurance operations for dealership. Analyzed and interpreted financial information and evaluated credit reports to assess eligibility for loans.
- **_Contract Negotiations:_** Negotiated contracts for all new and used vehicles, (approximately 75 per month.)

Sales & Marketing Experience

Sales & Leasing Consultant
MAZDA DEALERSHIP, New York, New York - 1992

- **_Sales:_** Responsible for selling and leasing new and used cars to individuals.
- **_Inventory:_** Monitored inventory levels of automobiles and stocked as needed.
- **_Client Development:_** Managed new business development and strategic planning to maximize growth and profitability. Personally managed account calls, follow-ups, presentations and negotiations.
- **_Customer Service:_** Assisted customers with selection of automobiles and provided information regarding dealership and services.

Sales & Leasing Consultant
NEW YORK TOYOTA, New York, New York - 1991

- **_Sales:_** Responsibilities were basically the same as those described above and included all areas of sales and customer service.

Bartender
STEVEN'S RESTAURANT & BAR, New York, New York - 1990 to 1991

- **_Sales:_** Sold food and beverages to customers in a restaurant & bar environment. Continuously upsold items to increase sales and profitability.
- **_Customer Service:_** Provided excellent service to customers by responding to requests, inquiries, and/or concerns.
- **_Training:_** Trained new employees in bar and inventory procedures.

Lynn Evans
1234 Northshore Drive
Wilkes-Barre, Pennsylvania 18773
(717) 399-0987

> In this type of Sales job, you must definitely be a Closer, a Relationship Builder, Hungry for Success, and a Team Builder.

Professional Objective & Profile

High-caliber, highly motivated Sales professional is seeking a position that will fully utilize more than 13 years of progressive experience encompassing positions in Sales and Client Relations. Desire a position that will provide a challenging opportunity to significantly contribute to a company's efficiency, organization, growth, and profitability.

Education

Associate of Science in General Business Administration
STATE COMMUNITY COLLEGE, Wilkes-Barre, Pennsylvania

> Illustrates ability to develop and sell business *and* close deals!

Professional Experience

Catering Sales Manager
PRESIDENTIAL HOTEL CONVENTION CENTER
Wilkes-Barre, Pennsylvania - 1988 to Present

- *Company Track Record of Success:* Began with Presidential Hotel in 1988 in Room Service, then advanced to *Banquet Server, Banquet Captain* and to current position in 1994 as *Catering Sales Manager.* Consistently advanced to positions of higher levels of authority and responsibility.
- *Sales & Profitability:* Responsible for selling catering services to organizations and businesses for major conventions for up to 1500 guests. Solicit and obtain new accounts as well as maintain existing clients. Generate more than $1 million in annual sales in Food & Beverage.
- *Account Management:* Manage new business development and strategic planning to maximize growth and profitability. Establish growth plans for catering services and personally manage account calls, presentations, and negotiations. Totally responsible for planning, coordinating and managing the PGA Senior Classic in 1994, 1995 and 1996. This involved coordinating Clubhouse and sky box activities, and arranging extensive catering services.
- *Client Relations:* Establish and maintain an exemplary network of business associates as a result of extensive interaction and strong communication with community businesses and organizations on an ongoing basis.
- *Meeting Planning:* Organize special meetings, reservations, menu planning/development, and requirements for convention facilities, which includes coordinating audio visual services. Coordinate special events and activities for individual clients.
- *Budget Management:* Assist in managing overall budget for catering services. Analyze and project budget needs and operate within budgetary guidelines.

Banquet Captain

- *Management:* Managed the organization and coordination of banquets.
- *Meeting Planning:* Worked closely with meeting planners to facilitate specific needs and requirements.
- *Supervision:* Supervised staff members and monitored overall job performances to ensure accuracy and adherence to standards and specifications.

Customer Service Representative & Secretary
MANUFACTURING & DISTRIBUTING, INC.
Philadelphia, Pennsylvania - 1984 to 1988

- *Accounting:* Prepared accounts receivable and accounts payable for company. Also responsible for payroll for up to 50 employees.

Lynn Evans
1234 Northshore Drive
Wilkes-Barre, Pennsylvania 18773
_____ **(717) 399-0987** _____

Date

Don Spielburg
Director of Sales
Johnson & Barrett Marketing Company
2983 Waring Street
Philadelphia, Pennsylvania 28883

> Be specific about where you heard of the job opening.

Dear Mr. Spielburg:

This letter is in response to the advertisement in Sunday's edition of *The Pennsylvania Newspaper* for a Sales Representative. I am confident that I can significantly contribute to your company's sales team and have enclosed a personal resume so you may review my credentials.

In addition to an Associate of Science Degree in General Business Administration, I also possess the following qualifications and areas of expertise.

- More than 13 years of experience encompassing positions in Sales, Customer Service and Meeting Planning.
- Strong sales skills with experience in soliciting and obtaining new clientele.
- Strong organization skills with experience in meeting planning.
- Dedicated to providing superior service to clients by responding to requests, inquiries, suggestions, and/or concerns.
- Demonstrated leadership, communication and negotiation skills.
- Proven ability to define issues, propose solutions, and implement changes.

I sincerely believe that, with my experience and career goals, I would be an asset to your organization. I would like to arrange a personal interview at your earliest convenience so we can discuss ways that I can significantly contribute to your company's organization, growth, and profitability.

Thank you in advance for your time and consideration. I look forward to speaking with you soon.

Sincerely,

Lynn Evans

Enclosure

RUSSELL STEVENSON

4545 Winthorpe Drive
Atlanta, Georgia 20034
(404) 998-5199

> This type of sales job requires that you be a Closer, Relationship Builder, Hungry for Success, and a Team Builder.

Professional Objective & Profile

High-energy, goal-oriented and motivated **Sales Executive** is seeking a position that will fully utilize 5 years of experience building and leading integrated sales operations for major companies. Desire a career opportunity that will provide a challenging avenue to significantly contribute to a company's efficiency, organization, growth, and profitability.

Education

Bachelor of Science - Major: Sociology - Minor: Marketing & Health
GEORGIA STATE UNIVERSITY, Atlanta, Georgia

Professional Sales Experience

Co-Owner & Sales Manager
GOLD PROMOTIONS, Atlanta, Georgia - August 1996 to Present

- *Ownership:* As Co-Owner, responsible for managing overall operations and administration of this company. Created and developed *Atlanta's Gold Party Pass* which cut costs for consumers and increased overall sales for businesses. Also, responsible for marketing and selling credit cards including Discover, LCI, ATT, Amoco and CitiBank.
- *Sales Management:* Direct and manage all facets of sales operations. Responsible for managing new business development and strategic planning to maximize growth and profitability. Establish growth plans for individual accounts and personally manage account calls, presentations, and negotiations.
- *Profitability:* As a result of effectively marketing *Atlanta's Gold Party Pass,* increased a premier nightclub's sales volume *(Atlanta Live)* by 100%. Coverage increased from $5 to $10 at the door, and the crowds increased from an average of 500 to 2000 customers nightly.
- *Promotions, Marketing & Advertising:* Create, develop and initiate innovative advertising and marketing strategies to increase business and overall profitability.
- *Client Relations:* Built company from ground up by calling on a variety of businesses and organizations including nightclubs, travel agencies, etc. Solicit and obtain new clientele.
- *Network Marketing Program:* Independently developed and launched a mini network marketing program on college campuses to market credit cards. Generated over 800 applications weekly.
- *Customer Service:* Provide superior service to clients in all business environments by effectively responding to inquiries, suggestions, requests, and/or concerns.
- *Personnel, Training & Supervision:* Interviewed, hired, trained and supervised 8 sales executives for specific territories. Trained sales executives in all areas of sales, marketing and customer service.

Account Executive
WORLDWIDE TRAVELER'S ASSOCIATION, Atlanta, Georgia - 1996

- *Sales, Marketing & Business Development:* Responsible for selling concierge services to business travelers. Utilized cold-calling, telemarketing and personal presentations to market services. Developed business opportunities and marketing strategies to maximize growth and profitability.

Marketing Manager
EXPERT REMODELING, INC., Dallas, Texas - 1992 to 1996

- *Sales & Marketing Management:* Directed and managed overall operations and assisted lead generation program for sales force in a 3-state area. Responsible for generating leads and developing business.
- *Personnel, Training & Supervision:* Interviewed, hired, trained and supervised sales staff. Independently staffed 5 separate in-store telemarketing programs in Sears stores. Generated over 800 leads monthly which resulted in overall sales up to $300,000.

Sales Management positions incorporate Closers, Relationship Builders, and Team Builders.

Erin Hamilton
2233 Lindell Drive
Omaha, Nebraska 66338
(535) 637-0987

Since this person is seeking a job in the health care industry, it's important to highlight any experience that deals directly with health care.

Professional Objective & Profile

Profit-oriented **Sales Manager** is seeking a position in health care that will fully utilize more than 20 years of experience building and leading integrated sales operations for diverse companies. Extensive background in and knowledge of health care sales, customer and member service.

Strong general management qualifications in strategic business planning, organizational reengineering, and process/productivity/quality improvement. Excellent experience in building underdeveloped territories to achieve maximum profitability.

Desire a position that will provide a challenging opportunity to significantly contribute to a company's efficiency, organization, growth, and profitability.

Summary of Qualifications

Health Care Sales:
Extensive experience in selling health care plans including Medicare Supplements and Long Term Care while working for the United Teachers Associates Insurance Company. In-depth knowledge of the health care industry, sales management, and customer and member service.

Sales Awards & Accomplishments:
- *Hired, trained and developed the No. 1 Salesperson in company* for 2 years in a row while at United Teachers Associates Insurance Company.
- Sales team produced more than *$1/2 million in premiums* during last year of employment at United Teachers Associates Insurance Company.
- Runner-up for *National Sales Manager of the Year.*

Business Planning & Development:
Have held full decision-making responsibility for developing annual financial objectives and preparing long-range strategic business plans. Skilled in strategic planning and development of an integrated sales, marketing and business development campaign targeted to specific market.

Training & Development:
Strong interpersonal skills. Empower associates to think and work independently, as well as in a team environment. Experienced in training and developing associates in all areas of sales, marketing, and customer service.

Client Relations:
Have held high-visibility public relations positions as the direct liaison to clients, community leaders and other business associates. Excellent ability to develop and maintain a strong working relationship between clients as a result of thorough attention and follow-up to accounts. Committed to providing excellent service which results in repeat business and referrals.

Education

NEBRASKA UNIVERSITY
Area of Concentration: Business Administration
Omaha, Nebraska

Licensure

Licensed in Life & Health Insurance

Professional Sales Experience

> This sales person *makes deals*! Do highlight specific sales increases!

Account Executive
PROGRESSIVE OFFICE SOLUTIONS
Omaha, Nebraska - 1995 to Present

- *Sales:* Responsible for selling reprographic services to businesses and organizations throughout Nebraska. Solicit and obtain new clients, as well as maintain existing accounts through cold calls, setting up appointments and contract negotiations.
- *Territory Development:* Generated new sales and built territory from zero to $35-40,000 monthly in sales revenue in just one year.
- *Account Management:* Responsible for managing new business development and strategic planning to maximize growth and profitability.

Sales Manager
PARTNERS INSURANCE COMPANY
Omaha, Nebraska - 1990 to 1995

- *Sales:* Responsible for selling insurance supplements to retired teachers throughout middle Tennessee. This included selling Medicare supplements and long-term health care plans to individuals.
- *Territory Development:* Restructured and built an underdeveloped territory to achieve an increase in revenue and overall profitability throughout Nebraska.
- *Account Management:* Established growth plans for individual accounts and personally managed account calls, presentations, and negotiations. Coordinated multimedia presentations for the President of retired Teachers' Groups in various cities throughout Nebraska.
- *Client Relations:* Provided information to clients regarding health care supplements and ensured strong working relationships between clients and company.
- *Personnel, Training & Development:* Recruited, interviewed, hired, and developed staff to achieve their maximum potential in sales.
- *Seminars:* Facilitated numerous seminars and classes to teach and train associates in all areas of sales, insurance, and customer service.
- *Supervision:* Monitored sales representatives' overall job performances to ensure accuracy and adherence to standards, rules, and regulations.
- *Business Networking:* Cultivated and maintained an exemplary network of business associates statewide as a result of extensive interaction and strong communication skills.
- *Advertising & Marketing:* Conceptualized, created, and developed innovative marketing and advertising strategies to promote company and its services.

Owner & Manager
TURNER REAL ESTATE INVESTMENT COMPANY
Omaha, Nebraska - 1980 to 1990

- *Management:* Managed overall operations of this company and responsible for coordinating and managing all aspects of real estate investments.

Sales Manager
THOMPSON'S INVESTMENT COMPANY
Omaha, Nebraska - 1975 to 1980

- *Sales Management:* Responsible for selling investments to clients. Managed independent portfolios for investors in municipal bonds.

This Sales Management position requires that you be a Closer, Relationship Builder, and Team Builder.

Rusty Kerrigan
7887 Blain Boulevard
Detroit, Michigan 77883
(808) 776-1277

Professional Objective & Profile

A multi-talented, profit- and achievement-oriented **Sales Manager** is seeking a position that will fully utilize an extensive background in sales and the cosmetics industry. Desire a career avenue that will provide a challenging opportunity to significantly contribute to a company's efficiency, organization, growth, and profitability.

Professional Experience

Director of Sales & Education
BEN'S SALON SERVICES
Detroit, Michigan - 1995 to Present

Sales & Education Management: Responsible for managing overall operations for sales and education. Guide and direct 14 sales representatives throughout Michigan.

Personnel & Training: Develop and implement training/education programs to instruct sales representatives in all areas of products, sales, merchandising, and customer service. Interview and hire sales representatives. Monitor overall job performances to ensure accuracy and adherence to company policies and procedures.

Promotions - Special Events: Hair Shows: Responsible for setting up major hair shows for up to 3,000 attendees. This involves designing promotional materials for shows and scheduling guest stylists from all over the U.S. Also, develop and coordinate in-salon contests to promote special hair products.

Client Relations/Customer Service: Provide excellent service to clients/customers through attentive follow-up to sales, and by responding to clients' requests, inquiries, suggestions, and/or concerns.

Salon Consultant
STATEWIDE ENTERPRISES - BEAUTY SUPPLY COMPANY
Tampa, Florida - 1992 to 1995

Salon Consultant: Consulted Salons regarding business as well as retail and merchandising. Worked in Tallahassee for one year and was promoted to a territory that achieved an annual $1 million in sales in Jacksonville.

Delivery Sales Representative
THE BAKING COMPANY, Tallahassee, Florida - 1988 to 1992

Delivery Sales: Responsible for delivering bakery products to restaurants and grocery stores.

Client Relations: Developed and maintained an excellent network of business associates as a result of extensive interaction and communication with businesses. Gained extensive retail and merchandising experience in this job.

Instructor - Air Assault School
UNITED STATES ARMY
United States including Hawaii, Japan, Korea, Philippines & Australia - 1984 to 1988

Instruction: Responsible for training a staff of 15. Each class contained 75-100 students. Strong leader and motivator of students. Taught classes in all areas of Air Assault.

Professional Honors & Awards

Numerous Recognition & Achievement Awards including the following:
Certificate of Appreciation for Exceptional Meritorious Service/Operation Desert Shield/Storm
Certificate of Achievement for Outstanding Achievement & Dedicated Service
Battalion Soldier of the Month (Several times)

Education
Bachelor of Science in Business Administration
MICHIGAN STATE UNIVERSITY, Detroit, Michigan

DOUGLAS EASTMAN
1299 Villa Road
Seattle, Washington 99932
(704) 563-1643

> This type of Sales job includes Closers, Relationship Builders, and Team Builders.

Professional Objective & Profile

High-Caliber **Sales Manager & Executive** with 10 years of experience building and leading integrated sales operations for major industry. Guide and direct companywide sales and marketing activities for 4-state territory. Strong general management qualifications in strategic planning to promote and increase sales and profitability. Self-motivated and self-directed with excellent decision-making skills, and ability to quickly identify opportunities and resolve problems. Seeking a position that will provide a challenging opportunity to significantly contribute to a company's efficiency, organization, growth, and profitability.

Sales Awards

Gold Seal Award for Outstanding Job Performance

Masters of Business Sales & Management Award

(Top 3% nationally in personal sales and crew sales, 5 years)

Top Sales Representative Award (Top 3% nationally, 7 years)

District Sales Manager of the Year, 1996, '94, '93

Field Sales Manager of the Year, 1992

Presidential Recommendation Award (4 Years)

Top Crew Manager Award (Top 3% nationally)

Professional Sales & Management Experience

District Sales Manager
NORTHWESTERN COMPANY, Seattle, Washington - 1986 to Present

- *Company Promotion:* Began in 1986 as a *Sales Associate,* and was promoted to *Field Sales Manager & Organizational Manager,* and then to *District Sales Manager* in 1991.
- *Sales & Profitability:* Responsible for strategic planning and development of sales force in district which includes Washington, Oregon and California. Continuously surpassed sales quotas. Have averaged over 27% growth per year over the past 7 years. Ranked in the top 1% of all sales managers nationally each year.
- *Personnel Recruitment & Training:* Responsible for planning, staffing and directing sales and marketing for district. Recruited, interviewed, hired, and trained sales managers and sales representatives. In 1995, interviewed over 3000 candidates for sales positions. In charge of training 50 sales managers and over 200 sales representatives.
- *Public Speaking - Training Seminars:* Facilitate advanced training seminars for sales managers and sales representatives which focus on leadership and motivation. Have completed over 600 hours conducting seminars in front of large groups.
- *Client Relations:* Establish and maintain excellent working relationships with Career Development Directors and Department Heads at 15 major universities throughout sales territory on an ongoing basis.
- *Accounting Operations:* In charge of all accounts receivable, outstanding invoices and collections.
- *Management:* As *District Sales Manager,* was responsible for managing overall sales and marketing of books for Northwestern Company in 4-state area. Guided and directed more than 50 sales managers and 200 sales representatives.
- *Direct Sales:* Began as a Sales Associate and was responsible for direct sales and marketing of books for Northwestern Company. Solicited and obtained new accounts through approximately 70,000 cold calls. Personally managed account calls, sales presentations and negotiations. Involved in over 20,000 "one-on-one" closing situations.

Education

Masters of Business Administration
Bachelor of Science in Political Science
WASHINGTON UNIVERSITY, Seattle, Washington
Eagle Scout Scholarship, Graduated with Honors, Delta Upsilon Fraternity

> Do include your education and any honors and special associations.

DOUGLAS EASTMAN
1299 Villa Road
Seattle, Washington 99932
(704) 563-1643

Date

Joanna Gilbert
President of Sales & Marketing
Progressive Company, Inc.
259 Court Street
Seattle, Washington 20282

> This letter is full of impressive achievements and accomplishments which will clearly *sell* Douglas to the employer!

Dear Ms. Gilbert:

Success- and profit-oriented . . . proven methods in sales management and direction . . . 10 years of experience in sales leadership and motivation . . . high energy . . . committed to surpassing company's expectations . . . are just a few of the many qualities I can offer your company.

It is my understanding that you are looking for a highly motivated, goal-oriented **Sales & Marketing Executive** to become a leader at Progressive Company, Inc. I believe that I can significantly contribute to your company's efficiency, profitability, and overall growth. For your review, I have enclosed a professional resume which will provide you with details concerning my background and qualifications.

As you will note in my resume, I am not a beginner, but rather a well-seasoned professional. In addition to a Masters of Business Administration from Washington University, I also have 10 years of experience guiding and leading extensive sales operations for the Northwestern Company. With territories including Washington, Oregon and California, I manage 50 sales managers and 200 sales representatives. I am completely responsible for the bottom line of my territory! This includes extensive personnel recruitment and training, and during 1995, I interviewed over 3,000 candidates for sales positions.

My success throughout my career is largely due to my outstanding sales and management skills, as well as to my ability to effectively design and incorporate innovative sales programs that yield company profitability. Due to my sales efforts, I have been successful in expanding the company in growth and profitability 25% over the past 7 years. In the past 4 years, I have increased revenue from an annual $400,000 in retail business to $2.5 million. I am confident that, with my experience and career goals, I would be an asset to your company.

I would like to request a personal interview at your earliest convenience so we can discuss ways that I can significantly contribute to your team of professionals. Please feel free to contact me at my home telephone number or address if you have additional questions.

Thank you in advance for your time and consideration. I look forward to speaking with you soon.

Sincerely,

Douglas Eastman

Resume Enclosed

DESMOND HOWARD
18 Clinton Ave.
Hickory, North Carolina 88768
(616) 444-7739

> This type of sales job requires a Closer, Relationship Builder, Hungry for Success, and Team Builder. In the very challenging automobile industry, you must be Hungry for Success to be successful!

Professional Objective & Profile

Career-minded individual desiring a business opportunity in marketing or management that will provide a challenging avenue to significantly contribute to a company's organization, growth, and profitability.

A successful track record of achievement has been accomplished with fifteen years of sales experience in a diverse background of businesses through self-motivation and self-discipline. Strong general management qualifications in strategic planning, account development, and quality assurance. Excellent experience in cold calling and developing client relationships. A goal oriented, self-starter, and independent thinker.

Education & Training

Bachelor of Business Administration, 1981
Emphasis: Marketing
DELTA STATE UNIVERSITY, Cleveland, Mississippi

> Do list any advanced training or seminars like the Dale Carnegie Course.

DALE CARNEGIE COURSE, 1986
Completed various industry sales and management courses.

Professional Affiliations

Certified Member of AFIP
(Association of Finance & Insurance Professionals)

Summary of Qualifications

Sales Experience:
Fifteen years total sales experience in Finance & Insurance Products, Office Equipment, Financial Supplies & Forms, and Automobiles.

Sales Management:
Skilled in building sales territories to maximize growth and profitability. Independently manage entire sales cycle from client identification, presentations, contract negotiations and final closings.

Sales Training:
Effectively trained other successful District Managers to develop and manage other districts.

Sales Awards & Honors:
Significantly increased sales through account development and new business in underdeveloped territories in Alabama, Georgia, and Tennessee for MS Diversified Corporation. Awarded *"Salesman of the Year"* in 1987 for Executive Business Products.

Client Relations:
Adept at developing and maintaining strong business relationships with clients. Excellent troubleshooter with ability to utilize creative problem-solving techniques to resolve issues.

Professional Experience

> Many Sales positions include Marketing duties also. Be sure to include this if applicable.

District Sales Manager of Finance & Insurance
ALL STATE DIVERSIFIED CORPORATION
Hickory, North Carolina - 1989 to Present

- *Sales:* Promote the sale of finance and insurance products to the automobile industry. Products include credit insurance, extended service agreements, and customer benefit packages.

- *Account Development:* Responsible for account development in established accounts. Service accounts includes tracking production, training, handling administrative problems, addressing claim problems and maintaining a positive relationship with the client. Provide superior service to customers with follow-up and attention to detail.

- *Marketing:* Responsible for soliciting new accounts within district and promoting/marketing new products to existing accounts. This includes continuously building a network of business contacts and developing relationships with key dealership personnel in prospective accounts. Also, present proposals, individual business plans, and negotiate contracts to prospective dealers.

- *Seminars & Sales Meetings:* Organized numerous seminars and sales meetings to provide ongoing training and information on finance and insurance products.

- *Computer Operations:* Utilize laptop computer to prepare sales call reports, proposals, and documents. Proficient in Windows and WordPerfect.

Sales Representative
EXECUTIVE BUSINESS PRODUCTS
Monroe, Louisiana - 1986 to 1988

- *Sales:* Responsible for selling office equipment throughout north central Louisiana.

Sales Representative
AMERICAN BANK PRODUCTS
Shreveport, Louisiana - 1985 to 1986

- *Sales:* Sold and marketed printed forms, supplies and advertising materials to financial institutions in West Louisiana and East Texas.

Sales Representative & F&I Manager
STRAIGHTWAY OLDSMOBILE
Jackson, Mississippi - 1982 to 1985

- *Sales:* Began as a new car sales representative and advanced to position of F&I Manager.

References

Available upon request.

DESMOND HOWARD
18 Clinton Ave.
Hickory, North Carolina 88768
(616) 444-7739

Date

Gary Miller
General Manager of Sales & Marketing
Jackson's Automobile Service
720 Sweetwater Street
Hickory, North Carolina 88768

> Explaining why you're seeking a new position can offer added insight to your potential employer regarding your situation.

Dear Mr. Miller:

I have reached a point with my current employer where advancement and an acceptable level of opportunity for growth do not exist in the immediate future. Therefore, I am seeking an organization that can utilize a highly motivated, goal-oriented sales and marketing professional.

Enclosed is a personal resume of my qualifications. In addition to a Bachelor of Business Administration from Delta State University, I also possess fifteen years of sales and management experience. My areas of expertise include the following:

- Self-motivated and self-disciplined with ability to work independently or in a team environment.
- Superb sales skills with proven track record of success in increasing sales and profitability.
- Strong interpersonal skills with ability to effectively communicate with diverse individuals and all levels of management and personnel.
- Demonstrated leadership, communication and negotiation skills.
- Proven ability to define issues, propose solutions and implement changes.
- Knowledge and experience of computer systems and applications.

I sincerely believe that, with my experience and career goals, I would be an asset to your organization. I would like to arrange a personal interview at your earliest convenience so we can discuss ways that I can significantly contribute to your team of sales professionals.

Thank you in advance for your time and consideration. I look forward to speaking with you soon.

Sincerely,

Desmond Howard

Resume Enclosed

This type of Sales job includes Closers, Relationship Builders, and Hungry for Success.

GARY MUMFORD
111 Sedwood Drive
Nashville, Tennessee 37215
(615) 355-9876

SALES/MANAGEMENT PROFESSIONAL

A top producer with a proven track record in *major account sales* and *new business development.* A seasoned Account Executive experienced in coordinating sales teams toward total customer satisfaction throughout the sales cycle. Characterized by superior decision-making skills, an ability to cultivate and maximize long-term client relationships, and a constant desire to excel.

PROFESSIONAL EXPERIENCE

ARCOT, Springfield, Tennessee - 1992 to Present
Major Account Sales Representative, 1994 to Present
Sell company products and services directly to end users. Target engineering consulting firms for additional market exposure. Negotiate annual contracts with repeat customers. Interview and recommend candidates for sales positions. Market company capabilities at industry trade shows.

   Major Accomplishments
- Negotiated first ever company contract with *The Home Depot.*
- Closed over $7.7 million in sales in 1996; $4 million in 1995; $2.5 million in 1994.
- Introduced 15 new accounts to company in 1996.
- Increased home center market share by more than 75% since 1994.
- Manage the following key accounts: *The Home Depot, J.C. Penney, COMP USA,* and *Jorgen's.*

Engineered Systems Sales, 1992 to 1994
Developed proposals for presentation to target accounts. Conducted market analyses. Member of sales team led by Vice President of Engineered Systems.

   Major Accomplishments
- Managed three accounts with annual sales of approximately $1.75 million: *Home Quarters, Hechinger,* and *Contractors' Warehouse.*

UNITED STATES MARINE CORPS, Camp Pendleton, California - 1988 to 1991
Director, Advanced Radar & Communications Systems
Completed a 4-year tour of duty achieving the rank of First Lieutenant. Rapidly advanced through a multitude of assignments. Briefed Senior, Allied Officers. Trained Marines in system methodology. Evaluated and promoted Marines.

   Major Accomplishments
- Supervised a crew of 20 Marines during *Operation Desert Storm.*
- Coordinated communications between various headquarters, involving over 500 people.
- Oversaw the fulfillment of hundreds of airstrikes and medical evacuations.
- Successfully planned and executed numerous deployments.

EDUCATION

BELMONT UNIVERSITY, Nashville, Tennessee
Bachelor of Science in Engineering Science & European History, 1987

Any military experience should be included as a regular job.

References Available Upon Request

In Marketing, it is especially important to be a Relationship Builder. Great deals depend not only on your creativity, but also on your ability to network and communicate with industry executives.

FRANCINE K. JENNINGS
5656 Gun Club Drive
New Orleans, Louisiana 27788
(555) 344-0099

In the entertainment industry, any experience in copyrights and contract negotiations is a plus.

Professional Objective & Profile

I am a highly talented **Marketing & Entertainment Industry** professional with 6 years of experience building and leading integrated marketing and promotions operations for entertainment agencies and production companies. Consistently successful in reviewing copyrights and negotiating contracts with entertainment artists and companies. Skilled in developing and spearheading innovative marketing and promotions programs that increase overall company profitability. Possess strong writing skills with experience writing and editing news releases, press kits, brochures, direct mail and feature articles.

I would like to obtain a **Marketing/Promotions** position in the **Entertainment Industry** that will fully utilize my strengths and talents in the marketing and entertainment industry, and where I can significantly contribute to the company's efficiency, organization, growth, and profitability.

Education

Bachelor of Music in Marketing & The Entertainment Industry
UNIVERSITY OF LOUISIANA, New Orleans, Louisiana

Summary of Qualifications

Track Record of Success:
Background exemplifies a successful track record of career accomplishments. Positions have encompassed *Entertainment Agent & Marketing Specialist, MTV Marketing Representative,* and *Entertainment Director.*

Business, Artist & Entertainment Relations:
More than 10 years of experience building and maintaining an exemplary network of business relationships with artists, entertainment and production companies, and executive entertainment staff members. Ability to effectively communicate with all types of individuals in both small and large corporate business environments.

Artist Development - Marketing & Promotions:
Successful background in developing and implementing strong marketing and promotions campaigns to promote artists and entertainment events. Have worked extensively with management companies and booking/talent agencies to coordinate promotions.

Music Industry Experience

Do specify the type of industry where you have gained experience, especially if you want another job in the same industry!

Entertainment Agent & Marketing Specialist
NEW ORLEANS ENTERTAINMENT AGENCY & SUE RECORDS
New Orleans, Louisiana - 1991 to 1993

- *Company Reorganization - Marketing:* Company was initially called Lasting Productions. Af[...] keting operations, revitalized the company into a significant leader in the marketplace. Was responsible for totally restructuring and reengineering marketing methods to more efficiently streamline operations and increase profitability for company.

- *Creative Writing & Editing:* Wrote and edited all promotional, advertising and publicity materials for agency and for more than 40 entertainment artists. This included press kits, brochures, news releases, feature stories, and direct mail.

Document any special skills that will relate to the job you're seeking.

Music Industry Experience

Continued

- *Layout & Design:* Responsible for designing layouts for written materials and coordinating print production.
- *Contract Evaluations:* Evaluated, analyzed, reviewed and negotiated contracts between artists and music venues and promoters.
- *Record Label Production & Artist Development:* Coordinated copyrights and licensing of the songs, etc. Responsible for developing and promoting the careers of artists in the entertainment industry. As a result of designing and implementing strategic promotions and publicity campaigns, and successfully producing a top quality album for a traditional jazz band, this band was nominated to perform in the *Southern Arts Federation's Jazz Forum National Showcase.* This involved extensive interaction with recording studio, musicians, artists, and managers. Coordinated album credits and release information.
- *Public Relations:* Communications liaison between the public and New Orleans Entertainment Agency. Provided information to the public regarding entertainers and special events. Served as agency liaison between agency artists and the *New Orleans Jazz Festival,* the *Family Roots Festival,* and the *French Quarter Festival,* which involved extensive interaction between community businesses and organizations.
- *Direct Mail - Computer Operations:* Developed, coordinated and maintained a comprehensive mailing list to promote jazz festivals and music concerts nationally and locally. Set up, updated and maintained direct mail lists on computer system.
- *Budget Management:* Analyzed and administered operating funds allocated for marketing and publicity. Analyzed budget variances and initiated appropriate strategies to more aggressively control expenditures.
- *Trade Shows & Special Events:* Arranged and designed booths, and facilitated trade shows and special events to promote agency and entertainment artists.

Marketing Representative
MTV: MUSIC TELEVISION
New Orleans, Louisiana - 1989 to 1990

- *Public Relations & Promotions:* As an Intern, directed overall promotions and marketing operations for MTV events at the University of Louisiana. Liaison between MTV Marketing Department in New York and the University of Louisiana. Instrumental in coordinating promotional campaigns to promote MTV.
- *Media Relations:* Coordinated all promotional, publicity, and marketing materials which consisted of news releases, brochures, and feature stories.

Entertainment Director
START RIGHT PRODUCTIONS
New Orleans, Louisiana - 1987 to 1990

- *Entertainment Productions:* Organized and booked music concerts and special events for the University of Louisiana, which involved scheduling all facets of production, lighting and stage crews, equipment, and entertainment personnel. Worked extensively with artists, celebrities, executive entertainment staff members, and entertainment production companies. Reviewed and negotiated contracts and copyrights with entertainment artists and companies.
- *Writing & Editing:* Wrote and edited promotional and advertising materials which consisted of news releases, brochures, flyers, and feature stories.
- *Marketing Management:* Chairperson, responsible for directing overall operations, marketing, and administration of this University in-house production company.
- *Entertainment Sponsors:* Solicited and obtained corporate sponsors for music events. Called on community businesses, organizations and agencies, and personally managed account calls, presentations and negotiations.
- *Budget Management:* Managed and administered a $700,000 annual operating budget.

FRANCINE K. JENNINGS
5656 Gun Club Drive
New Orleans, Louisiana 27788
(555) 344-0099

Date

John Macht
Director of Marketing & Promotions
Windfall Entertainment
2993 Overlook Street
New Orleans, Louisiana 98322

> Francine entices the reader, Mr. Macht, to read more right away, by identifying what the company needs.

Dear Mr. Macht:

High-growth companies such as Windfall Entertainment require leadership, talent and the ability to develop and expand business. With this in mind, I would like to come aboard as your new **Assistant Director of Marketing & Promotions.** I am confident that, with my background in marketing and promotions, I can significantly contribute to Windfall's team of professionals. I have enclosed a personal resume so you may review my credentials.

My areas of expertise and qualifications include the following:

- Six years of comprehensive experience in marketing and promotions encompassing positions as *Entertainment Agent & Marketing Specialist, Marketing Representative* and *Entertainment Director.*
- Excellent writing and editing skills with experience writing news releases, press kits, brochures, feature stories, and direct mail.
- Demonstrated leadership, communication and negotiation skills.
- Proven ability to define issues, propose solutions and implement changes.
- Knowledge of, and experience in, computer systems and applications.
- Strong interpersonal skills with ability to establish and maintain an exemplary network of business associates.

Mr. Macht, I am sure that I would be an asset to your organization, and would like to request a personal interview at your earliest convenience so we can discuss ways that I can significantly contribute to your team of professionals. I will be calling within a couple of days to arrange this interview.

Thank you in advance for your time and consideration. I look forward to speaking with you soon.

Sincerely,

Francine K. Jennings

Resume Enclosed

MARLA SOLOMON

4938 National Street
Gloucester, Massachusetts 39882
(722) 663-0987

OBJECTIVE

To obtain a challenging, achievement-oriented **Marketing** position that will fully utilize skills in Sales, Marketing, Customer Service, and Merchandising.

> This type of sales job requires a person who is Hungry for Success and is a Relationship Builder.

EDUCATION

Bachelor of Arts Degree in Speech Communications, 1993
UNIVERSITY OF MASSACHUSETTS, Gloucester, Massachusetts
Financed 75% of education through work and scholarships.

SUMMARY

> A brief summary of qualifications will quickly point out this candidate's key talents and skills.

- Solid organizational, interpersonal and communication skills.
- Ranked *#1 in District in Sales* while at High Fashion International. Strong sales, marketing and client relations skills.
- Proven ability to define issues, propose solutions, and implement changes.
- Demonstrated leadership, communication and negotiating skills.
- Experience in management and employee relations.

EXPERIENCE

> Marla wanted a position in the cosmetics industry, so it was important to highlight her experience in cosmetics in these two positions.

CLINIQUE, Boston, Massachusetts, 1996 to Present
AREA MARKETING SPECIALIST
- Promote and market Clinique's products by traveling to the different stores in the Boston area.
- Establish and maintain an excellent network of business relationships by providing superior service to customers, and by educating them regarding Clinique's products.

ENTERTAINMENT PHOTOS, Boston, Massachusetts, 1995 to 1996
MAKE-UP ARTIST & CUSTOMER SERVICE REPRESENTATIVE
- Responsible for providing make-up services to customers.
- Provided excellent service to customers by effectively responding to their requests, inquiries, suggestions, and/or concerns.

POSTAGE COMPANY, INC., Boston, Massachusetts, 1994 to 1995
ASSOCIATE AREA SALES REPRESENTATIVE
- Sold postage meters to area companies and increased sales by 37% within one year.
- Provided superior service to clients to ensure customer satisfaction.
- Generated sales through cold-calling and setting up appointments.

HIGH FASHION INTERNATIONAL, Boston, Massachusetts, 1992 to 1994
SALES DEVELOPMENT MANAGER/MERCHANDISER
- Managed overall operations and administration of retail store.
- Planned and implemented sales contests as motivational techniques for employees.
- Responsible for merchandising, marketing and advertising.
- Ranked #1 in District in sales, and instrumental in store being the #1 Store in District on several occasions.

MARLA SOLOMON

4938 National Street
Gloucester, Massachusetts 39882
(722) 663-0987

Date

Karen Taylor
Executive Vice President of Marketing
Cosmetics Techniques, Inc.
2083 Dover Street
Boston, Massachusetts 30029

Dear Ms. Taylor:

Experience in *Sales, Marketing, Customer Service, Merchandising, and Management* makes me an excellent candidate for the position of Marketing Assistant, which was advertised in the *Bostonian Newspaper* last week. As requested, I have enclosed a personal resume which will provide you with details concerning my qualifications.

As you will note, I am not a beginner, but rather a seasoned professional with diversified experience. My areas of expertise include the following:

> Emphasizing her experience in the cosmetics industry was important since she wanted a Marketing position in cosmetics.

- Hands-on experience in Marketing in the Cosmetics Industry.
- Extensive sales, marketing, and merchandising experience. Ranked #1 in District in Sales while at High Fashion International. High achiever and extremely goal-oriented.
- Ability to manage employees and motivate associates to achieve their maximum potential.
- Demonstrated leadership, communication and negotiating skills.
- Proven ability to define issues, propose solutions and implement changes.

I sincerely believe that, with my experience and career goals, I would be an asset to your organization. I would like to request a personal interview at your earliest convenience so we can discuss how I can best contribute to your team of professionals.

Thank you in advance for your time and consideration. I look forward to speaking with you soon.

Sincerely,

Marla Solomon

Resume Enclosed

A Marketing Executive must be a Closer, Relationship Builder, and Team Builder.

EDWARD M. SHEPARD

Executive Credentials

1234 Streetline Avenue
Atlanta, Georgia 30399
(404) 476-0012

EDWARD M. SHEPARD
1234 Streetline Avenue
Atlanta, Georgia 30399
(404) 476-0012

Executive Profile

A versatile, multi-talented **Senior Marketing Executive, Entrepreneur, Administrator** and **Leader,** with a proven track record of success including more than 20 years of experience building and leading integrated marketing, financial and data processing operations for major corporations. Consistently successful in developing and nurturing international and domestic client relationships. Conversationally fluent in Spanish and French with an extensive background in European travel.

Strong general management qualifications in business analysis and development, strategic planning and all facets of process/productivity/quality improvement. Talented in spearheading business opportunities; developing marketing strategies to maximize growth; integrating and reengineering operations to reduce costs and increase profitability; and effecting smooth company mergers and acquisitions.

Excellent leader and insightful mentor who is dedicated to team- and partnership-building. Proactive toward customer service and employee relations.

Desire a challenging career opportunity in **Marketing** involving leadership and partnership. Would like to become a full partner, with opportunities to expand and build a highly successful business.

Education   *Master of Business Administration*
HARVARD BUSINESS SCHOOL, Boston, Massachusetts, 1973

Master of Arts in Journalism
UNIVERSITY OF MASSACHUSETTS, Boston, Massachusetts, 1970

Bachelor of Science in Commerce - Bachelor of Arts in American History
MERCER UNIVERSITY, Boston, Massachusetts, 1968

Honors & Affiliations

- *Author of historical biography,* Ramey Faxon, *University of Mississippi Publishers. (1974)*

- *Director of the Winston Companies, (NYSE), Property & Casualty Insurance. (1990-93)*

- *Director of the Wind Corporation (NYSE), Work Uniform Manufacturing, Rental/Laundering and Sales. (1989-93)*

- *Member of the Omega Delta Kappa (National Leadership Fraternity) and Kappa Tau Alpha (Journalism Scholarship).*

- *Captain in the United States Army Transportation Corps, Virginia. (1972)*

Executive Experience

President & CEO
RETAIL SYSTEMS GROUP, Atlanta, Georgia - 1994 to 1996

- *Management - Marketing & Operations:* Managed overall marketing and finance operations for this company. Managed 1,250 employees nationwide, who were engaged in telecommunications and POS operations. Responsible for application design, including newly developed programs for gift registry, foreign office buying and corporatewide human resources management.
- *Information Systems:* Reengineered computer operations from mainframe to client/server technology. Designed and implemented new desktop applications and database management systems. Scope of operations: 1,800 MIPS; 3 terabytes of DASD; 10,000 desktops; 75,000 cash registers; nationwide proprietary telecommunications network.
- *Profitability:* Launched companywide long-term strategic marketing plans to outsource in-house functions performed by this division for Retail and accomplished a significant reduction in costs, thereby increasing overall profitability by 70% for company.

Vice Chairman & Board Member
FINE DEPARTMENT STORES COMPANY, New York, New York - 1982 to 1992

- *Company Track Record of Success:* Began with this national retailer in 1982 as *Executive Vice President of Strategic Planning & Human Resources.* Progressed to position of *Vice Chairman & Board Member* in 1986.
- *Financial Management:* Held full profit & loss responsibility for overall operations of 7 department store companies (a total of 138 stores and 38,000 employees in 14 states which then comprised 40% of the $10 billion in annual revenue).
- *Company Mergers:* Successfully spearheaded major company mergers to streamline operations and decrease costs.
- *Profitability:* Consistently met or surpassed financial goals without exceeding inventory plan.
- *Marketing Management & Market Development:* Worked closely with Principals of these stores to develop business opportunities and marketing strategies to maximize growth and profitability, to accomplish the mission of these businesses and to expand market penetration.

Executive Vice President of Merchandising & Marketing
1982 to 1986

- *Business Planning:* Conceptualized, designed and initiated strategic business plans and human resources activities to promote services for corporate and division executives. Activities included spearheading overall corporate strategic initiatives.
- *Marketing & Merchandising:* Helped reposition several department store companies through industry leading merchandising and marketing programs.
- *Human Resources Development:* Developed, organized and implemented complete corporate human resources programs including compensation, performance appraisal, and career development.

Principal - Partner
COCHRANE & COMPANY, INC., Chicago, Illinois - 1975 to 1982

- *Elected Partner in 1980:* Directed and managed various marketing projects for U.S. client companies in consumer packaged goods, advertising and food manufacturing.
- *International Relations:* Traveled throughout Europe to work on mergers for U.S. client companies.

EDWARD M. SHEPARD
1234 Streetline Ave.
Atlanta, Georgia 30399
(404) 476-0012

Date

Jacqueline Morris
President & CEO
Business Ventures, Inc.
9033 Peach Drive
Atlanta, Georgia 30399

Dear Ms. Morris:

> This Marketing Executive is seeking an executive position or partnership and will want to highlight his skills in all areas of Marketing, Sales, and Operations.

Are you looking for a highly motivated, goal-oriented executive and entrepreneur to become a leading partner in your organization? I am confident that, with my 20-plus years of experience and hands-on approach to business, I could significantly contribute to your company's efficiency, organization, growth and profitability. I have enclosed a personal resume; briefly summarized, my qualifications and expertise include the following:

- Experience as division President & CEO, Corporate Vice Chairman and Board Member at major corporations.
- Talented in restructuring and designing nationwide marketing, merchandising and financial programs that yield reduced company costs and increased profitability.
- Recent success as a CIO, including migrating from mainframe to client-server computer technology as well as managing nationwide telecommunications, point-of-sale networks, and large data center operations.
- Savvy marketing skills with ability to spearhead innovative campaigns to reposition operations to become more competitive and high-profile.
- Conversationally fluent in French and Spanish with international exposure to leading businesses and conferences in foreign cultures.
- Adept troubleshooter who can research and identify problems in operating systems or with employee relations. Very skilled in creative problem-solving techniques to resolve issues.
- Experienced in company acquisitions and mergers; successfully managed a series of large-scale integrations.
- Dynamic interpersonal, communication, writing and negotiating skills.
- Proactive leader who encourages and supports a teamlike work environment to increase employee morale, productivity and efficiency.

I sincerely believe that, with my experience, insightful perception, and commitment to success, I would be an asset to your organization and plan to contact you within a few days so we can discuss business opportunities.

Thank for your time and consideration.

Sincerely,

Edward M. Shepard

Enclosure

This type of Marketing position encompasses Relationship Builders, Creative Think Tanks, and Team Builders.

ELIZABETH Q. DUNAGAN
6767 West Hills Drive
Beverly Hills California 90210
(708) 888-6767

Closer, Relationship Builder

Professional Objective & Profile

Qualified, multi-talented **Director of Operations** with more than 20 years of experience building and leading multi-disciplinary operations for multimillion and billion dollar corporations. Desire a position with a leading company that will provide a challenging opportunity to significantly contribute to and improve the efficiency, organization, growth, and profitability.

Summary of Qualifications

Track Record of Success:
Background exemplifies a successful track record of career accomplishments which encompasses positions as *Area Director & Regional Training Director, Vice President & Director of Operations, General Manager and Catering Director & Supervisor.*

Management, Sales & Marketing:
Strong general management qualifications in strategic planning, business development, sales, marketing, public speaking, media & client relations, and leadership. Won numerous awards for outstanding leadership, marketing, and sales performances.

Employee Relations, Training & Team Building:
Developed and implemented numerous training programs to improve job performances. In-depth background in writing training manuals, and in facilitating programs to train all levels of management and personnel. Empower employees to think and work independently and in a team environment

Public Speaking & Public Relations:
Extensive experience in public speaking and public relations. Powerful motivational speaking skills. Background includes appearances on television & radio talk shows and at seminars.

Advanced Education & Training

GENERAL MILLS COLLEGE FOR EXECUTIVES, Cool Springs, Delaware
Areas of Concentration: Public Relations, Public Speaking, Media Relations, Motivational Speaking, Recruitment.

UNIVERSITY OF MARYLAND, College Park, Maryland
Area of Concentration: Business Administration

It's important to emphasize teambuilding experience, since this is an important part of a Marketing position.

Professional Experience

Area Marketing Director & Regional Training Director
BIG BOYS, INC., Beverly Hills, California - 1996 to 1997

- *Management:* Directed overall operations of Big Boy's Restaurants in specific region. Responsible for conducting ongoing analyses to evaluate the efficiency, quality and productivity of business operations which achieved more than $16 million annually.
- *Personnel:* Supervised more than 40 Managers and 500 employees. Delegated work responsibilities and monitored overall job performances to ensure accuracy and adherence to policies and procedures.
- *Marketing:* Developed and implemented innovative marketing strategies into everyday operations to increase business and overall profitability for company.
- *Training & Development:* Spearheaded the training operations which included training and developing management staff to achieve maximum potential in their performance.
- *Labor & Cost Control:* Effectively reduced labor and inventory costs through streamlining of operations and efficient utilization of inventory. Saved company more than $72,000 in one year.

Since Marketing Executives often wear more than one hat, briefly outline your comprehensive experience.

Professional Experience

Continued

Vice President of Marketing & Director of Operations
RESTAURANT MANAGEMENT GROUP
WEST COAST FOODS COMPANY
San Mateo, California - 1989 to 1996

- *Management:* Directed and managed overall operations of small restaurant chain which included 5 restaurants. Held direct P&L responsibility and managed the development of new units and nurturance of client relationships, core prospect marketing, all accounting/financial affairs and personnel.
- *Program Development:* Developed and implemented Training Programs for restaurant chain. Taught effective methods in guest services, team building, employee relations and restaurant management.

General Manager
Catering Director & Supervisor
QUAKER MILLS RESTAURANT GROUP - Red Lobster Restaurants
Los Angeles, California - 1981 to 1989

- *Management:* Directed and managed overall operations of area Red Lobster Restaurants, which achieved $60 million in a billion dollar corporation. Consistently increased revenue performance and profitability for company as a result of innovative, strategic marketing and development.
- *Business Development - Project Management:* Conceptualized, planned, and initiated the nationwide Catering Services for Red Lobster. Responsible for researching and analyzing potential catering markets, all accounting/financial affairs, competitive bidding, and entire project management. Managed new business development and strategic planning to maximize growth and profitability. Established growth plans for individual accounts and personally managed account calls, presentations, and negotiations.
- *Vendor & Client Relations:* Established and maintained an excellent network of business relationships as a result of extensive interaction between vendors and clients.
- *New Store Openings:* Opened the highest volume restaurant in Red Lobster's history in San Francisco, California. Served over 11,000 guests per week. In addition, responsible for managing the conversion of 17 stores to Red Lobster Restaurants in southern California. Directed all material planning, capital equipment acquisition, financial performance analysis and planning/development functions.
- *Quality Assurance & Control:* Investigated and monitored facilities; inspected Health & Sanitation operations, as well as operational methods, to ensure adherence to OSHA and other safety and health rules, regulations, and standards.
- *Budget Management:* Developed and administered operating budgets. Analyzed budget variances and initiated appropriate strategies to more aggressively control expenditures.
- *Inventory Control:* Responsible for monitoring inventory and efficiently controlled inventory by improving accuracy and streamlining handling procedures.

Area Supervisor
MORGAN STEAKHOUSE, Baltimore, Maryland - 1974 to 1981

- *Company Track Record of Success:* Began as a Manager in Training, and advanced to positions of higher levels of responsibility and authority due to outstanding job performance. This company was bought by General Mills Restaurant Group (listed above.)
- *Area Supervisor:* Responsible for full scale operations of 4 Country Steakhouse Restaurants in designated area and included all areas of management, training, supervision, inventory & purchasing, and customer service.

JOHNSON MILLIGAN

1897 Ridge Trail
Memphis, Tennessee 32876
(909) 676-3726

> It is okay to use the first person in the Executive Profile.

> This type of Sales & Marketing position encompasses Closers, Creative Think Tanks, Relationship Builders, and Team Builders.

Executive Profile

I am a high-caliber **Executive Sales & Marketing Director,** with more than 20 years of experience building and leading integrated sales and marketing operations for high profile nationwide retail companies. I place a strong focus on team building and employee relations, for without a unified force, businesses cannot excel. One of my greatest contributions to a company is my positive team approach toward staff members which leads to unified efforts and ultimate success. A proactive leader and motivator, I serve as a Mentor for my staff and take great pride in developing their skills and talents to their maximum potential so they can achieve optimum results. I create a team-oriented environment and introduce a participative decision-making style which results in high employee morale and company profitability.

My background exemplifies a successful track record of career accomplishments which include executive positions as **President, Vice President of Sales & Marketing,** and **Corporate Vice President** for leading retail industries. I am talented in reengineering and restructuring companies to position them in higher profile markets to increase sales and profitability. In addition, I have built and nurtured client/business relationships throughout my career and have established an exemplary network of business associates in the retail industry. Experienced in all facets of process/productivity/quality improvement, I am skilled in developing, introducing, and expanding new product lines into a competitive marketplace. With in-depth experience in conceptualizing and developing business opportunities and marketing strategies, I can maximize growth and profitability for integrated operations. I am an executive liaison with comprehensive analytical, planning, organizational and negotiation skills.

Education & Affiliations

Annual CEO U.S. Sales Conferences, Footwear Industries of America and U.S. Recruiting Committee
Franklin Academy, New York, New York, *Area of Concentration: Business Administration*

Executive Experience

Sales Manager National Accounts
BOOT & FOOTWEAR INC.
Memphis, Tennessee - 1996 to Present

- *Sales & Marketing Management:* Manage and direct overall national sales and marketing operations for company. Recognized by President of Boot & Footwear for outstanding performance and client relations skills. Responsible for strategic planning and development of integrated sales, marketing and business development campaigns targeted to consumers nationwide. Lead sales and marketing teams to redesign and improve sales and marketing management processes on an ongoing basis. Consult with different lines of footwear regarding long-term strategic planning and further business development and expansion and changing distribution base to broaden market expansion.
- *Team-Building - Employee Relations:* After taking over sales operations, created a team-oriented structure and introduced participative decision-making style, which has resulted in a successful sales and operations management team.

BEST SHOES, INC. - 1994 to 1996

- *Company Track Record of Success:* Served in 2 executive positions including, **President** and **Vice President of Sales Operations** for different divisions of Best Shoes, Inc.
- *Company Reengineering:* Recruited to direct an aggressive reorganization and profit/performance improvement sales program for Best Shoes, Inc. to make it marketable to other companies. Provided direction for long-range business focus to meet industry changes and requirements.

Executive Experience

President
FOOTWEAR COMPANY, 1995 to 1996

- *Management:* Launched a fine dress and casual shoe program to sell to major retailers and upscale independent stores. Led companywide reengineering and market positioning program to achieve revenue growth and profit improvement. Restructured all key departments which included personnel staffing and development. Held full financial and operating responsibility for this division.
- *Sales & Profitability:* Achieved 78% profitability as a result of designing and implementing new sales programs, which increased overall profitability for company.
- *Account Management:* Established growth plans for individual accounts and personally managed account calls, presentations, and negotiations.
- *Budget Management:* Managed, analyzed and projected budget for operating expenditures. Analyzed budget variances and initiated appropriate guidelines to more aggressively control expenditures.

Vice President of Sales Operations
FLACKS FOOTWEAR, A Best Shoes Company - 1995 to 1996

- *Sales Management:* Directed and managed overall sales operations for this Best Shoes company. Expanded the distribution base to department stores and fine independents nationwide, while also controlling markdowns. Developed and implemented innovative marketing strategies to increase sales.
- *Product Introduction:* Planned and directed the introduction of Flacks Footwear in stores nationwide. Successfully positioned brand as one of the leading products in the marketplace through high impact marketing, advertising and promotional strategies.
- *Profitability:* Increased sales revenue by **$5.5 million** and margins by 8.5%

Vice President of Sales & Marketing
ALL CHILDRENS' DIVISIONS - 1994 to 1995

- *Management:* Brought in to build up distribution to include major department stores and fine independents. Held full P&L responsibility for all children's divisions of Best Shoes, including *Toddler University, University Brands and Street Hot Athletics.*
- *Product Development - Marketing:* Coordinated market research activities, maintained competitor information, and managed product/service development and pricing strategy. Developed business opportunities and marketing strategies to maximize growth and expand market penetration.

Director of Sales & Marketing
NIKE, INC., Portland, Oregon - 1991 to 1993

- *Management:* Directed and managed overall sales, marketing and product development operations for Nike, Inc. Recruited to reengineer operations of division and achieve profitability through high volume.
- *Product Development:* Designed and developed product that was technologically advanced. Worked with vendors worldwide to produce the most advanced footwear, which resulted in Nike having the best sell-through at retails that they had achieved in many years. Achieved the first profit for a fiscal year.
- *Sales & Profitability:* Grew annual sales from $23 million to **$35.6 million. Company was on track to achieve $41 million in 1994. Drastically reduced markdowns.**
- *Product Development:* Developed and designed strategic marketing plans to introduce a men's casual line into the marketplace. Successfully promoted product to major department stores and upscale independent stores nationwide. Achieved sell-through at retail among the highest ever in men's and women's brands in industry.

> Throughout his resume, his accomplishments and the increases in profitability are highlighted. This is key information in all sales & marketing resumes.

Carrie Marshall

1800 Thoroughbred Court ~ San Antonio, Texas 78248 ~ (210) 999-0909

Multi-talented, multilingual **Executive in International Marketing, Sales, Contract and Materials Management,** with more than 20 years of experience planning, building, and leading integrated sales, marketing and management operations for international companies. Proven track record of success in all facets of international sales, which involves extensive contract negotiations with European and U.S. companies.

Strong general management qualifications in strategic planning, research & feasibility analysis, contract negotiations, organizational reengineering, and all facets of process/productivity/quality improvement. High-caliber executive liaison with international companies. Fluent in English, Italian, French and knowledgeable of Spanish. Highly successful in analyzing, planning, organizing and negotiating new business opportunities. Have held full decision-making responsibility for developing annual financial objectives and preparing long-range strategic business plans. Will Relocate.

Master's Degree in Law & Economics, NAPLES UNIVERSITY, Naples, Italy

Director of Material Management & Marketing
THE THOMPSON ENERGY COMPANY
An Aerospace Company, San Antonio, Texas - 1988 to Present

> A Marketing Executive is skilled as a Relationship Builder, Creative Think Tank, and Team Builder.

- **Company Track Record of Success:** Began with company in 1988 as a *Partner* and *Contract Manager* of an Italian Aerospace Company, which contracted with The Thompson Energy Company. Advanced to position of *Director of Material Management* in 1993.
- **Management:** Report directly to the President of the company, and hold full responsibility and decision-making authority for all company purchasing and subcontract negotiations to increase profitability. Also, in charge of managing subcontracts and material planning for company which achieves $125 million in annual sales, employs 1,500 non-union employees, and is one of the world's largest aircraft modification centers.
- **Marketing:** Responsible for directing all marketing operations for company.
- **Budget & Financial Management:** Analyze, manage and administer an $80 million budget for operating expenditures and capital asset projects. Responsible for financial performance analysis and business planning/development functions. Analyze budget variances and initiate appropriate guidelines to more aggressively control expenditures and increase productivity.
- **International & National Client Relations:** Established partnership of European company with the Thompson Energy Company, and on an ongoing basis, maintain an exemplary network of business associates as a result of interacting extensively with U.S. and European clients.
- **Quality Control:** Work closely with subcontractors to ensure adherence to ISO 9000, OSHA and all other Federal, State and local laws, rules and regulations.
- **Personnel:** Interview, hire, and manage 75 staff members. Delegate responsibilities and monitor job performances to ensure accuracy and adherence to policies and procedures.

Director of Marketing, Contracts & Programs (1978 to 1992)

- **Marketing & Business Development:** Responsible for managing new business development and strategic planning to maximize growth and profitability. Established growth plans for company and personally managed account calls, presentations and negotiations on an international and national level.
- **Sales:** Diversified market segments and customer base, introduced new product lines and expanded sales. Assisted in establishing company as one of the leading aircraft modification centers in the world through creative design and implementation of high-impact marketing, advertising and promotional strategies.

> If you write a one-page resume, but have a more extensive background, let the employer know you can furnish a more comprehensive portfolio.

A More Comprehensive Portfolio Available Upon Request

Carrie Marshall
1800 Thoroughbred Court
San Antonio, Texas 78248
(210) 999-0909

Date

Mr. John Henson
CEO and Director of Marketing
2983 Highlands Avenue
Westward Manufacturing
Redmond, Washington 98021

Dear Mr. Henson:

This is an effective way to network with companies. If this person doesn't have a need for you in his company but knows of a company that does, he will pass on your resume.

If you or anyone you know of could use a multilingual, multi-talented **Executive Marketing and Sales Management** professional with more than 20 years of experience in International Marketing, Sales, Contracts and Materials Management experience, please pass my resume on to them or call me.

My areas of qualifications and expertise include the following:

- Multi-talented, multilingual **Executive in International Marketing, Sales, Contract and Materials Management.**
- More than 20 years of experience planning, building, and leading integrated sales, marketing and management operations for international companies.
- Demonstrated abilities in all facets of international sales and marketing, which involves extensive contract negotiations with European and U.S. companies.
- Fluent in English, Italian, French and knowledgeable of Spanish.
- Highly successful in analyzing, planning, organizing and negotiating new business opportunities.

I will be calling you within a couple of days to arrange a personal meeting so we can discuss employment opportunities.

Thank you in advance for your time and I look forward to speaking with you soon.

Sincerely,

Carrie Marshall

Resume Enclosed

> This Sales & Marketing
> background involves skills
> as a Closer, Creative Think
> Tank, Relationship Builder,
> and Team Builder.

TAYLOR CUNNINGHAM

A Presentation

of

Professional Credentials

8989 Sedberry Road
Portland, Oregon 87878
(909) 888-2772

TAYLOR CUNNINGHAM

8989 Sedberry Road
Portland, Oregon 87878
(909) 888-2772

PROFESSIONAL OBJECTIVE & PROFILE

High-Caliber **Executive Marketing & Sales Manager** with more than 19 years of experience building and leading integrated sales and marketing operations for high profile companies. Strong focus on team-building and employee relations. Excellent leader who creates a team-oriented environment, which increases employee efficiency and productivity.

Skilled executive liaison with experience in strategic business planning, organizational reengineering, and in building and nurturing client/business relationships. Successful in leading business opportunities and marketing strategies to maximize growth and profitability. Experienced in employee training, development, supervision, and leadership. Excellent analytical, planning, organizational and negotiation skills. In-depth background in all facets of process/productivity/quality improvement.

Desire a **management and leadership** position in **Sales & Marketing** that will provide a challenging opportunity to significantly contribute to a company's efficiency, organization, growth, and profitability.

SUMMARY OF QUALIFICATIONS

Track Record of Success:
Background exemplifies a successful track record of career accomplishments which encompass positions as General Manager, District Sales Manager and Manager - Travel Agency Sales. Consistently advanced throughout career to positions of higher levels of responsibility and authority through outstanding job performance.

EDUCATION

Bachelor of Science in English
OREGON UNIVERSITY, Portland, Oregon

Associate of Liberal Arts
OREGON STATE COLLEGE, Portland, Oregon

ADVANCED TRAINING

UNIVERSITY OF OREGON
Sales Management & Marketing Strategy

LEARNING INTERNATIONAL - XEROX TRAINING CENTER
Challenges of Sales Management
Selling with Presentations
Sales Coaching
Professional Sales Negotiation
Account Development Strategies
Professional Selling Skills
Interpersonal Management Skills

DALE CARNEGIE COURSE, Portland, Oregon

Lots of strong, high-powered verbs are used throughout the resume to signify action!

PROFESSIONAL EXPERIENCE

General Manager
AIRLINE UNIFORM SERVICE
Portland, Oregon - 1995 to Present

- **Company Track Record of Success:** Began with company in 1995 in Cleveland, Ohio as *Service Manager* and was promoted to *General Manager* in 1996 and transferred to Portland, Oregon.
- **Management:** Manage and direct overall operations and administration of this major industrial uniform rental service and laundry.
- **Sales & Profitability: Increased annual sales by $250,000** in 1996 as a result of soliciting and obtaining new accounts and successfully maintaining existing clients, which increased overall profitability for company.
- **Marketing:** Successfully reengineered marketing operations and positioned company as a leader in the industry. As a result, company has achieved its most profitable year in its history.
- **Business Development & Account Management:** Responsible for managing new business development and strategic planning to maximize growth and profitability. Establish growth plans for individual accounts and personally manage account calls, presentations, and negotiations.
- **Client Relations:** Continuously establish and maintain an exemplary network of business associates as a result of extensive interaction and strong communication skills.
- **Customer Service:** Provide superior service to customers through attention to detail and follow-up on all sales. Effectively respond to clients' inquiries, requests, suggestions, and/or concerns.
- **Personnel, Training & Development - Supervision:** Interview, hire, train and develop employees in all areas of sales and customer service. Delegate responsibilities and monitor overall job performances to ensure accuracy and adherence to policies and procedures.
- **Quality Control:** Supervise all areas of quality control and review service and products to ensure the highest quality and compliance with standards and regulations.
- **Budget Management:** Manage, analyze and administer budget for operating expenditures and projects. Responsible for financial performance analysis and business planning/development functions. Analyze budget variances and initiate appropriate guidelines to more aggressively control expenditures and increase productivity.

District Sales Manager
CONTINENTAL AIRLINES, Cleveland, Ohio - 1989 to 1995

- **Sales Management & Profitability:** Managed and directed overall sales operations of this $100 million district. Exceeded all sales goals and increased local sales **more than $20 million** which significantly increased company profitability.
- **Supervision:** Managed and supervised employees including customer service representatives, sales representatives and administrative staff.

Manager - Travel Agency Sales
CONTINENTAL AIRLINES
Washington, D.C. and Winston-Salem, North Carolina - 1978 to 1989

- **Company Track Record of Success:** Began with USAir/Piedmont Airlines in 1978 and continued to advance to positions of higher levels of responsibility and authority.
- **Management:** Held full decision-making authority for region which exceeded $1.6 billion annually. Managed and directed national accounts, direct mail, and regional sales operations.
- **Public Relations:** Authorized spokesperson for airline. Liaison between media and airlines and responsible for providing information to the public, including release of information to the media.
- **Sales & Marketing:** Developed innovative marketing and business strategies and plans to maximize growth and profitability, expand market penetration and accomplish mission of company.

TAYLOR CUNNINGHAM
8989 Sedberry Road
Portland, Oregon 87878
(909) 888-2772

Date

Chad McNabb
Executive Director of Sales & Marketing
Corporate Companies of America
29883 Shoreline Boulevard
Portland, Oregon 87878

Dear Mr. McNabb:

A mutual friend, Mr. Robert Weston, mentioned that you are looking for a highly motivated, goal-oriented Sales Manager to become a leader for Corporate Companies of America. I am confident that with my background in sales, marketing and client relations, I can significantly contribute to your company's team of professionals. I have enclosed a personal resume so you may review my credentials.

In addition to a Bachelor of Science from Oregon University, I also possess more than 19 years of professional experience. My qualifications and areas of expertise include the following:

- Adept in all areas of sales management and customer service. Talented in designing and implementing innovative sales and marketing strategies that reposition operations to become more competitive and that yield significant company profitability.
- Financial and analytical expertise in budget development, forecasting, and management. Strong strategic and business planning qualifications.
- Demonstrated leadership, communication and negotiation skills.
- Proven ability to define issues, propose solutions and implement changes.
- Effective team-building skills with ability to empower associates to think and work independently, as well as in a team environment. Lead associates to achieve their maximum potential.

I sincerely believe that, with my experience and career aspirations, I would be an asset to your organization. I would like to request a personal interview at your earliest convenience so we can discuss how I can best contribute to your company's goals.

Thank you in advance for your time and consideration. I look forward to speaking with you soon.

Sincerely,

Taylor Cunningham

Resume Enclosed

In Banking, Sales & Marketing, professionals are Relationship Builders, Creative Think Tanks, and Team Builders.

Jessica Slovich

A Presentation

of

Sales & Marketing Credentials

9090 West Mercer Avenue
Cincinnati, Ohio 37001
(502) 888-0123

The Objective & Profile is a small story about the candidate. Use it as a powerful, attention-grabbing sales tool!

Jessica Slovich

Professional Objective & Profile

Highly motivated, goal-oriented **Sales & Marketing** professional with more than 15 years of experience building and leading integrated sales and marketing operations for major financial corporations. Consistently successful in developing, expanding and building sales territories to achieve maximum growth and profitability.

Strong general management qualifications in strategic planning, organizational reengineering and development, and process/productivity/quality improvement. Excellent experience in personnel training, development and leadership. Skilled public speaker and executive liaison.

Desire a position in **Sales & Marketing** that will provide a challenging opportunity to significantly contribute to a company's efficiency, organization, growth, and profitability.

Summary of Qualifications

This Summary of Qualifications clearly focuses on specific areas that are beneficial in a Sales & Marketing career.

Track Record of Success:
Background exemplifies a successful track record of career accomplishments which include more than 15 years of professional experience. Positions have encompassed *Sales Executive, Regional Sales Manager, Assistant Branch Manager, Associate Director of Business Development, and Administrative Assistant to President.*

Marketing & Sales:
Solid background in marketing and sales. Skilled in developing business opportunities and marketing strategies to maximize growth and profitability. Successful in accomplishing mission of expanding market penetration and increasing sales growth. Personally ranked #1 in sales volume for 3 years while at Winchester Bank, and ranked #1 in the number of new merchant accounts sold for 2 years.

Program Development:
Talented in developing, designing, and initiating companywide programs that yield company savings and profitability. For example, developed and implemented a Regional Merchant Bank Card Sales Program that was successful in achieving **$46 million in annual sales volume.**

Client & Public Relations:
Strong interpersonal skills. Easily establishes excellent rapport and makes effective sales presentations to all levels of management including top corporate executives and administrators. On an ongoing basis, establish and maintain an exemplary network of business associates through effective public relations and superior client/customer service.

Always quantify your achievements by using actual numbers and percentages.

Advanced Education & Training

CINCINNATI UNIVERSITY
Cincinnati School of Banking, (Graduate) Cincinnati, Ohio

Bachelor of Science in Secondary Education
Minor: Psychology & Sociology
OHIO TECHNOLOGICAL UNIVERSITY, Cincinnati, Ohio

AMERICAN INSTITUTE OF BANKING, Cincinnati, Ohio

When your company has been bought, merged, or reorganized, write a brief history to explain the situation. The reader will appreciate this.

Professional Experience

NOVA INFORMATION SYSTEMS
(WINCHESTER BANK until 1992), Cincinnati, Ohio - 1987 to Present

- ***Company History:*** Began working for Winchester Bank as a *Regional Sales Manager* in 1987. In 1992, Third Union National Bank bought Winchester. Continued working for Third Union as a *Regional Sales Manager,* and then in 1996, Nova Information Systems bought Portfolio from Third Union, and continued working for company in position of *Sales Executive.* A brief synopsis of responsibilities and positions is highlighted below.

Public Relations skills exemplify a Relationship Builder.

Sales Executive
NOVA INFORMATION SYSTEMS -1996 to Present

- ***Sales Management:*** Responsible for selling merchant bank card processing services which involves selling electronic processing equipment to businesses and organizations. Cross-sell commercial banking services in support of 54 Third Union National Bank branch offices throughout Ohio. Manage new business development and strategic planning to maximize growth and profitability.
- ***Account Management:*** Manage all aspects of multimillion dollar accounts in Ohio. Establish growth plans for individual accounts and personally manage account calls, presentations, and negotiations.
- ***Public Relations:*** Develop and maintain an exemplary network of business associates through extensive interaction and communication. Call on clients with the Bank's *Banking & Cash Management Departments, Commercial, Private* and present reports at the Quarterly Executive Consumer Sales Meeting.
- ***Client Services & Training:*** Provide excellent service to clients through attentive follow-up to accounts. Install electronic processing equipment for clients and train them in operations. Respond effectively to clients' inquiries, suggestions, requests, and/or concerns. Implement creative problem-solving techniques to resolve issues.

Regional Sales Manager
THIRD UNION NATIONAL BANK - 1992 to 1996

- ***Program Development:*** In charge of developing and initiating a Regional Merchant Bank Card Sales Program. This involved developing and maximizing commercial account leads.
- ***Sales & Profitability:*** Solicited, sold, and maintained Ohio's 5 largest accounts, which totaled $46 million in annual sales volume, and significantly increased overall profitability for Third Union. Achieved $12 million in new processing sales volume during 1995.
- ***Quality Control Committee:*** Selected as one of 5 members of the Quality Team for the purpose of creating and establishing quality guidelines for the FUNB of Ohio, which were submitted to corporate offices in Illinois.
- ***Personnel Training & Development:*** Developed and facilitated numerous training programs for Sales Representatives and bank personnel for 54 regional branch offices.
- ***Market Research & Analysis:*** Researched and conducted ongoing analyses of target markets to evaluate potential profitability ratios.

Regional Sales Manager
WINCHESTER BANK - 1987 to 1992

- ***Program Development:*** In charge of developing and administering a Regional Merchant & Agent Bank Card Sales Program for Winchester.
- ***Account Development & Management:*** Developed commercial and agent bank account leads, and managed and directed all facets of accounts.
- ***Sales & Profitability:*** Due to high sales, Ohio ranked 1st among 5 regions in the number of new merchant accounts signed during 1988-1990. Ranked #1 in sales volume for 3 years. Personally ranked #1 in the number of new merchant accounts sold during 1988-1990.

Having Personnel Training skills also denotes that you have team building skills, which can be beneficial in sales.

Jessica Slovich
9090 West Mercer Ave.
Cincinnati, Ohio 37001
(502) 888-0123

Date

Gregory Stewart
Director of Sales & Marketing
Eastern Bank
911 Washington Street
Cincinnati, Ohio 37001

> Expressing confidence in your Cover Letter will make the reader take notice!

Dear Mr. Stewart:

The ability to develop and expand banking services is one of my greatest strengths. Since you are now looking for a highly motivated, success-oriented **Sales and Marketing** professional, I believe this is the perfect time to arrange a meeting so we can discuss employment opportunities. I am confident that I can significantly contribute to your company's efficiency, organization, growth, and profitability. For your review, I have enclosed a personal resume which will provide you with details concerning my background and qualifications.

As you will note in my resume, I am not a beginner, but rather a seasoned professional with more than 15 years of experience building successful sales and marketing operations for major corporations. My expertise includes the following areas:

- Ability to research, analyze, and develop strategic sales and marketing plans that maximize growth and profitability.
- Personally ranked #1 in sales volume for 3 years while at Winchester Bank, and ranked #1 in the number of new merchant accounts sold for 2 years.
- Strong analytical, planning, organization and new business development skills.
- Proven ability to define issues, propose solutions and implement changes.
- Excellent skills in managing individual accounts which include account calls, presentations, and negotiations.

My success throughout my career is due largely to my strong commitment to success, and to my ability to prioritize multiple responsibilities. In addition, I am very talented in developing and designing companywide programs that yield company savings and profitability. I sincerely believe that, with my experience and career goals, I would be an asset to your organization.

I would like to arrange a personal interview with you at your earliest convenience so we can discuss ways that I can significantly contribute to your team of professionals. As I mentioned above, I will be contacting you within a few days to arrange a meeting.

Thank you in advance for your time and consideration. I look forward to speaking with you soon.

Sincerely,

Jessica Slovich

Resume Enclosed

This type of sales job requires skills as a Closer and Relationship Builder.

SCOTT HORTON
6633 Galbraith Drive
Milwaukee, Wisconsin 77665
(555) 553-6655

Professional Objective & Profile

A dynamic, results- and profit-oriented **Sales Representative** is seeking a position that will fully utilize more than 8 years of experience building and leading integrated sales operations for various corporations. Strong analytical and technical skills with special talents in building a territory to achieve maximum profitability. Desire a Sales position that will provide a challenging opportunity to significantly contribute to a company's efficiency, organization, growth, and profitability.

Education

Bachelor of Science in Business Administration
WISCONSIN UNIVERSITY, Milwaukee, Wisconsin

Community Affiliations

National Youth Sports Coaches Association

Professional Experience

Sales Representative
JOHNSON'S BEARINGS & SUPPLY, Milwaukee, Wisconsin - 1995 to Present

- *Sales:* Responsible for selling bearings and power transmissions to industries in the Milwaukee area. Solicit and obtain new clientele as well as maintain existing accounts.
- *Profitability:* Successfully built and grew the #1 client from $50,000 to $100,000 in sales annually which significantly increased profitability for company. Achieve $750,000 per year in sales, and maintain the highest gross profit percentage in Milwaukee and the second highest gross profit percentage in the company.
- *Account Management:* Responsible for managing new business development and strategic planning to maximize growth and profitability. Establish growth plans for individual accounts and personally manage account calls, presentations and negotiations.
- *Client Relations:* Consistently establish and maintain an exemplary network of business associates as a result of extensive interaction and strong communication skills.
- *Customer Service:* Provide excellent service to customers by attention to detail and thoroughly following up on all sales. Effectively respond to clients' requests, inquiries, suggestions, and/or concerns.
- *Consulting:* Provide consulting services to clients involving technical information about products.

Sales Representative
INDUSTRIAL PRODUCTS, Milwaukee, Wisconsin - 1994 to 1995

- *Sales:* Sold hydraulic and pneumatic seals to manufacturing companies. Responsibilities were basically the same as those described above and included all areas of sales and customer service.

Sales Representative
NABISCO FOODS GROUP, Milwaukee, Wisconsin - 1989 to 1994

- *Sales:* Responsible for selling Nabisco food products to businesses throughout middle Tennessee and southern Kentucky. Began this job part-time while in college and continued full-time thereafter.
- *Profitability:* Sales were at $600,000 when taking over territory, and in 1994, had achieved $1 million in annual revenue. Won 7 individual sales contests and 2 team contests. Achieved sales objectives 21 periods in a row and voted **Sales Representative of the Period.**

SCOTT HORTON
6633 Galbraith Drive
Milwaukee, Wisconsin 77665
(555) 553-6655

Date

To the Director of Personnel:

Are you looking for a highly motivated, goal-oriented **Sales Representative** to become a leader in your organization? I am confident that, with my strong sales and client relations skills, I can significantly contribute to your team of professionals. For your review, I have enclosed a personal resume which will provide you with details concerning my credentials.

In addition to a *Bachelor of Science in Business Administration* from Wisconsin University, I also possess more than 8 years of experience in sales. My areas of qualifications and expertise include the following:

- Proven track record of success in sales with outstanding sales skills and ability to develop and build territories to achieve maximum profitability.
- Extremely client relations-oriented with strong skills in establishing and maintaining an exemplary network of business associates as a result of extensive interaction and strong communication skills.
- Style which exhibits maturity, leadership, teamwork and the ability to interact with all types of individuals and all levels of management and personnel.
- Proven ability to define issues, propose solutions and implement changes.
- Demonstrated leadership, communication and negotiation skills.

I sincerely believe that, with my experience and career aspirations, I would be an asset to your organization. I would like to request a personal interview at your earliest convenience so we can discuss ways that I can contribute to your company goals.

Thank you in advance for your time and consideration. I look forward to speaking with you soon.

Sincerely,

Scott Horton

Resume Enclosed

You must be a Closer and a Relationship Builder in this type of position.

Melinda Michaels
22 Nordstern Drive
Chicago, Illinois 60699
(312) 777-4553

PROFESSIONAL OBJECTIVE & PROFILE

Highly motivated and goal-oriented **Sales** professional is seeking a position in sales that will fully utilize 11 years of experience at Motion Industries, Inc. in Inside and Outside Sales. Seeking a Sales position that will provide a challenging opportunity to significantly contribute to a company's efficiency, organization, growth, and profitability, while at the same time offering an avenue for career advancement and professional growth.

PROFESSIONAL EXPERIENCE

Sales Representative
MOVING INDUSTRIES, INC., Chicago, Illinois - 1985 to Present

- **Company Track Record of Success:** Began with Moving Industries in *Inside Sales* and advanced to position of outside *Sales Representative.* Responsibilities have been comprehensive and include the following areas of expertise.
- **Sales & Marketing:** Responsible for the sales and marketing of industrial supplies for this company which is an industrial distributor in Nashville and surrounding areas. In charge of soliciting and obtaining new clients as well as maintaining existing accounts. This involves managing new business development and strategic planning to maximize growth and profitability for accounts. Call on manufacturing companies, develop business opportunities and establish growth plans for individual accounts and personally manage account calls, presentations, and negotiations.
- **Profitability:** After taking over sales territory, succeeded in building and doubling sales the first 3 months, which significantly increased overall profitability for company.
- **Client Relations & Customer Service:** Establish and maintain an excellent network of business associates with clients as a result of strong communication skills and by providing excellent service, attention and follow-up to accounts.
- **Advertising & Marketing:** Create, develop and implement innovative marketing and advertising strategies to promote business and increase sales.
- **Inventory & Purchasing:** While in Inside Sales, provided support to outside sales staff, and was responsible for monitoring inventory level of industrial products, and purchasing as needed.
- **Vendor Relations:** Developed and maintained good working relationships with vendors and suppliers as a result of extensive interaction to effectively coordinate purchasing orders.
- **Computer Operations:** Utilized special customized computer software to track inventory. In charge of updating and maintaining inventory records in computers.

EDUCATION & ADVANCED TRAINING

MOVING INDUSTRIES, INC., Chicago, Illinois
Numerous Training Classes & Seminars including the following:

Sales	*Inventory & Purchasing*
Fluid Power School	*Power Transmission School*
Time Management	*Customer Service*

This position involves Closers and Relationship Builders.

BRIAN SHEAHAN

A Presentation

of

Executive Credentials

272 Forest Hills Drive
Great Lakes, New Jersey 07444
(201) 333-1234

An Executive Profile is a great way to summarize your background. Pack it with power!

BRIAN SHEAHAN
272 Forest Hills Drive
Great Lakes, New Jersey 07444
(201) 333-1234

EXECUTIVE PROFILE

High-caliber **International Marketing Executive** with more than 17 years of building and leading integrated marketing and business operations for major financial institutions. Consistently successful in developing and nurturing international and domestic client relationships. Talented in initiating and spearheading start-up operations of branch offices, and in positioning finance as a critical business partner, supportive of and responsive to the needs of large and diverse operating units. Proficient in leading business opportunities and marketing strategies/plans to maximize growth and profitability and accomplish mission of integrated operations.

Strong general management qualifications in financial market analysis, planning and all facets of process/productivity/quality improvement. Very skilled in developing financial objectives and preparing long-range strategic business plans. Excellent analytical, planning, organization, and negotiation skills. Skilled international executive liaison with experience interacting with high governmental officials. Fluent in French and English.

Desire an international career opportunity in **Marketing,** requiring **leadership and management** skills, that will provide a challenging avenue to significantly contribute to its efficiency, organization, growth, and profitability.

These action verbs signify strength, aggressiveness, and assertiveness. They are powerful and grab attention!

EXECUTIVE EXPERIENCE

<u>Vice President of Marketing</u>
TRANSATLANTIC INTERNATIONAL COMPANY
New York, New York - 1990 to Present

- *<u>Management:</u>* Hold full responsibility and decision-making authority for establishing policies and procedures for marketing ventures. Responsible for directing and managing overall operations and administration of marketing services for this international financial company which has 23 branches throughout the world. Conduct ongoing analyses to evaluate market conditions.
- *<u>Marketing:</u>* After reengineering and restructuring marketing services, company has been recognized as the **#1 financial institution in New York** in dealing with currencies. Responsible for the analysis and interpretation of financial information. Plan, develop and coordinate marketing strategies for team of brokers on an ongoing basis.
- *<u>Profitability:</u>* **Increased net profits by $3.5 million** in a 4-year period from 1990 to 1994, for this company, which nets **$50 million annually.** Continuously develop and expand services through strategic marketing and business planning efforts and increase overall profitability for company.

EXECUTIVE EXPERIENCE

- ***International Markets - Branch Openings:*** Responsible for coordinating and directing the opening of branch offices throughout the world which includes Europe and the Middle East. In the last 18 months have opened branches in Beirut, Lebanon and South Africa. Currently coordinating logistics and financial preparations to open branch in Moscow. Responsible for designing and implementing the various financial products and services for the branches. This involves extensive strategic planning and analyses for proposed projects and transactions. Structure transactions and negotiate financial agreements.
- ***International & Domestic Client Relations:*** Continuously establish and maintain an exemplary network of business associates throughout the world as a result of extensive interaction and strong communication skills.
- ***New Business Development:*** Responsible for managing new business development and strategic planning to maximize growth and profitability.
- ***Supervision:*** Supervise 6 Foreign Exchange Brokers. Oversee daily trading functions to ensure aggressive marketing operations. Delegate responsibilities and monitor performances to ensure accuracy and adherence to established policies and procedures.

Vice President of Foreign Exchange, New York, New York - 1989 to 1990
Finance Manager, London, England - 1983 to 1985
SEO FINANCIAL COMPANY

- ***Company Track Record of Success:*** Began with company in 1983 as a Finance Manager, based in London, England. In New York, progressed to position of Vice President of Foreign Exchange in 1989.
- ***Financial Management:*** Directed and managed overall foreign exchange operations. Generated trade ideas and worked closely with sales staff to execute trades.
- ***Client Relations:*** In London, was responsible for building and nurturing client relationships between London and Paris. Networked extensively with clients to build successful business ventures and to establish this company as one of the major foreign exchange companies in the business.

Trader
BANK ARAB FOR INVESTMENT INTERNATIONAL
Paris, France - 1987 to 1989

- ***Trader:*** Responsible for trading daily, weekly, and monthly floating rate debt and commercial paper, derivatives and private placements. Maintain portfolio database, credit ratings and dealer criteria. Established growth plans for individual accounts and personally managed account calls, presentations and negotiations.
- ***Financial Products:*** Responsible for trading all types of currencies for this international company. Responsible for portfolio analysis, generation of trade ideas, and assessment of financial products.

Director of Finance
BANACOR, Paris, France - 1985 to 1987

- ***Finance Program Development:*** Planned and initiated the responsibilities for this position that dealt with cross currencies in Europe. This involved designing and implementing company's policies and procedures into everyday operations. First company in Paris to implement these financial services into its business operations.

BRIAN SHEAHAN
272 Forest Hills Drive
Great Lakes, New Jersey 07444
(201) 333-1234

Date

Upkong Sanavongxay
Executive President of Marketing
International Division
London International Banking
29883 Grand Street
New York, New York

If you're seeking an International Marketing position, be sure to emphasize your international abilities, foreign language skills, and relationship building skills.

Dear Ms. Sanavongxay:

A mutual friend of ours, Philip DuMaurier, suggested that I submit my professional resume for the position of **International Marketing Director.** Philip confided that you have been looking for a highly motivated, goal-oriented **Marketing Executive** to become an integral member of your management team in London. I am confident that, with my experience in International Marketing and Financial Management, I can significantly contribute to your company's efficiency, growth, and profitability. I have enclosed a personal resume so you may review my credentials.

My background is comprehensive and includes the following areas of qualifications and expertise:

- Proven track record of success in marketing, management and client relations.
- Excellent skills in reengineering and restructuring marketing operations that have global impact and yield an increase in profitability for company. Strong strategic and business planning skills.
- Fluent in French and English with ability to build and maintain an exemplary network of business associates throughout the world. Experienced in interacting with high governmental officials and all levels of management and personnel in numerous foreign countries including Europe, the Middle East, Lebanon, South Africa and Russia.
- Throughout career have successfully analyzed and managed multimillion dollar budgets and initiated appropriate strategies through contract negotiations to more aggressively control expenditures.
- Empower staff members to think and work independently and in a team environment to accomplish mission of corporate objectives.
- Demonstrated leadership skills with ability to motivate staff to achieve highest objectives.
- Proven ability to define issues, propose solutions, and implement changes.

I sincerely believe that, with my experience and career goals, I would be an asset to your organization. I would like to request a personal interview at your earliest convenience so we can discuss how I can best contribute to your company's growth. I am open to discussing any business opportunity that's relevant to my background.

Thank you for your time and consideration. I look forward to speaking with you soon.

Sincerely,

Brian Sheahan

Enclosure

You must have skills as a Closer, Team Builder, and Relationship Builder for this position.

MATTHEW HARRISON

A Presentation

of

International Marketing Credentials

455 River Road Annex
St. Louis, Missouri 63021
(314) 644-4772

MATTHEW HARRISON

455 River Road Annex
St. Louis, Missouri 63021
(314) 644-4772

Professional Objective & Profile

High-caliber, results-oriented, **International Marketing Executive** with experience building and leading integrated marketing operations for international company. Talented in spearheading the development of an international marketing company. Strong expertise in leading business opportunities and marketing strategies to maximize growth and profitability for company.

Strong general management qualifications in market analysis and planning all facets of process, productivity and quality improvement. Skilled in developing financial objectives and preparing long-range strategic business plans. Executive liaison who enjoys the international market with flair for building and maintaining strong business relationships globally. Excellent background in training, development, personnel and leadership.

Desire an **International Marketing** position in leadership and management that will provide a challenging opportunity to significantly contribute to a company's growth, organization, and profitability.

Education

Master of International Business
ST. LOUIS UNIVERSITY, St. Louis, Missouri, 1994

Bachelor of Science Degree in Marketing
MARYVILLE UNIVERSITY, St. Louis, Missouri, 1992

Associate of Science Degree in Electronics - Phi Theta Kappa
ST. LOUIS COMMUNITY COLLEGE, St. Louis, Missouri, 1980

International Marketing Experience

International Marketing Manager
NATIONAL SURGICAL CORPORATION, St. Louis, Missouri - 1994 to Present

- *International Company Development:* Recruited from Health Care Instruments by National Surgical Corporation to spearhead the creation, development and implementation of an *International Marketing Department.* This has involved extensive strategic planning and analyses of foreign market and company products and has resulted in a successful venture forward to firmly establish this company in the international marketplace.
- *Management:* Direct and manage overall operations and administration of this international marketing department which achieves sales equal to 10% of domestic sales. Company achieves over $12 million in annual domestic sales.
- *Sales & Business Development:* Responsible for selling surgical microscopes to physicians and dentists throughout the world. Manage new business development and strategic planning to maximize growth and profitability. Call on physicians, dentists, hospitals and other health care centers to solicit and obtain new clientele. Establish growth plans for individual accounts and personally manage account calls, presentations, and negotiations. Structure transactions and negotiate financial agreements.
- *International Client Relations:* Travel extensively throughout the world and continuously establish and maintain an exemplary network of business associates as a result of thorough interaction and strong communication skills.
- *Advertising & Marketing:* Oversee the designing, writing and production of a variety of advertising and marketing materials including brochures, direct mail, newsletters and print ads.

Training and Personnel experience exemplify strong team-building skills.

International Marketing Experience

- **_Product Development:_** Work closely with engineers and manufacturing departments at company plant and assist in conceptualizing and creating new products. Responsible for modifying existing American products to meet international requirements.
- **_International/National Trade Shows:_** Facilitate international/national trade shows to promote products.
- **_Personnel & Supervision:_** Interviewed, hired and currently supervise 24 Distributors around the world. Oversee overall job performances to ensure aggressive marketing and sales operations.
- **_Training:_** Created, developed and facilitate training programs and accompanying manuals to train international and domestic Distributors in all areas of sales, marketing and product information.
- **_Marketing Research:_** Conduct demographic and marketing research to target clients in foreign markets.
- **_Budget Management:_** Develop and administer operating funds allocated for operations and general expenditures. Analyze budget variances and initiate appropriate strategies to more aggressively control expenditures. Design budget forecasting and analysis plans.

Senior Technical Support Specialist
HEALTH CARE INSTRUMENTS, St. Louis, Missouri - 1989 to 1994

- **_Technical Support:_** Led the technical support team and responsible for providing technical support to staff regarding field installation, maintenance and repair of products.
- **_Communications Liaison:_** Liaison between customers and company departments including sales, marketing, engineering, manufacturing and service.
- **_Troubleshooter - Customer Service:_** Researched and identified problems within customer service and/or systems, and implemented creative problem-solving techniques to resolve issues. Provided excellent service to customers by effectively responding to requests, inquiries, suggestions, and/or concerns.
- **_Program Development:_** Engineered and implemented a _Service Training Program_ for staff to utilize when installing and repairing products.
- **_Database Development:_** Created and utilized database files for customer information. This included scheduling of installations, costs, contact log and system specifications.

Technological Experience

Software Support Engineer
HONE & BABBAGE, St. Louis, Missouri - 1987 to 1988

- **_Software Support Engineer:_** Responsible for testing, installing, repairing and maintaining computer software on IBM mainframes.
- **_Systems Development:_** Built, implemented and maintained a database and library system.
- **_Troubleshooter:_** Investigated and identified problems within software and resolved problems. Utilized system documentation and manuals to identify and interpret software problems.
- **_Training:_** Trained customers in all areas of software and applications programs.
- **_Sales:_** Sold computer software to customers, which achieved maximum CPU performance.

Senior Field Service Engineer - Maintenance Development Engineer
STORAGE CORPORATION, Louisville, Colorado - 1975 to 1986

- **_Engineering:_** Responsible for installing, repairing and maintaining computer systems and applications for various clients. Performed maintenance on safety and engineering modifications.
- **_Training:_** Trained customers in computer systems.

MATTHEW HARRISON
455 River Road Annex
St. Louis, Missouri 63021
(314) 644-4772

Date

Mouhamed Ali
Executive Manager of International Sales
Piermont Corporation
2993 Lane Boulevard
St. Louis, Missouri 19933

Dear Mr. Ali:

> If you're constantly researching career possibilities, then you'll stay abreast of changes in domestic and international markets. Because Matthew explored his opportunities by reading trade and business magazines, he discovered a company that needed him!

I recently read in *Entrepreneur Magazine* that your company is expanding throughout northern Europe. With my direct experience in international sales, I am confident that I will become your next leader in **International Marketing.** My background in International Marketing directly parallels your needs and I would like to discuss this with you next week. I have enclosed a personal portfolio so you may review my background and credentials.

In addition to a *Master's of International Business Degree* from St. Louis University, I also possess more than 20 years of experience encompassing positions in management, sales, marketing and information systems technology. My qualifications and areas of expertise include the following:

- Experienced in spearheading the development, expansion and growth of an international marketing department for National Surgical Corporation throughout the world, which has achieved sales equal to 10% of domestic sales.
- Strong interpersonal skills with ability to effectively communicate with diverse cultures all over the world.
- Effective team-building skills. Responsible for recruiting, hiring, training and supervising distributors in foreign markets. Ability to motivate, lead and empower associates to achieve success.
- Proven track record in strategic planning, business analysis and development, and all facets of sales and marketing.
- Demonstrated leadership, communication and negotiation skills.
- Proven ability to define issues, propose solutions and implement changes.

I sincerely believe that, with my experience and career aspirations, I would be an asset to your organization. I would like to request a personal interview at your earliest convenience so we can discuss how I can best contribute to your company's goals.

Thank you in advance for your time and consideration. I look forward to speaking with you soon.

Sincerely,

Matthew Harrison

Resume Enclosed

This area of sales requires Closers, Relationship Builders, Hungry for Success, and Team Builders.

LEE R. CHUNG

632 Meadow Road
Chicago, Illinois 37211
(285) 333-9516

LEE R. CHUNG
632 Meadow Road
Chicago, Illinois 37211
(285) 333-9516

Professional Objective & Profile

Dynamic . . . multi-talented . . . expert international & national sales executive . . . experienced in developing and expanding markets with O.E.M. Manufacturers throughout the world . . . fluent in Mandarin Chinese, Taiwanese and English . . . are just a few of the many qualities I can offer your international company. An expert business professional, I welcome challenging opportunities to significantly contribute to a company's efficiency, organization, development, growth, and profitability.

Education

Master of Business Administration, M.B.A.
Marketing & Operations Management
ILLINOIS INSTITUTE OF TECHNOLOGY, Chicago, Illinois, 1992

Bachelor of Science in Industrial Engineering
UNIVERSITY OF WISCONSIN, Madison, Wisconsin, 1990

Summary of Accomplishments & Talents

> Stress any international sales experience, as well as foreign language skills, if you want an international sales position.

- **Track Record of Success:**
  Background exemplifies a successful track record of career accomplishments including 5 years of experience in international & national sales, marketing and account management.

- **International Sales Expertise:**
  Successfully initiated and developed several new markets for Pantene Electric Company (based in Chicago, Illinois area) throughout Israel, Jordan, Syria, Turkey, Lebanon, Iran and Pakistan. Strong interpersonal skills with ability to effectively communicate with diverse cultures all over the world.

- **Languages & International Background:**
  Fluent in Mandarin Chinese, Taiwanese and English. Born in Taiwan and educated in the United States. Well-traveled with extensive knowledge of, and experience in, the Middle East, Pacific Rim, and other regions and cultures throughout the world. Family members own and operate businesses in the Pacific Rim.

> Being able to develop and manage accounts clearly expresses that you're a Relationship Builder.

- **Account Development & Management:**
  Maintained multimillion dollar sales volume by establishing growth plans and managing more than 50 Original Equipment Manufacturers (OEMs) and Distributor accounts throughout the U.S., Middle East and North Africa.

- **Growth & Profitability:**
  Skilled in developing and expanding a company's sales operations on an international, as well as national basis, and increasing annual sales revenue and profitability for company. Consistently achieve and surpass annual goals by 15%.

If you were recruited for a certain position, state this and explain why.

Professional Experience

Marketing, Sales, & Production Manager
HALY AIR COMPRESSOR CORPORATION
Chicago, Illinois - 1995 to Present

- *Recruitment:* Recruited to direct an aggressive reorganization and initial sales program for international business division.
- *Sales & Profitability:* In charge of sales of Haly Air Compressor products to distributors, sales representatives and engineers. Solicit and obtain new clientele, as well as being in charge of maintaining existing clients through follow-up and service. Assisted in increasing overall sales volume by 52% in 1995, which substantially increased profitability for company.
- *Marketing:* Responsible for strategic planning and development of innovative marketing plans for the purpose of expanding sales and increasing profitability.
- *Vendor & Client Relations:* Interact extensively with vendors and clients, and consistently establish and maintain an exemplary network of business associates by providing superior service and attention to specific engineering needs.
- *Production:* By restructuring and reengineering production procedures, achieved a 20% increase in production in 1995.
- *Inventory Control:* Continuously monitor and review inventory of materials and supplies, and utilize efficiently in order to minimize and maintain inventory costs.
- *Purchasing:* Review and analyze needs for purchasing materials and/or new equipment, and purchase as needed.

International Sales Engineer
Manufacturing Engineering Department (Intern)

Always support your statements with actual numbers and percentages.

PANTENE ELECTRIC COMPANY
Batavia, (Chicago) Illinois - 1992 to 1995

- *Intern:* Began as an Intern in 1992 in the Manufacturing Engineering Department. Promoted to full-time, permanent management position due to superior job performance. As an Intern, responsibilities included the following:
- *System & Program Development:* Responsible for developing and implementing a new cost accounting system as a result of performing a Time Study on the Metal Plating Process.
- *Purchasing:* Analyzed cost expenditures and profitability ratios for purchasing a new oil applicator for punch press operations.
- *International Contract Negotiations:* After being promoted to position of *International Sales Engineer*, traveled worldwide and negotiated, and/or maintained multimillion dollar sales contracts for Pantene Electric Company with more than 50 Original Equipment Manufacturers (OEM) and distributor accounts including international clients throughout North Africa and the Middle East.
- *Market Analysis:* Researched and analyzed foreign markets. Identified potential markets and proposed new products to these markets based on technology trends and engineering needs.
- *Client Development:* Initiated and introduced product lines to foreign companies and provided direction for long-range business focus to meet foreign industry changes and needs.
- *Account Management:* Independently managed the entire sales cycle from client identification and account development through presentations, contract and price negotiations, and final sales closings.
- *International Trade:* Established and maintained cooperative working relationships with Foreign Embassies and Trade Delegations including regulatory agencies and import/export organizations and U.S. Trade Delegations.

Special Products Coordinator (Intern)
NATIONAL BANK OF CHICAGO, Chicago, Illinois - 1991

- *Quality Control Program:* As an Intern, developed and implemented a Total Quality Management Program for the Customer Services Group's communication process.
- *System Development:* Assisted the Special Products' Customer Services Group Management team in developing and implementing a System that provided special recognition and services for First Chicago's new customers as well as the existing, long-standing customers.

This supports his ability to close deals.

LEE R. CHUNG
632 Meadow Road
Chicago, Illinois 37211
(285) 333-9516

Date

Seunghye Chang
Executive Director for Pacific Rim
Seo Manufacturing Company
298 Lakeside Drive
Chicago, Illinois 37211

> Lee validated his statements about being perfect for the company by listing his direct experience that related to the needs of this company.

Dear Ms. Chang:

I am aware that the Seo Manufacturing Company is looking for an experienced **International Sales Representative** to expand its services throughout the Pacific Rim. I am perfect for this position, as my background directly parallels your needs. For your review, I have enclosed a personal resume which will provide you with details concerning my background and qualifications.

In addition to holding an *M.B.A. in Marketing & Operations Management,* I also speak fluent Mandarin Chinese, Taiwanese and English. My background also includes the following:

- Experience in manufacturing and international sales. While working for Pantene Electric Company, I successfully expanded the company by developing several new markets in Israel, Jordan, Lebanon, Syria, Turkey, Iran and Pakistan. As a result of my strategic market planning and client development, Pantene Electric became the first and only American company to supply products to the largest air conditioning manufacturer in Lebanon.
- Not only do I have experience throughout the Middle East and Africa, in addition, I was born in Taiwan, and presently have family members who own businesses throughout the Pacific Rim.
- My success throughout my career is largely due to my ability to develop and expand new markets on an international basis, and to effectively communicate with diverse cultures throughout the world.
- An excellent leader, team builder, relationship builder, and motivator of others, I am a strong decision maker and arbitrator when working with Foreign Embassies, Trade Delegations, and other import/export agencies of the United States Government.

I am confident that, with my experience and career goals, I would be an asset to your company. I would like to request a personal interview at your earliest convenience so we may discuss ways that I can significantly contribute to your team of professionals. I will follow up with a telephone call within a few days. I am single, with no dependents, and available to travel and/or relocate as needed.

Thank you in advance for your time and consideration. I look forward to speaking with you soon.

Sincerely,

> Let a company know if you're single and available to travel or relocate. This could help you win the job!

Lee R. Chung

Resume Enclosed

JOSE LOPEZ

3322 West 20th Street
Miami, Florida 33999
(305) 299-0088

> Closer, Relationship Builder, and Team Builder needed here.

Professional Objective & Profile

Dynamic, multi-lingual **International Sales & Marketing Representative** with more than 10 years of experience which includes building and leading international sales operations for major corporations. Desire a position in International Sales & Marketing that will fully utilize excellent talents in working with Latin American culture. Native Spanish speaker, with fluency in English, Portuguese, Italian and French. Extensive knowledge of Latin America, which includes its geography, citizens, and culture.

Experienced in spearheading projects to initiate sales in South America. Skilled in establishing growth plans for individual corporate accounts and managing account calls, presentations and negotiations. Strong general management qualifications in market analysis, business planning and development functions, client relations and service, and leadership. Totally service- and client relations-oriented with ability to successfully network with executive decision makers and all levels of management and personnel. Excellent analytical, organization, and negotiation skills.

Desire an **International Sales & Marketing** position that will provide a challenging opportunity to significantly contribute to a company's efficiency, organization, growth, and profitability.

> Use high-powered action verbs to sell yourself!

Summary of Qualifications

Track Record of Success:
Background exemplifies a successful track record of career accomplishments which encompasses positions in international sales and management. Have excelled in all facets of sales and business administration due to outstanding job performance and strong commitment to success.

International Sales Expertise:
Successfully initiated new markets for direct sales of products through television in Argentina, Brazil, Chile, Ecuador, Venezuela, Uruguay, Costa Rica and Netherlands Antilles. Multilingual and very talented in establishing and maintaining strong business relationships throughout Latin America as a result of thorough knowledge of language and culture.

Growth & Profitability:
Skilled in developing and expanding a company's sales operations on an international, as well as national basis, and increasing annual sales revenue and profitability for company. Have consistently achieved and surpassed sales goals.

Training & Development:
Experienced in training and developing new sales associates in all areas of sales and customer service. Build teams to increase effectiveness.

Employee Relations & Leadership:
Style exhibits maturity, high energy, sensitivity and teamwork with the ability to relate to a wide variety of people and all levels of management and personnel. Strong leader and motivator of others with ability to guide associates to achieve their maximum potential. Encourage and support a teamlike work environment which increases employee morale, efficiency and productivity.

Education

Bachelor of Science in Business Administration
INSTITUTO ALFREDO VAZQUEZ ACEVEDO
Montevideo, Uruguay, 1971

Each area of
expertise is
categorized to
make it easier to
scan and absorb.

JOSE LOPEZ

Professional Experience

Assistant Manager of Sales & Cargo & Operations Agent

AMR CORPORATION, Miami, Florida - 1992 to Present

- *Business Operations:* While working for AMR Corporation, a contracting company for airlines, have been responsible for various positions with Iberia Airlines and Flagship Airlines/American Eagle. A brief synopsis is highlighted below.
- *Management:* Assist in directing and managing overall sales and cargo operations. This involves managing parking operations for airlines, cargo loading, and radio communications. Review and monitor cargo to ensure adherence to weight and balance regulations.
- *Personnel & Supervision:* Assist in interviewing, hiring, training and supervising employees. Delegate responsibilities and monitor overall job performances to ensure accuracy and adherence to standards, rules and regulations.
- *Sales:* Responsible for selling tickets to passengers for Iberia and flagship airlines. Assist customers with flight scheduling and provide information on flight releases.
- *Passenger Services:* Provide superior service to passengers by effectively responding to requests, inquiries, suggestions, and/or concerns.

International Sales Representative

LOMBARDI MANAGEMENT, Santa Fe Springs, California - 1993 to 1996

- *International Sales:* Successfully conceptualized, initiated and developed several new markets for direct sales of various products through television in Argentina, Brazil, Chile, Ecuador, Venezuela, Uruguay, Costa Rica and Netherlands Antilles. Independently managed the entire sales cycle from client identification and account development through presentations, contract and price negotiations, and final sales closings. Structured transactions and negotiated financial agreements. Provided direction for long-range business focus to meet industry changes and needs.
- *Account Management:* Responsible for managing new business development and strategic planning to maximize growth and profitability. Established growth plans for individual accounts and managed account calls, presentations and negotiations.
- *Market Research:* Researched and analyzed foreign markets. Identified potential markets and expanded sales regions.
- *International Trade & Client Relations:* Established and maintained cooperative working relationships with foreign companies as a result of providing superior service, extensive interaction and strong communication skills.

Assistant Sales Manager

EL HOMBRE RENT A CAR, Miami, Florida - 1987 to 1990

- *Management:* Directed and managed overall sales operations for South America. Responsible for developing business opportunities and expanding territory.
- *International Client Relations:* Developed and maintained an exemplary network of business associates in South America due to excellent communication skills.
- *Marketing & Sales:* In charge of selling services including car rentals and leasing services to individuals and companies. Responsible for strategic planning and development of innovative marketing plans to expand sales and increase profitability.

Sales Representative

FOHLER CHRYSLER PLYMOUTH, Union City, New Jersey - 1982 to 1987

- *Sales & Profitability:* Sold new and used automobiles to customers. Solicited and obtained new clientele through cold-calling and appointment-setting. Continuously achieved and surpassed sales quotas which increased overall profitability for company.

Specify any specialties in trading and financial positions.

DENVER JOHNSON

6699 Forest Avenue
Dallas, Texas 75229
(214) 999-8822

This position requires a Closer, Relationship Builder, Creative Think Tank, and Team Builder.

PROFESSIONAL OBJECTIVE & PROFILE

High-caliber **Financial Vice President of Sales & Marketing** desires a position Trading, Banking, Investments or Proprietary Trading. Offering 9 years of experience building and leading operations in trading, marketing, product management, and client services. Exceptional skills in client services with proven ability to define issues, propose solutions, and implement changes which significantly contribute to the company's bottom line.

PROFESSIONAL EXPERIENCE

Vice President of Mortgage-Backed Securities Trading & Sales
SECOND NATIONAL BANK, Dallas, Texas - 1995 to Present

- **Company Track Record of Success:** Began as an *Investment Officer* and was promoted to *Vice President* within 1 year as a result of intense study of product and outstanding job performance.
- **Trading/Sales:** Hold full decision-making responsibility for directing, managing, selling, and analyzing mortgage-backed securities for an institutional sales force of 20. Trade, position, maintain and hedge a mortgage inventory with positioning capabilities of $75 million.
- **Product Management - Marketing:** Research, analyze, identify and select dealers. Create markets, determine best price and duration, and sell products to sales staff. This involves portfolio analysis, generation of trade ideas, and assessment of value in the mortgage-backed sector. Develop and implement innovative marketing strategies to promote and sell securities.
- **Specialties:** Specialize in Balloons, FFIEC's, 15-year Collaterals and CMO's. Assist in ARMS & Floaters as needed.
- **Proprietary Trading:** Provide analytical support to Trading Desk which consists of 4 sales representatives.
- **Education/Instruction:** Study and analyze the products and responsible for educating sales force on all aspects of the mortgage-backed market.

Assistant Portfolio Manager & Marketer
SMITH BARNETT, INC., New York, New York - 1993 to 1995

- **Company Track Record of Success:** Began as an Assistant Trader and was promoted to Assistant Portfolio Manager after one year due to intense study of the market and outstanding job performance.
- **Portfolio Management:** Held full decision-making responsibility for one national, 8 state-specific *open end municipal bond funds* and one *high-yield closed-end fund* listed on the New York Stock Exchange. Total assets exceeded $2.8 billion.
- **Trading:** Responsible for analyzing, identifying, and executing trades including bond swaps, derivatives, and private placements. Reconciled trading desk accounts daily.
- **Program Development:** Developed and initiated *Financial Futures Hedging Program.*
- **Market Analysis:** Analyzed markets including credit surveillance of all positions, evaluated bond pricing and assured compliance with prospectus and SEC requirements.
- **Client Relations:** Interacted extensively with institutional bond dealers and traders to evaluate market conditions.
- **Financial Reporting:** Wrote annual/quarterly reports for shareholders and boards of directors. Also, wrote marketing new releases for brokers.

EDUCATION

- *Bachelor of Arts in Political Science,* **UNIVERSITY OF WISCONSIN-MADISON,** Madison, Wisconsin, 1989
- **MILTON ACADEMY,** Milton, Massachusetts, 1981-1985

A More Detailed Portfolio Is Available Upon Request

DENVER JOHNSON

6699 Forest Avenue
Dallas, Texas 75229
(214) 999-8822

Date

Judith Berk
President of Banking Services
East Coast Financial Company
2998 Sunset Drive
Long Island, New York 39982

> The first sentence is used as an attention grabber.

Dear Ms. Berk:

Are you looking for a highly motivated, goal-oriented **Financial Industry Sales & Marketing** professional with a solid background in trading, marketing, product management and client service? I am confident that, with my experience and knowledge of investments, I could significantly contribute to your team of professionals. For your review, I have enclosed a personal resume, which will provide you with details concerning my credentials.

In addition to a *Bachelor of Arts in Political Science,* I also possess 9 years of experience which encompasses positions as **Vice President, Assistant Portfolio Manager, Trader and Sales Representative.** My areas of expertise and qualifications include the following:

> This detailed cover letter is an effective marketing tool and can help sell the candidate.

- Comprehensive knowledge of fixed rate pass-through mortgage backed securities. Skilled in generating trade ideas, selling trades to sales force, and executing trades.
- Strong general management qualifications including managing the sale of all newly originated second securitized mortgages.
- Proven track record of success as a Trader. Total assets exceeded $2.0 billion. Was responsible for trading daily, weekly, monthly floating rate debt, commercial paper, derivatives, and private placements.
- Ability to manage highly complex financial system and data.
- Strong analytical and technical skills; very adept at learning and comprehending new procedures quickly.
- Demonstrated leadership, communication and negotiation skills.
- Proven ability to define issues, propose solutions and implement changes.

I sincerely believe that, with my experience and career aspirations, I would be an asset to your organization. I would like to request a personal interview at your earliest convenience so we can discuss how I can best contribute to your company's goals.

Thank you in advance for your time and request. I look forward to speaking with you soon.

Sincerely,

Denver Johnson

Resume Enclosed

BILL J. KELLY
7877 Tropical Road, Nashville, Tennessee 37555 (615) 444-1166

> Executives in sales must be Closers, Relationship Builders, Creative Think Tanks, and Team Builders.

Executive Profile

A multi-talented, achievement-oriented **Sales & Marketing Executive** with over 17 years of experience which includes building and leading integrated financial operations for a worldwide organization. Consistently successful in positioning finance as a critical business partner, supportive of, and responsive to, the needs of large and diverse business operations. Seeking a career avenue in a **sales/marketing** consulting, contractual or full-time position that will provide a challenging opportunity to significantly contribute to a company's efficiency, organization, growth, and profitability.

> This Sales & Marketing professional has an in-depth background in Operations and Administration, which can be an asset in sales.

Executive Experience
Marketing & Sales Consultant
EQUITY MANAGEMENT, INC., Nashville, Tennessee - 1993 to Present

- *Marketing & Sales:* In charge of marketing financial products to individuals and businesses. Contact companies and solicit and obtain new business through innovative marketing and advertising strategies.

Owner, President & CEO
ELECTRIC SALES & SERVICE, INC., Rocky Mount, North Carolina - 1992 to 1993

- *Operations & Administration - Sales & Marketing:* Owned and operated this $10 million company - an industrial motor repair, new motor and construction electric business - in conjunction with River Associates of Chattanooga, Tennessee. Responsible for all sales, marketing, and client relations.
- *Operations Design - Cost Control:* Restructured and redesigned business procedures in order to streamline operations and reduce and maintain costs. Sold ownership in company.

President & CFO
KENNDELL, INC., Columbia, Tennessee - 1990 to 1992

- *Operations & Administration:* Responsible for overall operations and administration of this company - a Tobacco Dealer/Processor.
- *Sales & Company Profitability:* Investigated, researched and monitored Kenndell's North Carolina business operations, and sold this company after assessing profitability ratios. With the absence of the non-profitable company, Hail & Cotton surged forward to increase its overall profitability.
- *Chief Financial Officer:* Full P&L responsibility for this tobacco manufacturing company. Conducted ongoing analyses to evaluate the efficiency, quality and productivity of diverse operations.
- *Company Acquisitions:* Negotiated and coordinated the acquisition of the Tobacco Supply Company.
- *International & Domestic Relations:* Managed overall operations of national and international accounts with major U.S. Tobacco Companies and foreign monopolies. Established and maintained cooperative working relationships with regulatory agencies. Managed the interaction/communications with foreign and domestic clientele to coordinate sales and marketing of tobacco products. Clientele consisted of 90% foreign customers and 10% domestic customers. Experienced in import/export laws.

Executive Vice President & CFO

- *Company Acquisition:* Researched, planned, negotiated and coordinated the acquisition of Kenndell.
- *Financial Management:* Planned, staffed and directed financial affairs for this international company which produced annual sales of more than $35 million. Managed over $20 million in bank lines of credit. Consistently achieved all annual budget objectives with no cost overrides.

Education
Graduate School of Credit & Financial Management
HANDSIN UNIVERSITY, Palo Alto, California

Bachelor of Science in Accounting
INDIANA UNIVERSITY, Bloomington, Indiana

BILL J. KELLY
7877 Tropical Road
Nashville, Tennessee 37555
(615) 444-1166

Date

Terrence Rosenwood
Owner & President
Ringwald Financial Services Corporation
9822 Templeton Road
St. Louis, Missouri 02888

The first paragraph is packed with power punchin' verbs and adjectives, summarizing Bill's credentials in one sentence!

Dear Mr. Rosenwood:

Achievement- and profit-oriented . . . strong management qualifications in strategic planning . . . organizational reengineering and process/productivity/quality improvement . . . strong leader and motivator . . . talented in analyzing companies' operations and in identifying problematic areas . . . achieved excellent improvements in productivity, efficiency and quality within companies . . . are just a few of the many qualities I can offer your company.

I am seeking full-time employment or a position as a **Contract Sales & Marketing Consultant,** and have enclosed a personal resume so you may review my qualifications and expertise.

- I am a seasoned professional with a successful track record of career accomplishments that includes more than 17 years of experience.
- Throughout my career I have achieved the positions of *Owner, President & CEO, President & CFO, and Executive Vice President* for several major corporations.
- My success throughout my career is largely due to my strong business and financial analysis skills.
- One of my greatest strengths is in analyzing companies' operations and identifying areas which need improvement.
- I have launched a series of internal realignment and reorganization initiatives within international companies to meet demands and operational requirements, which have resulted in an increase in profitability for the company.

I sincerely believe that, with my experience and career goals, I would be an asset to your organization. I would like to arrange a personal interview at your earliest convenience so we can discuss ways that I can significantly contribute to your team of professionals. Please feel free to contact me if you have any additional questions concerning my qualifications.

Thank you in advance for your time and consideration. I look forward to speaking with you soon.

Sincerely,

Bill J. Kelly

Executive Summary Enclosed

JOHN VAUGHT
227 Mountain Road
Detroit, Michigan
(615) 833-2613

> In Medical Sales, you must be a Closer and Relationship Builder.

Professional Objective

A **Sales** position in Medical Sales that will fully utilize my excellent background in the health care industry.

Sales Experience

> In this resume, we have simply highlighted major responsibilities and achievements in a one-sentence description.

Sales Representative - Wound Closure Technician
NATIONAL SURGICAL CORPORATION
Detroit, Michigan - 1995 to Present

- Call on Surgeons in OB/GYN, General Surgery, Cardiovascular, and Peripheral Vascular Units.

- Demonstrate and sell wound closure techniques to Surgeons.

- 4th Quarter 1995: Achieved 4th in the Country, and No. 1 in the Southern Region in Sales.

- 1st Quarter 1996: Assigned to a new territory, which is the largest in the Southern Division. Achieved 93% of sales goal, which is the highest percentage achieved in the 4 previous quarters.

- Successfully converted Marshall Medical Center to 100% U.S. Surgical.

- 2nd Quarter 1996: As of May 1996, achieved 70% of sales quota.

Sales Representative
DUN & BRADSTREET CORPORATION
Atlanta, Georgia; Raleigh, North Carolina; and Columbia, South Carolina
1989 to 1995

- Self-directed and self-motivated. Worked independently from home with no direct supervision.

- 1995: Achieved 2nd in 1st quarter in National Sales Contest, which was 120% of annual objective, and 126% over prior year's sales.

- 1994: Achieved 106% of sales objective, which was 23% over prior year's sales.

- 1993: Achieved 3rd in Region in product sales.

- 1992: Achieved 100% of Club.

Sales Experience   *Continued*

The spacing and bullets make this resume easy to read.

- Ranked No. 1 in the country 8 months of the year, and achieved 3rd rank overall.
- First Quarter Regional Vice-President's Council, Representative of the Quarter.
- Wrote and edited Regional Newsletter for District.
- 1991: Regional Vice-President's Council, 3rd and 4th Quarters.
- 1990: Placed 4th in National Sales Contest.
- Third-Quarter Representative of the Quarter.
- Achieved 100% of Club.

Accomplishments are highlighted throughout this resume. This is a powerful way to keep someone's attention!

- Designed sales presentation visual which was used companywide.
- Achieved 5th for Presidential Citation.
- 1989: Awarded Rookie of the Month 3 times.

Sales Representative
BUSINESS SYSTEMS WORLDWIDE, Columbia, South Carolina
March 1989 to September 1989

Sales Representative
BUSINESS MACHINES COMPANY, Knoxville, Tennessee
April 1988 to February 1989

Sales Training

- **NATIONAL SURGICAL CORPORATION,** New York, May 1995
  Areas of Emphasis: New Products & Laptop Computer Training.
- **NATIONAL SURGICAL CORPORATION,** New York, October 1995
  Graduate - Areas of Emphasis: Anatomy, Physiology, & Aseptic Techniques, Sales Presentations. Methods included Classroom, Role Play and Animal Laboratory.
- **TARGET ACCOUNT SOLUTION SELLING PROGRAM,** Parsippany, New Jersey, 1993
- **DUN & BRADSTREET SALES TRAINING,** Greensboro, North Carolina, 1989
- **LANIER BASIC SALES SCHOOL,** Greenville, South Carolina, 1989
- **MITA SALES TRAINING,** Atlanta, Georgia, 1988

Education & Academic Affiliations

Bachelor of Business Administration
EAST TENNESSEE STATE UNIVERSITY, Johnson City, Tennessee, 1987
Four-year Basketball Scholarship   *Basketball Captain 1986 - 1987*
All Southern Conference Freshman Team, 1983   *Four-year Letterman*

Shawn Raymond

6099 Sherwood Drive
Portland, Oregon 66553
(553) 778-9982

> This position requires Closers, Relationship Builders, Hungry for Success, and Team Builders.

Professional Objective & Profile

Dynamic, profit- and results-oriented **Medical Sales Specialist** with more than 7 years of experience building and leading integrated sales and marketing operations for major medical corporations. Proven track record of success in leading and building business opportunities and marketing strategies to maximize growth and profitability. Especially talented in reengineering and repositioning sales operations to increase market share and revenue. Excellent analytical, planning, organization and negotiation skills. Executive liaison with physicians, medical centers and hospitals with ability to develop and nurture strong client relationships.

Desires a challenging opportunity in **leadership and sales management** to significantly contribute to a company's efficiency, organization, growth, and profitability.

Summary of Sales Awards

- *President's Club, Medical Sales Award, 1996*
- *Sales Leader, Medical Sales Award, 1996*
- *Representative of the Quarter , Medical Sales Awards, 1996, 1995*
- *Cardiovascular Alliance Teamwork Award, Medical Sales Award, 1996*
- *Regional Gold Awards, Medical Sales Awards, 1996, 1995*
- *Circle of Merit Awards, CGA Pharmaceuticals, 1993, 1992*
- *Innovation Panel Awards, CGA Pharmaceuticals, 1992, 1991*
- *Business Team of the Year, 1990*

> Highlighting Sales Awards lends credibility to this candidate's statements.

> Always mention specific, provable, successful results when possible!

Professional Medical Sales Experience

Angioplasty Sales Specialist
MEDICAL SALES COMPANY
Portland, Oregon - 1993 to Present

- **Sales:** Recruited to Medical Sales Company to direct an aggressive reorganization of sales operations and initiate high-volume sales in the highest dollar-potential market in the country. Responsible for expanding business and selling medical devices to hospitals throughout Oregon.
- **Profitability & Sales Accomplishments:** After successfully reengineering sales operations, increased revenue from **$225,000 year to $1.7 million annually** in just 2½ years. This was the fastest revenue growth in the nation. Achieved **#1 in sales** in the U.S. in 1996. Sold the largest single order - $213,300 - in Medical Interventional Vascular history. Recipient of the 2 highest Medical Sales Awards - the **President's Club and Sales Leaders,** 1996.
- **Account Management & Business Development:** Responsible for managing new business development and strategic planning to maximize growth and profitability. Establish growth plans for individual accounts and personally manage account calls, presentations and contract negotiations.
- **Client Relations/Service:** Continuously establish, nurture and maintain client relationships as a result of extensive interaction and strong communication skills. Provide superior service to clients through attention to detail and follow-up on all sales. Elected to *Medical Consumer Advocacy Council, 1995 - 1996.*

Professional Medical Sales Experience

Continued

- **Contract Systems Development:** Designed and implemented 3 major innovative contracts for physicians that became models for Medical's contracting department. Led the southwest region in innovative contract signings and negotiated and won 4 major accounts in 3 years.
- **Physician Education Training:** Responsible for planning, coordinating and attending physician education meetings nationally and internationally. Educate physicians on coronary angioplasty/stenting procedures as related to Medtronic equipment.
- **Columbia/HCA Steering Committee:** Communications liaison between company and the Columbia/HCA Steering Committee. Provide information to the committee regarding new medical products, practices and procedures.
- **Diversity Council:** Appointed to serve as *Representative of the U.S. Cardiovascular Sales Force* on the *Medtronic Diversity Council.*
- **Marketing:** Conceptualized and designed innovative marketing and sales materials for utilization by other sales representatives.
- **Employee Supervision:** Supervise and manage Clinical Specialist. Delegate responsibilities and monitor overall job performances to ensure accuracy and adherence to company policies.

Medical Sales Representative
GCA PHARMACEUTICALS
Summit, New Jersey - 1991 to 1993

- **Sales:** Responsible for selling pharmaceuticals to physicians and hospitals. Led sales cycle from initial client consultation through presentations, price negotiations and closings. Solicited and obtained new clientele, as well as maintained existing accounts.
- **Business Development:** Hired to reposition and grow market share in New Jersey. Developed business opportunities and marketing strategies within the Summit, New Jersey area. Expanded market penetration and provided direction for long-range business focus to meet industry changes.
- **Profitability & Sales Accomplishments:** Won **Circle of Merit Awards,** 1992-1993 and Innovation Panel Awards, 1991-1992. Reengineered sales operations and improved market share from the lowest ranking of 9th to 2nd. Expanded market penetration of **Lotensin by 295%** during a period of budgetary downsizing.
- **Systems Development:** Created, developed, and incorporated a new system to record sales call information, which efficiently increased district productivity.
- **Research & Marketing:** Coordinated market research activities and surveys. Developed and implemented innovative marketing strategies to penetrate market and expand sales.

Cardiovascular Sales Specialist
STEPHENS PHARMACEUTICALS
Philadelphia, Pennsylvania - 1990 to 1991

- **Sales, Profitability & Accomplishments:** Responsible for selling pharmaceuticals to physicians and hospitals. Built market share from 14% to 28% for LOZOL in one year, which was the highest market share in the nation. Achieved **#2 market share in the nation for ANSAID,** in the *highly* competitive market of non-steroidals. Won **Business Team of the Year Award** in 1990.

Education

Bachelor of Arts in Communication Arts
Major: Public Relations - Minor: Real Estate
THE UNIVERSITY OF WEST FLORIDA, Pensacola, Florida, 1985

Julie Simms
4449 Ashley Lane
Louisville, Kentucky 88998
(616) 444-0987

Closer, Relationship Builder, and Team Builder.

AREAS OF EXPERTISE

- **National Sales**
- **Contract Administration**
- **Customer Service**
- **Sales Management**
- **Corporate Presentations**
- **Budget Control**

PROFESSIONAL EXPERIENCE

1984 - Present

REGISTER COMPANY, Louisville, Kentucky
Manager, National Account Sales (September 1995 to Present)
Manage overall sales program for Corrigan National Account, which is the company's largest customer, and which includes a contract for 345 acute care facilities.

- Manage and direct all facets of this major account which achieves $45 million in annual sales.
- Redesigned and restructured business plans in order to streamline operations and increase efficiency, productivity, and profitability for company.
- Coordinated the installation of a new computer system for data management.
- Guide and direct 5 National Account Coordinators, and 1 National Account Manager, 76 Account Managers, 2 Consultants & Support Staff.
- Manage and direct the Standardization Program.

National Account Director (1993 to September 1995)
Dallas, Texas
Managed all sales and activities for a $5,000,000 major national account. Documented management, process improvement, workflow analysis, and outsourcing. Negotiated, renewed, and administered contracts. Developed, prepared, and delivered corporate level presentations to president, vice president, divisional managers, and function heads. Hired, trained, supervised, and evaluated staff. Created and managed quarterly and annual budgets.

- Increased profitability by 28%.
- Revitalized and expanded sales volume by 23%.
- Worked with engineers to identify needs and modify inventory control system to enhance service.
- Reorganized and improved order operations to increase production.
- Received performance-based promotions.

Continued

Account Executive Dayton, Ohio (1992)
Negotiated accounts of $100,000 or larger. Developed and delivered presentations to executive staff of vendor performance reports.
- Consistently met or exceeded quota.

Major Account Representative (1990 - 1991)
Promoted to work with major accounts. Contracted $200,000 new business.
- Increased new business by 25% of volume.
- Earned 100+ Club and the John Darragh Bonus 1991 Sales Year.

Account Representative (1987 - 1989)
Created and implemented yearly marketing and sales plans. Presented, implemented, and administered Forms Management.
- Increased volume by 200%.
- Achieved 100+ Club and Quota Plus Status.

Sales Representative (1985 - 1986)
- Achieved 100+ Club Status by selling 166% of quota (first year eligible).
- Increased sales by expanding new business by 59% (second year).

Special Account Assistant (1984)
After college graduation, worked in sales and product training.
- Completed a one-year program in 4 months.

1982 - 1984   **CABLEVISION,** Fairborn, Ohio
Territorial Manager (1984)
Generated sales through cold calling and prospecting new leads. Prepared marketing and promotions for sales and rental programs. Made credit collections.
- Completed undergraduate degree in 5 years while attending school at night and working full-time.
- Received performance-based promotions.

Customer Service Representative (1983)
Scheduled installation and service. Resolved customer concerns and provided comprehensive customer service.

EDUCATION   **(Self-financed college education 100%)**

WRIGHT STATE UNIVERSITY, Dayton, Ohio
Master of Science in Economics
Completed 24 Hours toward M.S. Degree, 1984

Bachelor of Science in Marketing 1984

WRIGHT STATE UNIVERSITY, Dayton, Ohio

> Keep action verbs close to the beginning of the sentence to add more power!

Relationship Builder, Closer,
and Team Builder

Haley Meyers

A Presentation

of

Professional Credentials

1234 West End
Boise, Idaho 07719
(908) 888-0987

Haley Meyers

1234 West End
Boise, Idaho 07719
(908) 888-0987

Summarize your background in your Professional Objective & Profile.

Professional Objective & Profile

*A **Territory Sales & Marketing Manager** who is an achievement- and goal-oriented business professional with experience building and leading integrated sales and marketing operations for major company.*

Self-directed and self-motivated with strong general sales and account management qualifications in strategic planning and marketing.

*Desire a **Marketing** position that will provide a challenging opportunity to significantly contribute to a company's efficiency, organization, growth, and profitability. Planning to relocate to New York on a permanent basis to be with friends and family.*

Explain any plans to move to the city where you're targeting your job search.

Summary of Qualifications

- Supervised the sales and distribution for the first *Sports Illustrated Daily* at the 1996 Summer Olympic Games.

- Prepared a marketing analysis to introduce *People Español Magazine* into a chain of 140 bookstores.

- At Barnes & Noble Bookstore, manage a new venture with *Time, Entertainment Weekly, Sports Illustrated, Fortune,* and *People* magazines. Analyze weekly title strategies in all Barnes & Noble Bookstores across the country through direct distribution.

- Manage the sales and forecast market trends of *Fortune* and *Money* magazines in all CompUSA and Egghead Softwares across the country.

- Strong interpersonal skills with ability to effectively communicate and network with all levels of management and personnel. Excellent leader and motivator of others.

Education

<u>Bachelor of Science in Business Administration</u>
UNIVERSITY OF IDAHO
Boise, Idaho
Specialization: Marketing
Concentration: Communications

Summarize your responsibilities in your job description. Don't leave an employer guessing about what your responsibilities were.

Professional Experience

Territory Manager
TIME WARNER, INC.
Boise, Idaho - January 1996 to Present

- *Sales Management:* Guide and direct overall sales operations for central Idaho for *Time Warner Magazines*. Sell profitable display positions for *Time Warner Magazines* in major retail stores.
- *Marketing:* Responsible for managing new business development and strategic planning to maximize growth and profitability. Execute marketing plans for individual accounts and personally manage account calls, presentations and negotiations.
- *Client Relations:* Provide superior service to clients through in-depth attention and follow-up to accounts. Effectively respond to clients' requests, inquiries, suggestions, and/or concerns.
- *Advertising & Promotions:* Assist District Manager and Key Account Manager in conceptualizing, developing and implementing innovative marketing and promotional campaigns in stores. Coordinate specific advertising and promotional activities with retail groups.
- *Personnel, Training & Supervision:* Supervise and lead a team of Store Merchandisers. Delegate work assignments and communicate opportunities in the marketplace.

Advertising Assistant
THE SALTSMAN GROUP
Boise, Idaho - February 1995 to April 1995

- *Advertising:* This was an Internship that involved assisting in the development and implementation of strategic advertising campaigns for clients.
- *Program Development - Research:* Reviewed syndicated research sources for clients and developed a Competitive Spending Analysis Program.
- *Media Relations:* Established and maintained a good working relationship with media personnel including radio, TV and print advertising to negotiate contracts and business planning.

Marketing Assistant
MATTEL TOYS, INC.
Boise, Idaho - May 1994 to August 1994

- *Marketing & Product Development:* This was an Internship that involved assisting in the development of new doll lines. Assisted Product Managers and Designers with the 1995 Toy Presentations.
- *Research & Analysis:* Conducted research and analyzed market needs, and utilized Lotus software to create spreadsheets and graphs. Analyzed monthly statistics and developed strategies to more aggressively compete with market.

Sales Associate
THE GAP, Boise, Idaho - 1989 to 1992

- *Sales:* Sold merchandise to customers in retail environment.
- *Merchandising & Marketing:* Arranged and designed floor displays to enhance merchandise and increase sales. Implemented company's marketing and advertising campaigns into everyday store operations.
- *Customer Service:* Assisted customers with merchandise selection and effectively responded to requests and inquiries.

Haley Meyers
1234 West End
Boise, Idaho 07719
(908) 888-0987

Haley is sending her letter and resume to a company without any knowledge as to whether they're hiring or not. This is a good way to establish a connection. You can always follow up with a phone call and begin networking with the company. Get to know them!

Date

Kathryn Perez
Director of Marketing & Sales
Reader's Entrepreneur Magazine Company
2993 5th Avenue
New York, New York 20022

Dear Ms. Perez:

Are you interested in a highly motivated, goal-oriented **Marketing & Sales** professional to become an effective leader at *Reader's Entrepreneur Magazine Company*? I can significantly contribute to your company's team of professionals. For your review, I have enclosed a personal resume which will provide you with details concerning my background and qualifications.

In addition to a Marketing Degree from the University of Idaho, I also possess experience as a *Territory Manager* for *Time Warner, Inc.* Based in Boise, I am responsible for managing and marketing the magazine industry throughout central Idaho. This involves managing new business development and strategic planning for retail accounts. I have developed and executed several successful promotions for *Time, In-Style,* and *Sports Illustrated* magazines.

My success is largely due to my strong creative skills, as well as to my ability to prioritize multiple responsibilities. I am very skilled in establishing new business opportunities and marketing strategies to maximize growth and profitability for companies. I sincerely believe that, with my experience and career goals, I would be an asset to your organization.

I would like to request a personal interview at your earliest convenience so we can discuss how I can significantly contribute to your team of professionals. I am planning to relocate to the New York area on a permanent basis to be with family and friends.

Thank you in advance for your time and consideration. I look forward to speaking with you soon.

Sincerely,

Haley Meyers

Resume Enclosed

Closers, Relationship
Builders, and Team Builders.

PAT DOOGAN

A Presentation

of

Professional Sales Credentials

876 Brighton Beach
New Orleans, Louisiana 44776
(504) 456-9876

PAT DOOGAN

876 Brighton Beach
New Orleans, Louisiana 44776
(504) 456-9876

Professional Objective & Profile

Dynamic **Pharmaceutical Sales Representative** with over 7 years of experience building and leading integrated sales operations for pharmaceutical and medical companies. Consistently successful in building and expanding territories to achieve #1 in sales growth in region, and #1 in sales growth for specific products in nation.

Seeking a **sales** position that will provide a challenging opportunity to significantly contribute to a company's efficiency, organization, growth, and overall profitability.

Education   **Bachelor of Science in Education**
TEXAS CHRISTIAN UNIVERSITY
Fort Worth, Texas, 1989
Athletic Trainer, Athletic Scholarship

> Think carefully about which achievements, skills, and competencies you want to highlight. You want to communicate the right message, and an increase in profitability *is* the right one!

Summary of Qualifications

Track Record of Success:
Background exemplifies a successful track record of career accomplishments which encompass positions as *Pharmaceutical Sales Representative, Biological Account Executive, Medical Equipment Sales Representative and Athletic Trainer.* Consistently advanced throughout career to positions of higher levels of responsibility and authority.

Profitability:
Dynamic, results-oriented sales professional who consistently achieves and surpasses sales quotas, which significantly increases overall profitability for company. For example, in 1996, achieved #1 in sales nationally for 2 pharmaceutical products, and #1 in sales growth in the region.

Client Services:
Skilled in developing extensive network of business associates in the pharmaceutical and medical industries. Proven track record in establishing and maintaining new accounts, which increase sales and profitability for company.

Pharmaceutical Educational Seminars:
Experienced in organizing and coordinating numerous seminars that feature notable speakers pertaining to new and unique pharmaceutical drugs.

Fund-Raising & Special Events:
Coordinate and organize numerous fund-raising events for the Hemophilia Organization, which involves volunteering at camps and special events.

Leadership:
Strong leader and motivator of others. Self-directed and self-motivated with ability to guide associates to achieve their maximum potential.

Professional Experience

Pharmaceutical Sales Representative
Biological Account Executive
BAYER CORPORATION - PHARMA BIOLOGICAL COMPANY
Bryan College Station, Texas - 1990 to Present

- *Company Track Record of Success:* Began working for Bayer Corporation in Bryan College Station, Texas, as a Sales Representative. Was promoted to Territory Sales Specialist and transferred to Austin, Texas and San Antonio. In 1996, advanced to Biological Account Executive and transferred to New Orleans. A brief overview of responsibilities is highlighted below.
- *Sales & Profitability:* Responsible for selling oncology pharmaceuticals to hospitals and physicians' offices. Surpassed sales quotas in 1996, and achieved *#1 in sales for 2 products, and #1 in sales growth* in the region. Achieved *$1 million in sales* for each product in only 6 months. Responsible for growing territory by soliciting and obtaining new accounts. Strong presentation, negotiation and closing skills.
- *Public Speaking & Education:* Coordinate numerous seminars and special meetings that feature notable public speakers who educate and provide information regarding pharmaceutical drugs to clients.
- *Client Relations:* Continuously establish and maintain an exemplary network of business associates through extensive interaction and outstanding communications. Effectively build clients relations through comprehensive presentations and sales meetings.
- *Customer Service:* Provide superior service to customers through attentive follow-up to sales and by effectively responding to requests, inquiries, suggestions, and/or concerns.
- *Territory Sales Specialist:* Responsible for calling on peer leaders/physicians in each pharmaceutical specialty.
- *Pharmaceutical Sales Representative:* Initially, responsible for selling pharmaceuticals to different pharmacies, hospitals and physicians' offices.

Medical Equipment Sales Representative
WALKER'S MEDICAL COMPANY
Fort Worth, Texas - 1989 to 1990

- *Sales:* Responsible for selling medical physical therapy equipment to companies and organizations. Solicited and obtained new accounts and was responsible for signing the Dallas Cowboys as a major client.
- *Client Relations:* Networked with major clients throughout the Dallas/Fort Worth areas and established an excellent rapport with businesses and organizations.

Athletic Trainer
HOUSTON OILERS
Houston, Texas - 1988 to 1989

- *Athletic Trainer:* This was an Internship while in college. Provided rehabilitation services to football players who sustained injuries during games. This involved using different types of medical equipment to administer treatments.

Closers, Relationship Builders, and Creative Think Tanks.

Tina Waldrup
4499 Kingston Lane
Kansas City, Kansas 29992
(405) 887-9988

Professional Objective & Profile

High-caliber **Pharmaceutical Sales Representative & Territory Manager** with experience building and leading integrated sales operations and increasing revenue for major pharmaceutical company. Consistently successful in building and expanding territory with proven track record of surpassing market share goal. Totally service- and client relations-oriented with ability to successfully network with leading decision makers and all levels of management and personnel.

Desire a sales position that will provide a challenging opportunity to significantly contribute to a company's efficiency, organization, growth, and profitability.

Education

Bachelor of Science in Sociology
Minor: Office Management & Psychology
KANSAS STATE UNIVERSITY
Kansas City, Kansas, 1995
Dean's List
Chi Omega Sorority

In all Sales & Marketing positions, these areas of Accomplishments and Qualifications are a must!

Summary of Accomplishments

Track Record of Success:
Background exemplifies a successful track record of career accomplishments which encompasses position as *Territory Sales Manager* for Bannon Laboratories, Inc. Dedicated, steady employee who has consistently advanced throughout career to positions of higher levels of responsibility and authority.

Sales & Marketing:
Dynamic, results-oriented sales professional who consistently achieves and surpasses sales goals and achieves top range of market share. Ranked #2 in Sales for pharmaceutical product in 1996. Strong presentation, negotiation and closing skills. Talented in conceptualizing and developing marketing strategies that will benefit customers and increase overall sales.

Client Services:
Skilled in developing an extensive network of business associates in the pharmaceutical and health care industries. Proven track record in establishing and maintaining new accounts, which increases sales and profitability for company.

Leadership:
Strong communication skills with ability to motivate and inspire associates to achieve their maximum potential.

Professional Experience

This signifies that this person affected strong results, which is what you want to stress in your resume!

Territory Sales Manager
BANNON LABORATORIES, INC.
Kansas City, Kansas - 1995 to Present

- *Sales Management:* Responsible for managing overall sales territory development throughout Kansas and for selling pharmaceutical drugs to hospitals, pharmacies, wholesalers, purchasing groups and physicians.

- *Market Share Increase & Profitability:* In just 5 months, have surpassed 1997 company goal of 23.6% market share in Kansas to 29.9%. Increased Kansas's market share goal of 20.8% to 20.9% in 5 months, and increased surrounding market share goal of 25.8% to 27.4% in 5 months.

- *Account Management:* Establish growth plans for individual accounts and personally manage account calls, presentations, and negotiations.

- *Public Speaking & Education:* Educate health care professionals regarding specific pharmaceutical drugs and provide information regarding the company and its services.

- *Marketing:* Conceptualize, develop and present innovative marketing strategies to increase sales and profitability. Currently designing a marketing plan to sell pill cutters in conjunction with pharmaceutical drugs for dialysis patients.

- *Client Services:* Provide superior service to clients by following up on all sales and by effectively responding to requests, inquiries, suggestions and/or concerns.

- *Client Relations:* Continuously establish and maintain an exemplary network of business associates through extensive interaction and outstanding communications.

Assistant Manager
BASKIN ROBBINS, Kansas City, Kansas - 1987 to 1991

- *Management:* Began with this company as a *Customer Service Representative* and was quickly promoted to Assistant Manager. (This was a part-time position while attending college.) Assisted in managing overall operations and administration of store.

- *Personnel & Supervision:* Assisted in interviewing and hiring employees. Delegated responsibilities and monitored overall job performances to ensure accuracy and adherence to company rules and regulations.

- *Employee Relations:* Encouraged and supported a teamlike work environment, which increased company morale, productivity and efficiency. Served as communications liaison between employees and upper management.

- *Customer Service:* Provided excellent service to customers which ensured customer satisfaction, repeat business and referrals.

- *Inventory:* Assisted in monitoring inventory levels of food and beverages.

Tina Waldrup
4499 Kingston Lane
Kansas City, Kansas 29992
(405) 887-9988

Date

Jeremiah Caldwell
Executive Sales Manager
Bristol Meyers Corporation
2983 Hillsboro Avenue
Kansas City, Kansas 29992

> This Cover Letter reflects someone who has the ability to build relationships and close deals.

Dear Mr. Caldwell:

Are you looking for a highly motivated, goal-oriented **Pharmaceutical Sales Representative** and **Territory Manager** to become a leader in your organization? I am confident that, with my experience and career goals, I can significantly contribute to your company's team of sales professionals. I have enclosed a personal resume so you may review my credentials in detail.

In addition to a Bachelor of Science in Sociology from Kansas State University, I also possess more than 2 years of experience as a Territory Sales Manager for Bannon Laboratories, Inc. My qualifications and expertise include the following:

- Excellent sales management skills with experience in expanding sales territories to increase sales and profitability for company.
- Solid organizational, management, interpersonal and communications skills with a proven track record of making sound decisions.
- Strong troubleshooting skills with ability to research and identify problems and implement creative problem-solving solutions.
- Style which exhibits maturity, high energy, sensitivity, teamwork, and the ability to relate to a wide variety of professionals.
- Demonstrated leadership, communication and negotiating skills.
- Proven ability to define issues, propose solutions and implement changes.
- Computer literate with knowledge and experience in various computer systems and applications.

I sincerely believe that, with my experience and career goals, I would be an asset to your organization. I would like to request a personal interview at your earliest convenience so we can discuss ways that I can significantly contribute to your company's goals. I am available to relocate if needed.

Thank you for your time and consideration. I look forward to speaking with you soon.

Sincerely,

Tina Waldrup

Resume Enclosed

FRANK CHAPMAN
888 14th Street NE
Oklahoma City, Oklahoma 73667
(405) 332-1234

> Closers and Relationship Builders.

PROFESSIONAL OBJECTIVE & PROFILE

Experienced **Sales** professional is seeking a position that will fully utilize experience in *Sales, Customer Service, Lithographics, Printing, and Management.*

EDUCATION

Associate of Arts Degree in Liberal Arts
CENTRAL COLLEGE, Chicago, Illinois

PROFESSIONAL EXPERIENCE

1983 to
June 1997

Customer Service & Sales Representative
GRAPHICS, INC., Oklahoma City, Oklahoma
- **Sales:** Responsible for selling offset printing to businesses. Solicited and obtained new clientele, as well as maintained existing accounts.
- **Business Development & Account Management:** Responsible for managing new business development and strategic planning to maximize growth and profitability. Established growth plans for individual accounts and personally managed account calls, presentations and negotiations.
- **Client Services:** Provided excellent service to clients by effectively responding to requests, inquiries, suggestions, and/or concerns. Very talented in preventing problems by thoroughly assessing projects before initiation. Successful in minimizing costs by 45% and saving money for the company and clients as a result of attention to detail and effective planning. Major clientele consisted of First American National Bank and Sanford Corporation.
- **Cost Estimates:** Provided cost estimates to customers regarding customized jobs.
- **Trouble-Shooter:** Assisted clients in developing specifications for customized jobs. Researched and identified problems within jobs and/or customer service and implemented creative problem-solving techniques to resolve issues.

> Citing concrete results makes this candidate more credible and believable!

1981 to 1983

Production Director
JOHNSON ADVERTISING AGENCY, Oklahoma City, Oklahoma
- **Management:** Managed and directed all production services for advertising agency.
- **Print Production:** Directed production of print materials and print media including newspapers and magazine advertisements.
- **Personnel & Supervision:** Interviewed, hired, trained and supervised staff members. Delegated work responsibilities and monitored overall job performances to ensure accuracy and adherence to specifications, policies and procedures.

REFERENCES

Available Upon Request.

Closers, Relationship Builders, Team Builders, and Creative Think Tanks.

Leticia Dallas
6633 Queen Hill Drive
Seattle, Washington 33838
(776) 776-6776

Professional Objective & Profile

Established, successful **Sales & Marketing Manager** with 8 years of experience building and leading integrated operations in Sales, Marketing and Property Management. Consistently successful in designing and implementing sales and marketing programs which yield company savings and profitability.

Strong general management qualifications in strategic planning, organizational reengineering and all facets of process/productivity/quality improvement. Excellent background in personnel training, development, supervision, and leadership. Skilled executive liaison who is self-directed and self-motivated.

Desire a **Sales Management** position that will provide a challenging opportunity to significantly contribute to a company's efficiency, organization, growth, and profitability.

Education *Bachelor of Science in Marketing*
WASHINGTON STATE UNIVERSITY
Seattle, Washington, 1988

Summary of Qualifications

Track Record of Success:
Background exemplifies a successful track record of career accomplishments and encompasses positions as *Sales Manager, Assistant Property Manager, Divisional Computer Trainer, and Leasing Manager.* Consistently advanced throughout career to positions of higher levels of responsibility and authority.

Management Expertise:
Excellent background in managing and directing overall sales and leasing operations. Have held full decision-making responsibility for developing annual financial objectives and preparing long-range strategic business plans. High energy, goal-oriented with assertive decision-making skills.

Client Relations:
Solid interpersonal and communications skills with proven track record of establishing and maintaining an excellent network of business relationships as a result of extensive interaction between corporate businesses and agencies.

Sales, Marketing & Advertising:
Superb sales experience with skills in creating and developing innovative marketing & advertising campaigns that maximize growth and profitability for companies. Responsibilities have included managing new business development and strategic planning. Developed, directed and monitored comprehensive communications and advertising programs for companies. Established growth plans for individual accounts and personally managed account calls, presentations, and negotiations.

Budget Management:
Managed a $600,000 monthly budget for Gibbs Residential. Skilled in reviewing and analyzing budget variances and initiating appropriate recommendations to more aggressively control annual expenditures. Consistently achieved all budget objectives.

Professional Experience

Sales Manager
GIBBS RESIDENTIAL
Seattle, Washington - 1991 to Present

- *Company Track Record of Success:* Began with *Gibbs Residential* in 1991 as an *Assistant Property Manager.* Progressed to position of *Sales Manager* when company started the corporate housing division in 1995. Responsibilities have been comprehensive and include the following positions and job duties.
- *Sales & Account Management:* Responsible for directing overall sales and marketing operations for company. Independently manage entire sales cycle from client identification and account development through presentations, contract and price negotiations and final sales closings. Establish growth plans for individual corporate accounts and personally manage account calls, presentations and negotiations.
- *Corporate Apartment Design:* In charge of designing and setting up furnishings for corporate clients. This includes renting furnishings, as well as monitoring and maintaining inventory of 120 units in Seattle.
- *Client Relations:* Responsible for the development/nurturance of client relationships. Continuously establish and maintain an exemplary network of business relationships as a result of extensive interaction and strong communication skills.
- *Customer Service:* Provide superior service to customers by effectively responding to requests, inquiries, suggestions, and/or concerns.
- *Marketing:* Responsible for strategic business planning, development of integrated sales, core prospect marketing, research and analysis. Create and develop innovative marketing campaigns targeted to potential clients.
- *Company Liaison - Employee Relations:* Liaison between 13 properties in Seattle, and responsible for communicating information regarding company policies and procedures.
- *Inventory & Purchasing:* Monitor inventory levels of furnishings and purchase as needed for corporate apartments.

Assistant Property Manager

- *Management:* In this position, was responsible for managing overall operations which included leasing, sales and marketing for an 886-unit residential complex.
- *Budget Management:* Developed and administered a $600,000 monthly budget. Analyzed budget variances and initiated appropriate strategies to more aggressively control expenditures. Responsible for P&L.
- *Sales & Marketing:* Assisted Manager in developing strategic marketing and sales plans to maximize growth and profitability.

Divisional Computer Trainer

- *Computer Trainer:* Installed computer hardware and software in 17 properties within Division, and responsible for training staff members in all areas of computer operations. Provided support to staff as needed on-site.

Leasing Manager
WASHINGTON OUTDOOR ADVERTISING, INC.
Seattle, Washington - 1989 to 1991

- *Management:* In charge of managing overall leasing operations for this advertising company.
- *Sales & Account Management:* Researched and identified potential clients and personally managed account calls, presentations and negotiations. Solicited and obtained clientele by calling on advertising agencies, corporate offices and local businesses. Strategically chartered over 600 locations for advertisers on a daily basis.

Bryce Stevens
7846 Right Street
Pittsburgh, Pennsylvania 15299
(412) 909-7867

Closers, Creative Think Tanks, and Relationship Builders.

Professional Objective & Profile

High-caliber, experienced **Sales & Marketing Representative** is seeking a position in Sales that will fully utilize 10 years of experience in professional sales and marketing. Extremely successful in building and expanding sales territories and increasing revenue. Totally service- and client relations-oriented, with ability to successfully network with major executive decision makers and all levels of management and personnel.

Desire a **Sales & Marketing** position that will provide a challenging opportunity to significantly contribute to a company's efficiency, organization, growth, and profitability.

Education

Associate of Science in Business Administration
Major: Administrative Management
ROBERT MORRIS COLLEGE, Pittsburgh, Pennsylvania

Professional Experience

Regional Forms Sales Representative
HENSON PRINTING SYSTEMS, Pittsburgh, Pennsylvania - 1991 to 1997

- *Sales & Marketing:* Design, market and sell business forms to professionals in the medical industry. Solicit and obtain new clients as well as maintain and build existing accounts.
- *Profitability:* Increased territorial sales from $1.2 million to $1.6 million in 1996 and significantly increased overall profitability for company. Consistently achieve and surpass sales quotas. Achieved *Salesperson of the Month* in February 1997.
- *Account Management:* Responsible for managing new business development and strategic planning to maximize growth and profitability. Establish growth plans for individual accounts and personally manage account calls, presentations and negotiations.
- *Customer Service & Client Relations:* Provide excellent attention and superior service to clients by effectively responding to requests, inquiries, suggestions, and/or concerns.
- *Promotions:* Responsible for introducing and promoting new electronic software product on the market that expanded sales by 300%.
- *Company Merger:* Instrumental in assisting in streamlining of sales operations when Janson Systems, Inc. merged with Henson Printing Systems in 1994.

Marketing Coordinator
JANSON SYSTEMS, INC., Pittsburgh, Pennsylvania - 1988 to 1991

- *Sales Support:* Provided sales and administrative support to 2 Sales Managers and 10 Sales Consultants. Assisted sales staff by preparing sales presentations, proposals and training materials.
- *Meetings & Event Planning:* Organized and coordinated special events which included trade shows and seminars.

Sales Assistant
MARRIOTT CORPORATION, Pittsburgh, Pennsylvania - 1987 to 1988

- *Marketing & Sales:* Provided sales and administrative support to the Director of Marketing and the Director of Sales. Involved in all facets of opening the Pittsburgh Airport Marriott.
- *Meetings & Event Planning:* Organized and coordinated sales meetings for large corporations.

Bryce Stevens
7846 Right Street
Pittsburgh, Pennsylvania 15299
(412) 909-7867

Date

Arthur Lake
Director of Sales & Marketing
Zip Printing Industry
2998 Starns Boulevard
Pittsburgh, Pennsylvania 15299

Look for career jobs by reading trade magazines and journals. You can often pick up good leads for a new job by reading business articles.

Dear Mr. Lake:

I recently read an article in *Success Magazine* describing your company as "the company of the future." I am interested in joining the "company of the future," and feel confident that, with my sales and marketing experience, I could significantly contribute to your team of sales professionals. I have enclosed a personal resume which will provide you with details concerning my credentials.

In addition to an *Associate of Science in Business Administration,* I also possess 10 years of experience in sales and marketing. My areas of qualification and expertise include the following:

- *Salesperson of the Month,* Henson Printing Systems, February 1997.
- Consistently achieve and surpass sales quotas by more than 34%, which increases overall profitability for company. Ability to expand and develop client base.
- Easily establish excellent rapport and make effective sales presentations to all levels of decision makers including top corporate executives and administrators.
- Solid organizational, management, interpersonal and communications skills with a proven track record of making sound decisions.
- Skilled in planning, coordinating, and organizing special events, trade shows and seminars.
- Demonstrated leadership, communication and negotiating skills.
- Proven ability to define issues, propose solutions and implement changes.

I sincerely believe that, with my track record of success and future goals, I would be an asset to your organization. I would like to request a personal interview at your earliest convenience so we can discuss how I can best contribute to your team of sales professionals.

Thank you in advance for your time and consideration. I look forward to speaking with you soon.

Sincerely,

Bryce Stevens

Resume Enclosed

> Closers, Relationship Builders, and Team Builders.

Victoria Raven
6565 Oaklane Road
Sante Fe, New Mexico 88763
(676) 876-0987

Professional Objective & Profile

Self-directed and self-motivated **Department Sales Manager** is seeking a position as **Sales & Merchandise Coordinator** that will fully utilize an extensive background in Retail Management, Merchandising, Promotions, Sales, and Customer Service. Desire a position that will provide a challenging opportunity to significantly contribute to a company's efficiency, organization, growth, and profitability.

Education

Bachelor of Science in Mass Communications
Area of Emphasis: Graphic Arts
NEW MEXICO STATE UNIVERSITY
Sante Fe, New Mexico, 1989

Associate Degree in General Studies
NEW MEXICO STATE COMMUNITY COLLEGE
Sante Fe, New Mexico, 1985

Professional Experience

> Define how you progressed within a company. It indicates a person who is goal-oriented.

Department Manager
JEWELS DEPARTMENT STORE
Sante Fe, New Mexico - 1986 to Present

- **Company Track Record of Success:** Began as a *Sales Associate* in 1986 and quickly advanced to *Associate Department Manager,* and then to *Department Manager*. Transferred to Nashville in 1995, and assumed responsibilities of *Department Manager for Ladies' Shoes & Handbags*. Responsibilities are comprehensive and include the following areas of expertise.
- **Management & Supervision:** In charge of managing overall operations and administration of the Ladies' Shoes, & Handbags Department, which includes a $2.2 million inventory. Interview, hire, train, schedule, and supervise up to 16 associates. Train associates and monitor overall job performances to ensure accuracy and adherence to company's policies and procedures.
- **Profitability:** Consistently surpass sales quotas by 27% and achieve significant profitability for company.
- **Client Relations - Customer Service:** Committed to providing superior service to clients by responding to their requests, inquiries, suggestions, and/or concerns. Superior service results in repeat business.
- **Life Styling Team:** Member of *Life Styling Team* who is responsible for organizing and coordinating outstanding floor and window displays that include merchandise from all the departments of the store to enhance visual impact of departments.
- **Employee Relations:** Interact effectively with Buyers and Management Team to communicate needs, to plan inventory levels, and to develop effective merchandising and marketing strategies for department.
- **Special Events & Meeting Planning:** Plan, organize and facilitate special events and meetings each month with vendors to educate customers and sales associates regarding merchandising and products.
- **Visual Merchandising & Product Seminars:** Facilitate *Merchandising & Product Knowledge Seminars* for associates in order to educate them on new products and marketing strategies.
- **Advertising & Marketing:** Create, develop and proof print ads for advertising and marketing.
- **In-Store Promotions:** Assist in creating, developing and implementing in-store promotions for the purpose of advertising special sales and events and to increase profitability.
- **Inventory:** Monitor inventory levels of merchandise, and responsible for markdowns. Identify slow sellers and assess needs for future merchandise.

Victoria Raven
6565 Oaklane Road
Sante Fe, New Mexico 88763
(676) 876-0987

Date

Carmen Springwater
Executive Director of Marketing & Merchandising
Highlands Department Store
982 Desert Road
Santa Fe, New Mexico 88763

Dear Ms. Springwater:

I am interested in obtaining the position of **Marketing & Merchandising Coordinator** for Highlands Department Store, which was advertised in today's *Santa Fe Newspaper.* As requested, I have enclosed a personal resume which will provide you with details concerning my background and qualifications.

As you will note in my resume, I am not a beginner, but rather a seasoned professional with 10 years of experience at Jewels. Currently a Department Manager for Ladies' Shoes, & Handbags, I have the necessary qualifications you're seeking, with additional talents as well. I have an extensive background in management which includes sales, visual merchandising, seminars, special events and meeting planning. I sincerely believe that, with my experience and career goals, I would be an asset to Highlands Department Store.

I would like to request a personal interview at your earliest convenience so we can discuss ways that I can significantly contribute to your team of professionals. Please feel free to contact me if you have any additional questions concerning my qualifications.

Thank you in advance for your time and consideration. I look forward to speaking with you soon.

Sincerely,

Victoria Raven

Resume Enclosed

BART THOMPSON
3107 Southlake Drive
Las Vegas, Nevada 29867
(515) 345-6789

Closers, Relationship Builders, and Team Builders.

PROFESSIONAL OBJECTIVE & PROFILE

A highly professional and achievement-oriented **Sales Associate** is seeking a position that will fully utilize an extensive background in customer service, sales, client relations and merchandising. Self-directed and self-motivated with ability to work well independently or as a team member. Desire a career position that will provide a challenging opportunity to significantly contribute to a company's efficiency, organization, growth, and profitability.

EDUCATION

Bachelor of Business Administration
NEVADA STATE UNIVERSITY
Las Vegas, Nevada, 1993

PROFESSIONAL EXPERIENCE

Sales Associate
K-MART DEPARTMENT STORE - ELECTRONICS DEPARTMENT
Las Vegas, Nevada - 1984 to Present

- *Company Track Record of Success:* Began at Kmart part-time at age 16 as a *Sales Associate* while in high school, and continued working there while pursuing Bachelor's Degree and afterwards. Responsibilities are comprehensive and include the following areas of expertise.
- *Management:* Assist management staff in the overall administration and operations of the Electronics Department.
- *Sales:* Responsible for selling electronics merchandise to customers in retail environment.
- *Supervision:* Supervise employees and delegate work responsibilities. Monitor employees' overall job performances to ensure adherence to company policies and procedures.
- *Employee Training:* Train new sales associates in all areas of sales, merchandising and customer service.
- *Employee Relations:* Work closely with Managers to input data into computer systems, and to maintain a highly organized, efficient operation. Encourage and support a teamlike work environment among coworkers which increases employee efficiency and productivity.
- *Merchandising:* Responsible for arranging and designing floor displays in Electronics Department to enhance merchandise and increase overall sales and profitability.
- *Customer Service:* Committed to providing superior service to customers by assisting them in their selections, and by responding to their requests, inquiries, suggestions, and/or concerns.
- *Vendor Relations:* Continuously establish and maintain an excellent network of business relationships with vendors and suppliers as a result of extensive interaction and communication.
- *Inventory & Ordering:* Monitor and review inventory levels of merchandise, and responsible for ordering specific items as needed.
- *Computer Operations - Invoicing:* Utilize computer system to prepare invoices for more than 200 orders of film on a daily basis.

JANICE CHAPMAN

18 NW American Boulevard
Roswell, Georgia 30076
(770) 677-0987

> Closers, Relationship Builders, and Team Builders.

PROFESSIONAL OBJECTIVE & PROFILE

A self-directed and self-motivated **Retail Store Sales Manager** is seeking a **Sales Management** position that will provide a challenging opportunity to significantly contribute to a company's efficiency, organization, growth, and profitability.

Over 2 years of experience in building and leading integrated sales operations for an exclusive women's apparel store. Strong general management qualifications in strategic planning, organizational reengineering and process/productivity/quality improvement. Excellent experience in personnel training, development and leadership.

PROFESSIONAL EXPERIENCE

STORE SALES MANAGER, CACHET, The Limited, Inc.
Atlanta, Georgia - 1993 to Present

- *Company Track Record of Success:* Began with company in 1993 as a *Sales Associate* and advanced to *Assistant Manager* in 1994. In June 1995, was promoted to *Co-Sales Manager,* and then in August 1995, progressed to current position of *Store Sales Manager.* A brief synopsis of responsibilities is highlighted below.
- *Management:* Responsible for overall administration and operations of a store that achieves $1 million annually in revenue. Conduct ongoing analyses to evaluate the efficiency, quality, and productivity of business operations.
- *Sales:* Direct and guide sales operations which involves selling exclusive women's apparel to customers in retail environment.
- *Customer Service:* Provide superior service to in-store customers by assisting them with merchandise selection, and by responding to requests, suggestions, and/or concerns.
- *Client Relations:* Establish and maintain an exemplary network of business relationships on an ongoing basis through effective communication and excellent service.
- *Personnel, Recruitment, Training & Supervision:* Recruit, interview, hire, train and supervise associates. Also responsible for training and developing Co-Sales Managers. Fully accountable for personnel scheduling, job assignments, performance reviews and daily supervision. Monitor overall job performances to ensure accuracy and adherence to company policies and procedures.
- *Budget Management:* Analyze budget variances and initiate appropriate recommendations to more aggressively control annual expenditures. Design budget forecasting and expense analysis plans.
- *Marketing & Merchandising:* Implement company's marketing and advertising strategies into everyday operations. Create and design floor displays to effectively enhance merchandise and increase sales.
- *Employee Relations:* Empower employees to think and work independently and as team members. Encourage and support teamlike work environment, which increases employee efficiency and productivity and decreases employee turnover.

EDUCATION

Bachelor of Science in Movement Exercise/Science
SOUTHWEST UNIVERSITY, Orange, California
GPA: 3.8/4.0

Closers, Relationship Builders, and Team Builders.

Sarah Fennel
9987 Morningside Drive
San Antonio, Texas 99339
(615) 661-5002

Professional Objective & Profile

Desire a **Sales or Marketing** position that will fully utilize my background in Merchandising, Sales, Customer Service, and Office Administration. A self-starter who works well independently or as a team member. Committed to achieving success in a progressive environment that promotes professional advancement and career growth.

Education
Bachelor of Science in Home Economics
Major: Family & Child Development
SOUTHWEST TEXAS STATE UNIVERSITY, San Marcos, Texas

Professional Experience

March 1996
to October 1996

Petite Sales Specialist
DILLARD'S DEPARTMENT STORE, San Antonio, Texas
Responsible for selling merchandise to customers in retail environment. Provided excellent customer service by assisting them in their selection, and by effectively responding to requests, inquiries, suggestions, and/or concerns. Designed and arranged floor displays in order to enhance merchandise and increase sales. Achieved and maintained daily sales quota and received a salary increase after 3-month evaluation due to outstanding job performance.

October 1994
to March 1996

Sales Specialist
JEWELS COMPANY, San Antonio, Texas
Responsibilities were basically the same as those described above, and was responsible for all facets of selling merchandise to customers in retail environment. Received an increase in salary following a 90-day evaluation due to outstanding job performance.

August 1994
to October 1994

Receptionist
ADIA PERSONNEL SERVICES, San Antonio, Texas
Worked in several office and receptionist positions for this temporary agency while seeking a full-time, permanent position. Answered phones and coordinated messages for staff members. Also, typed and filed business correspondence. Received an increase in salary after 3 months of work.

March 1994
to May 1994

Administrative Assistant
COUNTRY CLUB ENTERPRISES, San Antonio, Texas
Provided office support to a country music company that worked with country music artists and promoters.

June 1993
to May 1994

Teacher
KINDERCARE LEARNING CENTER, San Antonio, Texas

MIA CARRERA
87 West 50th Street
New York, New York 10024
(212) 777-3332

> Closers, Relationship
> Builders, and Team Builders.

Professional Objective & Profile

High-caliber **Sales Executive & Manager** with an extensive background building and leading integrated sales operations for a worldwide organization. Consistently successful in identifying and implementing innovative sales and marketing strategies which significantly increase profitability. Extremely talented in project development from initial conceptualization to completion of a viable, business operation.

Strong general management qualifications in strategic planning, business development, organizational reengineering and process/productivity/quality improvement on an international basis. Excellent experience in all facets of sales, account management, and business development. Skilled in international relations and executive liaison. Seeking a **Sales Management** position that will provide a challenging opportunity to significantly contribute to a company's efficiency, organization, growth, and profitability.

Summary of Qualifications

Track Record of Success:
Background exemplifies a successful track record of career accomplishments and includes more than 15 years experience in Sales, Management, Entrepreneurial Ventures, Project & Business Development, and Advertising.

International Sales Management:
Conceptualized, designed, and spearheaded international sales for the largest brake manufacturer in the world, Benendo America, Inc., which has international headquarters in London, England. Held full decision-making responsibility for developing annual sales objectives, and for preparing long-range strategic business plans all over the world. Sold over $2.2 million in Mexico alone as a result of excellent sales abilities, client relations and service.

Domestic & International Client Relations:
Skilled and talented in communicating effectively with foreign cultures and businesses. Developed and maintained an exemplary network of client relationships all over the world.

> Use high-
> powered
> buzzwords that
> demonstrate
> action.

Business Development:
Entrepreneurial-minded with proven methods in conceptualizing, developing, and administering innovative business ideas and marketing strategies which have proven successful in significantly increasing company profitability. Successfully developed and initiated the Chrysler Motorcraft and Ford Motorcraft of Mexico.

Project Development:
Spearheaded project to develop and coordinate an independent television station in Tennessee with business partner. Also, developed and launched successful newspaper which focused on agricultural products and services.

Education

OAKLAND COMMUNITY COLLEGE, Union Lake, Michigan
Area of Concentration: Business Administration

NEWARK COMMUNITY COLLEGE, Newark, New Jersey

Executive Sales & Management Experience

International Sales - Key Account Manager
BENENDO AMERICA, INC. - International Headquarters in London, England
New York, New York - 1986 to 1996

- *International Sales & Profitability:* Spearheaded, conceptualized, developed, and initiated international sales strategies for company. Planned and directed international sales for Benendo America, Inc., the largest brake manufacturer in the world. Successfully increased annual sales in the U.S. and international markets.
- *Business & Program Development:* Talented in identifying new business opportunities. Conducted on-going analyses to evaluate the efficiency, quality and productivity of business operations, and developed a series of aggressive sales and marketing strategies to expand business and increase sales. Managed new business development and strategic planning.
- *Product Knowledge:* In-depth knowledge of, and experience in, the automotive industry in relation to the brake industry. Managed multidisciplinary operations within the company with full responsibility for strategic planning, technology, equipment/material resources and performance/analysis improvement.
- *International Client Relations:* Established and maintained a worldwide network of excellent business relationships which included clients in Mexico, Europe, Middle East and Asia. Worked with clients from conceptualization of product line to customer distribution.
- *Marketing & Advertising:* Led companywide marketing and product development activities for company on an international basis. In charge of updating and revising product line catalogues.
- *Distributorship:* Negotiated and organized distributorship in Mexico for the development and implementation of a warehouse for distribution operations.
- *Inter-Company Relations:* Technical liaison between engineering department and manufacturing department in relation to launching of product lines.
- *Troubleshooter:* Skilled in researching, investigating and identifying problems within product lines, or within client relations. Very creative in problem solving.

Quality Control & Engineering Experience

Quality Control Engineer
JOHNSON COMPANY, Romulus, Michigan - 1971 to 1975

- *Quality Control:* This company manufactured wheels for automobiles. Responsible for administering tests to ensure adherence to quality standards and regulations, as required by O.E.M. customers.

Entrepreneurial & Project Development Experience

Owner & Manager
THE PROFESSIONAL AUTO REPAIR COMPANY, Newark, New Jersey - 1979 to 1985

- *Operations & Management:* Managed overall operations and administration of this company, which included 2 independent automobile repair shops.
- *Sales & Account Management:* Responsible for soliciting and obtaining clients, and for maintaining established accounts. Built and expanded company to achieve significant profitability.
- *Personnel & Supervision:* Interviewed, hired, trained and supervised employees. Delegated work responsibilities, and monitored and evaluated employees' overall job performances.

Owner & Construction Project Manager
CC ENTERPRISES, INC., Newark, New Jersey - 1975 to 1978

- *Management:* Managed construction projects which included residential subdivisions. Owned and managed numerous rental properties in surrounding areas.

Philip Meredith
555 Breckinridge Road
Denver, Colorado 70023
(408) 444-7720

> Closers, Relationship Builders, and Team Builders.

PROFESSIONAL OBJECTIVE & PROFILE

A dedicated, committed **Sales Manager** is seeking a position in sales management. Strong general management qualifications in sales, business development, strategic planning, personnel and merchandising. Desire a **Sales Management** position that will provide a challenging opportunity to significantly contribute to a company's efficiency, organization, growth, and profitability.

SUMMARY OF QUALIFICATIONS

> Convey that you're a profit-oriented, results-oriented salesperson!

TRACK RECORD OF SUCCESS: More than 16 years of progressive experience with major companies. Consistently advanced to positions of higher levels of responsibility and authority.

SALES/PROFITABILITY: No. #1 Sales Representative in the Nation while working for Freeman Trailer Corporation. Consistently increased profitability for company by maintaining high percentage sales ratios.

MANAGEMENT: Experienced in developing business and managing all facets of major accounts for Freeman and John's Trucks & Trailers of Colorado.

TROUBLESHOOTER: Adept at identifying problematic areas within a sales territory and implementing creative solutions to resolve problems.

BUSINESS COMMUNICATIONS: Established and maintained an exemplary network of business relationships throughout the nation as a result of extensive interaction and strong communication skills.

PROFESSIONAL AFFILIATIONS

- Car & Truck Rental & Leasing Association of Denver
- Denver Traffic Club
- Colorado Trucking Association
  Board of Directors (past 7 years) - Elected by peers

VOLUNTEER   Y. M. C. A., Denver, Colorado
YOUTH SOCCER PROGRAM COORDINATOR
Volunteer with the Youth Soccer Program as well as serving on other committees.

EDUCATION   **KENT STATE UNIVERSITY,** Kent, Ohio
Bachelor of Science in Education, 1979

Philip Meredith
Page 2

This resume shows off special talents and displays true self-confidence, which makes it sure to win interviews!

PROFESSIONAL EXPERIENCE

Sales Manager
JOHN'S TRUCKS & TRAILERS OF COLORADO
Denver, Colorado - 1996 to May 1997

- *Sales & Operations Management:* Responsible for initiating and managing sales operations for Colorado. Sold new and used semi-trailers to clients. Held full P & L responsibility and decision-making authority. Responsible for the development/nurturance of client relationships, core prospect marketing, cost estimates, and complete operations management.
- *Store Opening:* In charge of opening this one-person store, which was the only location in Tennessee. Responsible for coordinating and organizing all operations, including warranties, service, titles, and repairs.
- *Territory Development - Account Management:* Responsible for managing new business development and strategic planning to maximize growth and profitability. Established growth plans for individual accounts and personally managed account calls, presentations, and negotiations.
- *Customer Service:* Provided superior service to customers by effectively responding to requests, inquiries, suggestions, and/or concerns.
- *Contract Negotiations:* Negotiated and initiated service and finance contracts for clientele.
- *Advertising & Marketing:* Created, developed and implemented innovative marketing and advertising strategies to promote business and increase sales.
- *Market Research:* Conducted demographic and marketing research to target potential clients.
- *Budget & Financial Management:* Full responsibility for analyzing and managing budget and for financial analysis/reporting. Also responsible for state and local taxes.
- *Computer Operations:* Utilized computer system to input data regarding inventory and client information.

Territory Sales Representative
FREEMAN TRAILER CORPORATION
Denver, Colorado - 1981 to 1996

- *Management:* Managed all facets of the Denver Territory which included all merchandising, personnel and sales.
- *Sales Accomplishment:* Recognized as the **Top Sales Representative** in the nation in 1994 and second in the nation in 1995.
- *Sales:* In charge of selling new and used semi-trailers, plus parts and service for company.
- *Account Management:* In charge of administration and operations of accounts; oversaw that all work was completed. Followed up to ensure total client satisfaction.
- *Human Resources/Training:* Assisted in interviewing, hiring, training and supervising sales staff.
- *Territory Development:* Responsible for researching companies and soliciting and obtaining new clientele.
- *Marketing & Advertising:* Developed and implemented aggressive marketing strategies in order to promote new and used trailer sales as well as parts and service programs.
- *Pricing:* Responsible for establishing effective pricing to maintain profitability.
- *Profitability:* Exceeded all company guidelines for gross margins in new and used trailer sales.

JASON PELFREY
7676 Woven Road
Dallas, Texas 22443
(660) 897-0098

> Closers, Relationship
> Builders, Creative Think
> Tanks, Team Builders.

Professional Objective & Profile

High-caliber, dynamic **Sales & Marketing Executive** with more than 25 years of experience building and leading integrated sales and marketing operations for international and domestic markets. In-depth background in industrial sales, manufacturing and quality control. Talented in planning and developing new manufacturing and corporate facilities which yield company profitability.

Extremely personable with high energy and self-direction. Strong general management qualifications in strategic and tactical planning, organizational reengineering, recruitment, training and development, and all facets of process/productivity/quality improvement. Excellent background in developing annual financial objectives and preparing long-range strategic business plans to maximize growth and profitability. Skilled executive liaison who is very client/customer service-oriented with ability to develop and maintain a strong network of client relationships.

Desire a career opportunity in **sales in leadership and management** that will provide a challenging opportunity to significantly contribute to a company's efficiency, organization, growth, and profitability.

Education

OHIO STATE UNIVERSITY, Newark, Ohio
Area of Concentration: Sales Management

UNIVERSITY OF TOLEDO, Toledo, Ohio
Area of Concentration: Industrial Technology

Professional Affiliations

American Society of Quality Control
Society of Plastic Engineers
American Standards for Testing & Materials

Sales, Marketing & Management Experience

Factory Sales Representative
SETTING CORPORATION, Dallas, Texas - 1997 to Present

- **Sales & Business Development:** Responsible for selling of factory direct home improvement products which includes siding, windows and other materials to individual homes and businesses. Responsible for managing new business development and strategic planning to maximize growth and profitability. Establish growth plans for individual accounts and manage account calls, presentations and negotiations.
- **Client Relations:** Continuously establish and maintain an excellent network of business associates as a result of extensive interaction with clients and strong communication skills.

Operations Manager
US PLASTICS, Houston, Texas - 1994 to 1997

- **Plant Development:** Spearheaded the development and initiation of a recycling plant in Texas for the Texas Valley Authority. Directed all material planning, recruitment and staffing operations, capital equipment acquisition, financial performance analysis and business planning/development functions.
- **Sales & Marketing:** Responsible for conceptualizing, developing and implementing innovative marketing and sales strategies to increase business and profitability.

Sales, Marketing & Management Experience

President
CORREY PLASTICS, Dallas, Texas - 1992 to 1994

- **Management:** As Owner and President, was responsible for managing overall operations of this plastic molding company. Founded, built and expanded this company to achieve significant profitability in the marketplace. Responsible for all operations, personnel, budget, sales and marketing, and client relations.
- **Sales & Marketing:** Managed sales and marketing operations and solicited and obtained clientele.
- **Business Planning Development & Negotiations:** Built business from ground up through successfully negotiating contracts. Prepared job bids and negotiated costs of materials and labor.
- **Company Acquisitions:** Negotiated purchasing and financing contracts to purchase facilities including an $800,000 plant facility and responsible for all financial/business planning functions as well as all inventory including capital equipment acquisition, raw materials and supplies, molds, etc. Analyzed and established strategic plans and objectives regarding facilities, equipment, space allocations, and utilization. Worked closely with vendors and suppliers to design plant including electrical and plumbing.
- **Budget Management:** Managed, analyzed and administered budget for operating expenditures. Responsible for financial performance analysis and business planning and development. Analyzed budget variances and initiated appropriate guidelines to aggressively control expenditures.
- **Federal & State Grants:** Prepared applications and presentations and submitted to obtain state and federal grants, loans and tax abatements.
- **Production/Accounting Programs:** Responsible for setting up basic accounting programs with spreadsheets to track production and inventory.

Vice President, Marketing
BBCI CORPORATION, Dallas, Texas - 1989 to 1992

- **Management:** Co-owner of company which manufactured packaging products. Held direct P&L responsibility for company operations.
- **International & Domestic Sales & Marketing:** Generated all international and domestic sales and built company to **$5 million** in 4 years. Responsible for strategic planning and development of an integrated sales, marketing and business plan targeted to specific industries.

Owner & Sales Agent
HANEY INSURANCE AGENCY, Dallas, Texas - 1985 to 1989

- **Management:** Established a new personal lines insurance agency that ranked **74th out of 2700** agents nationally. As Owner, was totally responsible for business development, international and domestic sales and operations.

Sales Manager
VVC SALES COMPANY, Dallas, Texas - 1982 to 1985

- **Sales Management & Profitability:** Managed overall sales operations for this company that sold used recreational vehicles. Generated **74% of all sales** and increased overall revenue from **$300,000 to $1.2 million annually.**

References available upon request

JASON PELFREY
7676 Woven Road
Dallas, Texas 22443
(660) 897-0098

Date

Debbie Milton
Executive Sales Manager
Sawyer Company
2983 Red Valley Road
Dallas, Texas 22443

> The cover letter is the first thing an employer reads, so make sure it's enticing and exciting!

Dear Ms. Milton:

I am a highly motivated, goal-oriented **Sales & Marketing Executive** and I would like to become your next **Sales Manager** at Sawyer Company. I am confident that with my extensive background in Sales, Marketing, Customer Service and Management, I can significantly contribute to your company's growth and profitability. I have enclosed a personal resume so you may review my credentials.

As you will note, I am not a beginner, but rather a seasoned professional with more than 25 years of experience. My qualifications and areas of expertise include the following:

- Proven track record of success in generating sales and increasing profitability through developing business opportunities and marketing strategies that maximize growth and expand market penetration.
- Financial and analytical expertise in budget development, forecasting and management.
- Overall management experience in all areas of company development, recruitment and staffing, developing/nurturing client relationships, financial business planning, capital equipment acquisition, contract negotiations and services. Track record of making sound business decisions.
- Effective team-building skills. Empower associates to think and work independently and in a team environment, which increases employee morale, productivity and efficiency.
- Proven ability to define issues, propose solutions and implement changes.
- Comprehensive knowledge of manufacturing and quality control.
- Knowledge and experience in computer systems and applications including Microsoft Windows, Excel, Word and DOS.

I sincerely believe that, with my experience and career aspirations in sales, I would be an asset to your organization. I would like to request a personal interview at your earliest convenience so we can discuss how I can best contribute to your company's goals.

Thank you for your time and consideration. I look forward to speaking with you soon.

Sincerely,

Jason Pelfrey

Resume Enclosed

Closers, Relationship Builders, and Team Builders.

SEAN WILLINGHAM
7877 Georgetown Road
Washington, DC 77665
(776) 887-9987

Professional Objective & Profile

An achievement- and success-oriented professional is seeking a position in **Marketing** that will fully utilize an extensive background in Sales, Marketing, Management, Purchasing, Finance and Customer Service.

Education

Bachelor of Science in Marketing
GEORGETOWN UNIVERSITY, Washington, DC

DALE CARNEGIE PUBLIC SPEAKING COURSE
Washington, DC

MARYLAND STATE UNIVERSITY
Area of Concentration: Aerospace Engineering & Math
Baltimore, Maryland

Honors

Eagle Scout Award and God & Country Boy Scouts Award

Professional Experience

Manager
Promoted from Assistant Manager in 1993
DC INTSY-PRINTS
Washington, DC - 1986 to Present

- *Company Promotion:* Began at Intsy-Prints as an *Assistant Manager,* and was promoted to *Manager* in 1993. Responsibilities are comprehensive and include the following areas of expertise.
- *Management:* In charge of overall administration and operations of store.
- *Sales & Marketing:* Responsible for sales and marketing of printing services to in-store customers, as well as to clients outside the store.
- *Client Relations:* Continuously establish and maintain an exemplary network of business associates as a result of extensive interaction and contact.
- *Team Building - Employee Relations:* Encourage and support a teamlike work environment which increases employee morale, productivity, and efficiency.
- *Customer Service:* Committed to providing superior service to clients by responding to their requests, inquiries, suggestions, and/or concerns. Organize and produce complex printing orders as needed.

Account Representative
BUSINESS CARDS
Washington, DC - 1985 to 1986

- *Sales & Marketing:* Responsible for soliciting and obtaining clients by calling on companies and setting up appointments with individuals.
- *Customer Service:* Provided excellent service to clients by assisting them and by offering information regarding the company and its services.

Johnny Humphries
1818 West Hills Ave.
Jacksonville, Florida 45372
(555) 988-1234

Closers, Creative Think Tanks, Relationship Builders, and Team Builders.

Professional Objective

Desire a management opportunity in **Sales & Marketing** that will provide a challenging avenue to significantly contribute to a company's efficiency, organization, growth, and profitability.

Professional Experience

President & Co-Owner - Sales & Marketing Director
JENSON INC., Jacksonville, Florida - 1995 to Present

- *Management:* As President and Co-Owner, responsible for directing the overall administration and operations of business, which processes recycled paper and sells to paper mills. Hold full decision-making responsibility for developing annual financial objectives and preparing long-range strategic business plans, which includes sales/marketing, client/owner relations, inventory and purchasing, finance/accounting, and cost estimating.
- *Personnel & Supervision:* Interview, hire, train and supervise staff members. Delegate responsibilities and monitor overall job performances to ensure accuracy and adherence to policies and procedures for more than 12 employees.
- *Sales - Account Management:* Responsible for direct sales of products to manufacturers and paper mills. Establish growth plans for individual accounts and personally manage account calls, presentations, and negotiations. Grew customer base from zero to 35 in the first year.
- *Marketing & Research:* Prepare feasibility studies; research and investigate markets to determine profitability ratios, and develop innovative marketing strategies to solicit and increase business by 25% within the first year, and expanded business from a regional to an international market.
- *Business Planning & Development:* Build business through networking and negotiating contracts, and increased profit margin by 10% the first year and by 15% the second year.
- *Budget Management:* Manage, analyze, and project budget for operating expenditures within company. Analyze budget variances and initiate appropriate guidelines to more aggressively control expenditures.

Vice President
HADINE, INC., Coral Springs, Florida - 1989 to 1995

- *Management:* Managed operations and administration of this retail bicycle business, which involved Sales, Customer Service, Advertising and Marketing and Human Resources. Business started with one location and expanded to 3 locations within the first 1½ years. Responsible for overall sales operations of 3 locations. Consistently achieved and surpassed sales goals by 20%, which increased profitability by 35% over a 6-year period.
- *Merchandising, Advertising & Marketing:* Created and implemented effective marketing and advertising campaigns which increased the company's customer base by 35% the first 2 years and by 65% the next 4 years through print advertising and direct mail.
- *Buyer:* Responsible for volume purchasing for 3 locations and decreased product cost by 25%.

Education

Master of Business Administration
FOREST COLLEGE, Lake Forest, Illinois, 1989

Bachelor of Science in Business Administration
Area of Concentration: Marketing
FOREST COLLEGE, Lake Forest, Illinois, 1987

Higher education might be a primary qualification for employment, so make sure it stands out on your resume.

Johnny Humphries
1818 West Hills Ave.
Jacksonville, Florida 45372
(555) 988-1234

Date

Tyler Dickson
South Town Recruiting Firm
2083 Palm Trees Avenue
Jacksonville, Florida 45372

> Explore all options to find a job, including recruiting firms.

Dear Mr. Dickson:

Is your recruiting firm looking for a highly motivated, goal-oriented **Sales & Marketing** professional? I am confident that I can significantly contribute to a company's team of professionals, and have enclosed a personal resume so you may review my qualifications and background.

In addition to a Bachelor of Science Degree in Business Administration, I also possess 10 years of progressive experience. My areas of expertise and qualifications include the following:

- Strong executive management background with proven techniques in all areas of sales, marketing, customer service, management, personnel, and finance.
- Financial and analytical expertise in budget development, forecasting and management.
- Ability to effectively restructure operations that yield company savings and profitability.
- Effective team-building skills with special talents in motivating, leading and empowering associates to achieve their maximum potential.
- Outstanding client relations skills with ability to network with community businesses, organizations, and agencies. Strong commitment to providing superior service in all business environments.
- Demonstrated leadership, communication and negotiation skills.
- Proven ability to define issues, propose solutions, and implement changes.

I sincerely believe that, with my experience and career goals, I would be an asset to an organization. I am open to discussing positions that are relevant to my background.

Thank you in advance for your time and consideration. I look forward to working with your recruiting firm.

Sincerely,

Johnny Humphries

Resume Enclosed

DUSTIN GEORGE
9090 White Drive
Oakland, California 90909
(415) 676-0983

> Closers, Relationship Builders, Creative Think Tanks, and Team Builders.

Professional Objective

Highly motivated, goal-oriented **Sales & Marketing** professional with over four years of experience in responsible Marketing, Sales and Customer Service positions. Desire a **Sales & Marketing** position that will provide a challenging avenue for career growth and professional advancement.

Education

Bachelor of Science Degree in Marketing
OAKLAND UNIVERSITY, Oakland, California, 1993

Professional Experience

Director of Production Sales
WYNDALL COMMUNICATIONS, INC.
Oakland, California - 1996 to Present

- Increase distribution of the company's unique music publications through retail and nontraditional distribution channels.
- Oversee the creation of the *Ancillary Products Division* and develop integrated marketing programs with retailers to optimize product sales and positively impact residual music sales.

Account Executive
TEN ENTERTAINMENT, INC.
San Diego, California - 1995 to 1996

- Developed sales of radio promotions and marketing services to companies involved in, or seeking involvement in the country and/or Christian music marketplace.
- Presented innovative marketing strategies to clients and potential clients to penetrate their target audience by utilizing national radio specials, localized remote broadcasts, contests and various other promotional and marketing opportunities.
- Brought in major corporate sponsorship partner for the first time in the history of an 11-year-old annual live broadcast event produced by Huntsman Entertainment, Inc., which was centered around the CMA Awards Show.

Marketing Assistant/Consultant
MOUNTAIN SOFTWARE, INC.
Portland, Oregon - 1992 to 1993 and 1994 to 1995

- Began as a Marketing Assistant at Mountain Software, Inc. from 1992 to 1993. In 1994 worked for Mountain as a Marketing Assistant and Consultant.
- Developed and implemented effective direct mail marketing campaigns, designed marketing materials, and established follow-up telemarketing contacts.

Remember, you have to know how to write your resume *better* than your competitors!

Professional Experience   **Continued**

- Provided qualified leads for sales department. Annual sales figures were the highest ever achieved in the company's history during my tenure. Updated, maintained, and enhanced the sales lead database.
- Determined print advertising placement, targeting trade journals and professional publications.
- Assisted with marketing efforts and represented company's products and services at industry trade shows.
- Analyzed financial statements and sales forecasts to recommend annual marketing budget.
- Assumed several additional duties previously the responsibility of the Vice President of Marketing.
- From 1992 to 1993, assisted the Sales Manager and Vice President of Marketing in targeting potential leads for the sales of accounting software.

Assistant Director of Marketing & Public Relations
GOSPEL MUSIC ACADEMY
Los Angeles, California - January 1994 to May 1994
- This was a post-college Internship, responsible for supporting and assisting the Director of Marketing & Public Relations.
- Assisted in coordinating and organizing the annual Gospel Music Week and Dove Awards Presentation.
- Handled customer information center operations.
- Managed cash handling and sales accounting.

Marketing Consultant
DANA CORPORATION - ALCOILS DIVISION
Portland, Oregon - Summer 1991
- Performed extensive research to develop new markets for company products.
- Organized and implemented a telemarketing and direct mail promotion.

Store Manager
FORSYTHE COMPUTERS
Portland, Oregon - Summer 1990
- Supported customer service and retail sales for authorized IBM reseller.

Intern
FORSYTHE COMPUTERS
Portland, Oregon - Summer 1989
- Handled retail sales and customer service. Assisted in computer network installations. Organized the product information filing systems for sales and technical support personnel.

RANDY CRAWFORD

1987 Total Street
Houston, Texas 77543
(887) 334-0098

Closers, Relationship Builders, and Team Builders.

Professional Objective & Profile

A dynamic, empowered and experienced **Area Sales Manager** is seeking a position that will fully utilize an in-depth, extensive background in sales. Desire a **Sales** position that will provide a challenging opportunity to significantly contribute to a company's efficiency, organization, growth, and profitability.

Education

Bachelor of Science in Business Administration
TEXAS UNIVERSITY, Houston, Texas
Graduated Cum Laude

Summary of Qualifications & Accomplishments

- *Track Record of Success:*
  Background exemplifies a successful track record of career accomplishments and includes more than 20 years of experience in sales.

- *Sales Accomplishments:*
  Recipient of numerous sales awards throughout career including, *Sales Award* for being the *No. 1 Salesman at McKesson Drug Company;* Recipient of the *National Sales Award* for obtaining the most new business at General Electric Company.

Experience in training seminars and sales meetings is a plus!

- *Advertising & Business Planning:*
  Skilled in setting goals and in planning and developing short- and long-term plans to achieve goals. Successfully develop innovative marketing and advertising strategies to promote sales and increase profitability.

- *Training Seminars & Meetings:*
  Experienced in developing and facilitating numerous sales seminars and meetings for the purpose of introducing new products, and for motivating employees.

- *Management, Training & Supervision:*
  Skilled and experienced in managing, training and supervising sales associates in all areas of sales and customer service.

- *Employee Relations:*
  Ability to create a teamlike work environment through strong leadership, guidance, encouragement and support of employees. This results in increased efficiency and productivity, which results in overall company profitability.

RANDY CRAWFORD

Energize your resume with strong descriptions about your work experience.

Area Manager
TEXAS WHOLESALE DRUG COMPANY
Houston, Texas - 1992 to Present

- *Sales Management:* Responsible for sales of pharmaceutical supplies to pharmacies, independent drug stores, and state hospitals throughout Texas. Solicit and obtain new accounts, as well as manage and maintain existing clients.
- *Client Relations:* Develop and maintain an exemplary network of business associates as a result of in-depth interaction and superior service. Liaison between company and State Hospitals, Pharmacies, and independent retail drug stores.
- *Profitability:* Successfully obtained 20 new accounts for Texas Wholesale Drug Company, and increased overall profitability for company.
- *Troubleshooter:* Adept at researching and identifying problems within clients' accounts, and very creative in implementing problem-solving solutions.

Manager of Operations & Contract Sales
PARTNER MANAGEMENT SERVICES
Houston, Texas - 1984 to 1992

- *Management:* Managed overall operations for Partner Management Services, which provided mobile CT scanners to hospitals.
- *Clientele & Contract Negotiations:* Called upon hospital administrators and radiologists to solicit and obtain clientele. Negotiated contracts after analyzing and approving credit for new accounts.
- *Employee Relations - Personnel & Supervision:* Interviewed, hired, trained, supervised and evaluated 15 employees. Developed and implemented an annual written Employee Appraisal System that enhanced employee morale and resulted in increased efficiency and productivity.
- *Site Preparation:* Coordinated and prepared locations for new service in hospitals.
- *Profitability & Collections:* Increased profitability for company as a result of an excellent track record for collecting outstanding balances on difficult accounts.

General Manager
TEXAS WHOLESALE DRUG COMPANY, Houston, Texas - 1983 to 1984

- *Management:* Responsible for overall operations of this company which shipped 75,000,000 drug orders annually.
- *Employee Relations:* Identified and resolved employee relations problems, and encouraged and supported a teamlike work environment, which resulted in improved job performance and efficiency.
- *Personnel, Training & Supervision:* Recruited, interviewed, hired, trained and supervised 35 employees.
- *Inventory & Shipping:* Responsible for monitoring and tracking inventory, and for all shipping.

District Manager
GENERAL ELECTRIC COMPANY, Houston, Texas - 1969 to 1983

- *Company Track Record of Success:* Began with this company in 1969 as a Territory Manager, and was consistently promoted throughout tenure. In 1974, was promoted to District Manager, and was responsible for sales and marketing in Texas.
- *Sales:* Solicited and obtained new clients by calling on hardware distributors, food distributors, and merchandisers. Sold home electrical supplies. Received *National Sales Award* for new business.
- *Sales Training:* Trained Distributors in all areas of products, sales and customer service.
- *Event Planning:* Responsible for planning and developing special company events.

Sales Representative
MCKESSON DRUG COMPANY, Houston, Texas - 1958 to 1969

- *Sales:* Responsible for selling pharmaceutical supplies and health and beauty aids to retail drug stores and hospitals. Received Sales Award for being *No. #1 Sales Representative* in Company.

Beth Shelley
2323 Penn Drive
Little Rock, Arkansas 33882
(818) 889-2222

> Closers, Relationship Builders, and Team Builders.

Professional Objective

To obtain a self-motivating **Sales** position that involves extensive relationship-building and team-building.

Education

Bachelor of Arts
Major: English
Minor: Economics
JAMES MADISON UNIVERSITY
Harrisonburg, Virginia, 1995

Relevant Coursework

> If you don't have an extensive background, it's helpful to list relevant coursework that might be an asset in a sales career.

Communication	*Technical Writing*
Marketing	*Public Speaking*
Management	*Problem Resolution*

Qualifying Work Experience

8/96 to Present **W. WATER COMMUNITIES**
Little Rock, Arkansas
Sales Assistant
- Organized presentations for the sale of vacation condominiums.
- Coordinated the sale of condominiums.
- Scheduled appointments with personal referrals.
- Presented condominiums to prospective buyers.
- Maintained favorable relations with clientele.

9/95 to 8/96 **GREAT RESORTS**
Springfield, Virginia
Sales Assistant
- Organized presentation for the sale of vacation condominiums.
- Presented several condominiums to prospective buyers.
- Assisted in the training of new employees.

Summer 1995 **FRANKLIN BUILDER**
Springfield, Virginia
Secretary
- Organized and filed accounts.
- Answered phones and scheduled appointments.
- Met clients for viewing of homes.

References

Available upon request.

Closers, Creative Think Tanks, Relationship Builders, and Team Builders.

EDDIE THOMPSON
8899 North Valley Drive
Columbus, Ohio 66335
(444) 333-9988

Professional Objective & Profile

High-caliber **Sales & Marketing** professional with 7 years of experience building and leading integrated sales operations for major corporations. Consistently successful in building territory volume to increase sales and profitability. Strong general management qualifications in strategic business planning, and in creating innovative promotional campaigns.

Desire a **Sales** position that will provide a challenging opportunity to significantly contribute to a company's efficiency, organization, growth, and profitability.

Education

Bachelor of Science in Business Administration
UNIVERSITY OF OHIO, Columbus, Ohio, 1989

Summary of Qualifications

Track Record of Sales & Management Success:
Background exemplifies a successful track record of career accomplishments and encompasses positions as Sales Representative for Nabisco Biscuit, Inc., and Co-Manager of Piggly Wiggly Supermarket.

Management & Marketing:
Skilled in managing overall sales operations, and in conducting ongoing analyses to evaluate the efficiency, quality, and productivity of sales. Ability to conceptualize, design and implement innovative marketing strategies by partnering with accounts in order to co-advertise and co-market, to increase sales and overall profitability.

International Marketing & Management:
Participated in a study tour of Europe, which focused on studying international marketing and management. Gained valuable experience in studying European economics and in interacting with foreign cultures.

Territory Development:
Skilled in building and expanding territory that results in an increase in sales and profitability. Grew sales volume from $1.8 million to $2.8 million annually for Nabisco Biscuit, Inc.

Professional Sales Awards, Honors & Accomplishments:
- *Selected as 1 of 4 Sales Representatives out of 1200 nationwide selected to attend a Nabisco Management Meeting in Chicago to provide feedback concerning reorganization in the company regarding new positions and sales levels.*
- *Selected as Team Captain of "Go For Gold" Contest 3rd Quarter, 1996.*
- *Currently in Lead for Sales Representative of the Year, 1996.*
- *Sales Representative of the Year for Columbus Branch, 1995, Nabisco Biscuit.*
- *#1 & #2 Highest Selling Kroger Store (of Nabisco Products) in the Nation.*
- *Achieved Largest Sales Volume & Percentage of Sales Increase.*
- *Increased annual sales from $1.8 million to $2.8 million.*
- *Increased average sale from $67,000 to $217,000 per account.*
- *Recognized for Superior Merchandising by Progressive Grocer, Piggly Wiggly.*

An impressive list of accomplishments like this is sure to get an employer's attention!

Professional Sales Experience

Sales & Marketing Representative
Super District
NABISCO BISCUIT, INC.
Columbus, Ohio - 1992 to Present

Began as a Sales Representative with Nabisco in 1992 in Chattanooga, and was promoted and transferred to a Super District in Columbus in 1993. A brief synopsis of responsibilities and accomplishments is highlighted below.

- *Marketing & Analysis Team:* One of 4 Sales Representatives out of 1200 nationwide selected to participate in a management meeting in Chicago for the purpose of analyzing and providing feedback regarding company reorganization which includes new positions and sales levels within the company.
- *Sales:* Responsible for selling and servicing Nabisco products to 13 retail accounts in West Columbus. Territory includes 3 Kroger Supermarkets which maintains 61% Nabisco Cookie/Cracker market share, as compared to 51% national average, top 3 H.G. Hill Supermarkets, and #1 Sam's Wholesale Club.
- *Profitability:* Grew business from *$1.8 million to $2.8 million in sales.* Increased average sale of $67,000 per account to $217,000 per account. Ranked as the #1 & #2 highest selling Kroger stores in the nation for Nabisco products due to strategic business planning and marketing at local level. Increased sales by 58% at Sam's Wholesale Club, which moved from #3 to the No. #1 Unit in Columbus for Nabisco.
- *Special Project Development - Promotions & Marketing:* Aggressive partnering with individual accounts to create, develop and implement partnership strategies and campaigns to promote both the store and Nabisco products. Responsible for selling the partnering concept to Nabisco management, and for negotiating marketing strategies between Nabisco and accounts. Utilize visual aids for negotiations to illustrate campaigns and to show the benefits and increase in sales resulting from promotions.
- *Management:* Manage 3 full-time Merchandisers. Responsible for supervising and training, in addition to evaluating overall job performances to ensure adherence to company standards and personal expectations.
- *Customer Service - Client Relations:* Provide superior service to customers by responding to requests, inquiries, suggestions, and/or concerns. Continuously establish and maintain an excellent network of business relationships as a result of extensive interaction and communication.

Co-Manager
PIGGLY WIGGLY SUPERMARKET
Chattanooga, Tennessee - 1989 to 1992

- *Management:* Responsible for co-managing a $5 million supermarket operation.
- *Personnel, Training & Supervision:* Interviewed, hired, trained and supervised 48 staff members. Responsible for scheduling employees and delegating work responsibilities.
- *Program Development:* Developed and spearheaded Customer Service and Quality Programs, and implemented these into everyday store operations.
- *Cost & Labor Control:* Increased profit margin by 2% as a result of efficiently controlling costs and increasing sales by 18%.

Relationship Builders and
Team Builders.

Vickie Holden

8756 Robin Bird Lane, Boston, Massachusetts 02134 (787) 213-0213

PROFESSIONAL OBJECTIVE & PROFILE

A self-motivated and self-directed **Sales** professional is seeking a position that will fully utilize experience in print advertising, sales, client services, supervision, and market analysis. Desire a sales position that will provide a challenging opportunity to significantly contribute to a company's efficiency, organization, growth, and profitability.

SUMMARY OF QUALIFICATIONS

- *Track Record of Success:*
  Background exemplifies a successful track record of career accomplishments including 7 years of experience in Sales, Management, and Supervision.
- *Sales & Marketing:*
  More than 3 years of experience in sales and sales support for magazine print advertising and real estate which includes: *Thomas Nelson Publishers Magazine Division, Eagle Communications, Publisher of Business Boston* and *Boston Life Magazines,* and for *Century 21 Hayworth Homes.*
- *Communications & Leadership:*
  Strong interpersonal skills with ability to effectively communicate with diverse individuals and all types of businesses and organizations. Excellent leader with proven ability to research and define issues, propose creative solutions and implement effective changes.

EDUCATION

Associate Degree in Liberal Arts
SADDLEBROOK COLLEGE, Mission Viejo, California

PROFESSIONAL EXPERIENCE

Sales Representative & Sales Assistant
BIN RAMON PUBLISHERS, Boston, Massachusetts - February 1996 to July 1996
- *Sales & Sales Support:* Responsible for selling magazine print advertising for 4 magazines. Provided support to Account Executives by conducting research and assisting in calling on clients. Established and maintained an excellent network of business relationships as a result of effective communication skills.
- *Project Management:* Assigned to sell all print advertising for the *Boston Symphony 50th Anniversary Commemorative Magazine,* which consisted of 6 full-page ads. Solicited and obtained clients by personally managing account calls, presentations and negotiations.
- *Marketing Research:* Conducted demographic and marketing research to target potential clients.

Sales Assistant & Office Manager
EAGLE COMMUNICATIONS, *Boston Life Magazines,* Boston, Massachusetts - 1 Year
- *Sales Support:* Provided support to Account Executives and assisted in soliciting and obtaining new clients.
- *Office Administration:* Managed all facets of office administration and operations, which included preparing Accounts Receivable and bookkeeping.

Real Estate Sales Agent
CENTURY 21, Boston, Massachusetts - 1 Year
- *Sales:* Sold commercial and residential real estate to individuals and businesses. Managed sales calls, presentations and negotiations.

STEVE TIRRELL
1808 Hobbs Road
West Hills, New Jersey 00227
(201) 887-9988

Closers, Relationship Builders, and Team Builders.

OBJECTIVE	Seeking a position which will utilize my experience in sales and information management systems and my proven skill in organization.

EDUCATION	**New Jersey University,** New Jersey *Business Administration* **Aquinas Junior College,** New Jersey *Business Administration*

Even if you don't have a degree, list any higher education and college experience.

SPECIALTY **TRAINING**	• Sales Training through Corporate Office of TAB Products Corporation • Dale Carnegie Course

HIGHLIGHTS OF PROFESSIONAL EXPERIENCE

March 1990 - **Present**	**BEST OFFICE SYSTEMS, Family-Owned Business,** West Hills, New Jersey *Sales/Service Representative* Responsible for territory encompassing Nashville areas for company offering records management/filing systems, office systems, and office furniture/space planning services. Develop accounts and meet with company management to evaluate, suggest, and develop systems to improve the efficiency of their operations. *Clientele:* Large and medium manufacturing companies, large insurance corporations and insurance agencies, hospitals and medical offices (physicians and dentists), and federal government offices and facilities.
June 1976 - **December 1990**	**TAB CORPORATION,** Nashville, Tennessee *Sales Representative* Responsibilities were basically the same as those listed above and included the following areas. *Clientele:* Clients included the same as those above in addition to independent Aerospace/Defense department supporting companies, colleges, and universities. • Developed records management/filing systems to improve the organization of information in these companies/accounts. • Developed magnetic media storage systems. • Designed work stations and made recommendations to improve the working environment and better organize the operations of Data Processing/Word Processing Departments. • Designed total open office furniture plans using new ideas and techniques to better utilize office space. • Average sales volume was $350,000 - 450,000 annually.

Don't list personal data on your resume, except for availability to travel or relocate.

PERSONAL DATA	• Single and willing to travel and/or relocate.

STEVE TIRRELL
1808 Hobbs Road
West Hills, New Jersey 00227
(201) 887-9988

Date

Charles Stengel
Director of Sales & Marketing
Dreamscape Corporation
82 Downey Place
Springtown, New Jersey 00228

Dear Mr. Stengel:

If your organization has need of the services of a capable and proven successful **sales performer,** then I am that person who can complement and complete your team. Attached is my resume for your review and consideration.

As you will note, I have been associated with the same company for the past eight years. At this time, and due to reasons I will discuss with you personally, I have decided to seek a new association which offers new challenges and opportunities to progress in my career. The ideal situation will require flexibility and versatility and will encourage the utilization of my strengths and skills.

My background reflects certain personal qualities which I feel will be of value in my future with your company. I am a self-motivated and energetic person who is success- and accomplishment-oriented, and who is able to interact with people of all ages and from diverse backgrounds, developing mutual respect; I am able to work independently and to make appropriate and timely decisions; I am a team player, as well as a leader who is able to develop loyalty and commitment to others; and I am skilled in problem identification and resolution and capable of developing innovative directions for fulfilling the demands of various situations. I feel confident you will find I have much to contribute to your long-range goals and objectives.

My true potential cannot be fully appreciated without the benefit of a personal interview; therefore, I would like to meet with you in order to discuss how my assets may be best utilized to our mutual advantage.

Sincerely,

Steve Tirrell

References Available at Interview

Use high-powered, charged words to grab attention on your resume, as we have in the descriptions here.	**DILLON G. McCRAVE** **8811 West 50th** **New York, New York 10001** **(212) 999-3333**	Closers, Relationship Builders, Creative Think Tanks, and Team Builders.

Executive Career Profile

High-caliber *Executive,* with over 15 years of experience building and leading integrated sales and marketing operations for major labels in the Music Industry. Positions have encompassed *Senior Vice President, Sales & Marketing, reporting to CEO,* and *Vice President, Sales & Marketing, reporting to CEO.* Consistently successful in developing and spearheading innovative sales and marketing programs that launch and grow the careers of artists and increase overall company profitability. In-depth background in all aspects of sales, marketing, artist/manager relations, distribution and product development.

Self-directed, focused, and self-motivated. Strong general management qualifications in strategic business planning, organizational reengineering and process/productivity/quality improvement. Excellent leader and mentor who empowers employees to achieve their maximum potential. Skilled Public Speaker and Executive Liaison with domestic and international companies.

Seeking a career opportunity that will provide a challenging avenue to significantly contribute to a company's efficiency, organization, growth, and profitability.

Executive Experience

Senior Vice President, Marketing & Sales (Reporting to CEO)
SONG COMMUNICATIONS
New York, New York - 1992 to Present

Promoted to *Senior Vice President, Marketing & Sales* in 1995 from position of *Vice President, Marketing & Sales.* Past and current accomplishments with company are highlighted below.

Management - Marketing & Sales: Direct and guide overall marketing and sales operations for an *Executive* staff of 1 *Vice President* and 4 *Executive Directors.* Responsible for 20 staff members and 15 Artists. As Vice President, responsible for 6 *Directors/Managers* and 40 marketing and sales staff members. Create and implement administrative policies and procedures into daily working operations.

International & Domestic Sales: Conceptualize, create, develop and implement innovative marketing and sales strategies for more than 100 releases annually, which achieve sales objectives in Domestic, International and Mainstream markets. In charge of all sales, marketing, and distribution of 4 major Labels on an international scale.

Executive Liaison - Public Relations: Excellent Public Speaker and Company Liaison between Virgin Records America and Virgin International. Liaison between Distribution and all retail channels. Oversee, organize and coordinate Trade Marketing, Sales Conferences & Seminars, and Trade Conventions.

Company Profitability: After restructuring and reengineering international and domestic marketing operations, tripled general market sales in the first year of the new distribution arrangement, as Senior Vice President. Increased sales from *$12 million to $32 million (166% increase)* between 1992 & 1994.

Business Management & Client Relations: Established and maintained an exemplary network of business relationships with special market accounts, such as *McCellan, Publishers Work* and *Starsound,* which resulted in more than 500,000 units sold in the first 6 months as a result of partnering with these major companies. Expanded and grew national accounts by several hundred percent as a result of superior management and client relations.

Continued

Program Development: Conceptualized, developed and spearheaded a strategic partnership with *American Airlines Advantage Incentives* to become the first music label to offer frequent flyer travel awards with music promotions and purchasing.

Artist Development: Developed and implemented the industry's most successful *New Artist Development Program,* which launched the careers of major new artists, and succeeded in achieving more than 100,000 initial units per title. Developed retail sales for *RK Wynn* from *350,000 units to 1 million, Cary Johnson* from *150,000 to 400,000* in sales, *Newsboys* from *25,000 to 400,000* in sales and several new artists over 6 figures on their debuts.

Media Promotions: Increased exposure of artists and revenue through TV, Print and Radio for *Cary Johnson and the Parable Group* by developing the first national *SpokesArtist* arrangement, which resulted in the largest consortium of independent specialty retailers (320 outlets in the U.S. & Canada). Placed *Cary Johnson (Star Song)* on *Raymond's Global Mission Program,* which was seen by over 1 billion viewers in over 40 countries and resulted in XXEA's filming of a music video, which Star Song used for artist and company promotions.

Promotions & Sales Profitability: Created and incorporated a Direct Sales approach as an independent record company, which launched *DC Talk* to Gold/Platinum status and increased general market sales for Star Song and Forefront Artists by more than 100%. Successfully developed apparel division to achieve over $6 million in annual CCA sales between 1992 and 1994.

Budget Management & Analysis: Analyzed and prepared Marketing & Sales budgets, and have held full decision-making responsibility for developing annual financial objectives, preparing long-range strategic business plans, and preparing future years' budgets based on previous expenditures and changes in organizational operations.

Vice President, Marketing & Sales (Reporting to President/CEO)
JOINT RECORDS, INC., New York, New York - 1991 to 1992

Marketing & Sales: Managed and directed overall Marketing & Sales operations for more than 10 artists. Responsible for all trade, mainstream, international, and ancillary market sales for the Label. Developed a strategic, comprehensive, CCA/Mainstream marketing plan which drove sales to near Platinum levels.

Budget Management: In charge of managing budget and operating within budget guidelines.

Pop Artist Development: Built sales from zero to $7 million through liaison with the new Geffen/Uni Distribution System during the first year. Liaison between Geffen Records Marketing & Sales Division and Reunion.

Vice President, Sales
WINSLOW CORPORATION, New York, New York and California - 1980 to 1991

Company Track Record of Success: Began as a *Regional Sales Representative,* and was promoted to *Regional Sales Manager* in 1983. In 1985, promoted to *National Sales Director,* and then in 1987 to position of *Vice President, Sales.*

Management: Managed all domestic sales, including in-house product and 6 outside labels for over 30 artists. In charge of day-to-day distribution to over 5000 retail outlets. Managed all sales, trade marketing, conventions, administration, and budgeting. Supervised 7 Managers and 38 staff members.

Education

SPEEDS COMMUNITY COLLEGE, Garden City, New York
Area of Concentration: Business Administration

DILLON G. McCRAVE
8811 West 50th
New York, New York 10001
(212) 999-3333

Date

Addressee
Company
Street Address
City, State, Zip

Are you looking for a highly motivated, goal-oriented **Marketing & Sales Executive** to effectively manage direct marketing and sales operations in your organization? I believe that I can significantly contribute to your company's efficiency, organization, growth, and overall profitability. For your review, I have enclosed a personal resume which will provide you with pertinent details concerning my background and qualifications.

As you will note in my resume, I am not a beginner, but rather a well-seasoned professional with more than 15 years of experience in Executive Management, Administration, Sales, Marketing, and Product Development in the music industry. My success is due to my ability to prioritize multiple responsibilities and to effectively create and design innovative marketing and sales strategies that yield company growth and profitability. For example, while at Song Communications, as *Senior Vice President,* I was a key component in increasing sales from *$12 million to $32 million (166% increase)* between 1992 and 1994. My products have won 12 Gold and 11 Platinum Industry Sales Awards. I have been successful throughout my career due to my comprehensive knowledge of the recording and video industry, as well as my commitment to excellence and success. In addition, I have excellent employee relations skills due to my ability to effectively guide associates to achieve their maximum potential. I sincerely believe that, with my experience and career goals, I would be an asset to your organization.

I would like to request a personal interview at your earliest convenience so we can discuss ways that I can significantly contribute to your team of professionals. Please feel free to contact me at my home telephone number or address if you have any additional questions.

Thank you in advance for your time and consideration. I look forward to speaking with you soon.

Sincerely,

Dillon G. McCrave

Personal Portfolio Enclosed

Closers, Relationship Builders, and Team Builders.

KENNETH BLUMFIELD
6655 Maple Street
Palo Alto, California 77665
(777) 333-3456

EXECUTIVE PROFILE

High-caliber Entrepreneur, **Sales Executive & Manager,** with more than 20 years of experience building and leading integrated business operations. Consistently successful in directing start-up operations and in positioning finance as a critical business partner, supportive of and responsive to the needs of large and diverse operating units. Talented in leading and developing business opportunities and marketing strategies/plans to maximize growth and profitability, and accomplish mission of integrated operations.

Strong general management qualifications in strategic planning, sales, marketing, and all facets of process/productivity/quality improvement. Excellent background in recruitment, development, and leadership. Very skilled in developing annual financial objectives and preparing long-range strategic business plans. Excellent analytical, planning, financial, organizational, and negotiation skills. Skilled executive liaison.

SUMMARY OF ADVANCED TRAINING & EDUCATION

EDUCATION

Master of Science in Accounting (Pursuant)
(Completed half of Master's Program)
UNIVERSITY OF SOUTHERN MISSISSIPPI
Hattiesburg, Mississippi

Listing higher education and advanced training illustrates an industrious person who is always learning and moving forward.

Bachelor of Science in Business Administration
UNIVERSITY OF SOUTHERN MISSISSIPPI
Hattiesburg, Mississippi, 1975

Graduate
DEAN WITTER REYNOLDS, INC.
NATIONAL SALES TRAINING SCHOOL

Graduate
UNITED STATES ARMY ROTARY WING AVIATION SCHOOL
Hunter Air Field, Savannah, Georgia, 1969

LICENSURE

Securities 7, 65, 63, 24, Series 3 Commodities License

Airline Transport Pilot
Airplane Multi-Engine Land, SA 227
Commercial Privileges, Airplane Single Engine Land
Rotorcraft-Helicopter, Instrument Helicopter

MILITARY

UNITED STATES ARMY - Active Duty, 1968 to 1971
Served as Helicopter Pilot in Vietnam.

UNITED STATES ARMY NATIONAL GUARD
INDIVIDUAL READY RESERVE (Currently in inactive Reserves).

Hard-hitting language conveys that you're a dynamic performer. Notice how we used power descriptions to explain job functions in each category.

PROFESSIONAL EXPERIENCE

Branch Manager & Principal
BRIGHT INVESTMENT GROUP, INC.
Chicago, Illinois and Palo Alto, California - 1996 to Present

- **Management:** Manage overall operations and administration of daily trading operations for 2 offices located in Palo Alto, California and Chicago. Conduct ongoing analyses to evaluate the efficiency, quality and productivity of operations. Direct all business planning and development, financial performance analysis, and marketing functions.
- **Business Development:** Responsible for managing new business development and strategic planning to maximize growth and profitability. Establish growth plans for individual accounts and personally manage account calls, presentations and negotiations.
- **Personnel & Recruiting:** Recruit, interview and hire staff members for offices. Delegate responsibilities and monitor overall job performances to ensure accuracy and adherence to policies and procedures.
- **Budget & Finance Management:** Manage, analyze and administer budget for operating expenditures. Responsible for financial performance analysis and development functions.

Stock Broker
DEAN REYNOLDS, INC., Jackson, Mississippi - 1994 to 1996

- **Trading:** Responsible for trading all types of stocks and investment plans including bonds, securities, equities, mutual funds, IRAs, FDIC-insured CDs, and tax-deferred annuities.
- **Business Networking:** Established and maintained an exemplary network of business associates as a result of extensive interaction and strong communication skills.

President
WEST STREET ESPRESSO, INC.
Memphis, Tennessee; Jackson, Mississippi; and Williamsburg, Virginia - 1991 to 1994

- **Owner & Management:** Managed and directed overall operations and administration of 5 stores in areas listed above. Full responsibility for establishing company's policies and procedures, and for all core prospect marketing, entire project design and development. Administered all financial affairs (budget development, capital equipment acquisition, financial analysis/reporting and contract negotiations).
- **Marketing & Advertising:** Conceptualized, developed and implemented corporate strategic marketing and advertising plans that increased revenue and overall profitability for company.
- **Budget Management:** Analyzed and managed budget for operating expenditures. Analyzed budget variances and initiated appropriate guidelines to more aggressively control expenditures. Established budget guidelines and operated within budgets.

Sales Manager
DIRECT MAIL SERVICES, Jackson, Mississippi - 1984 to 1991

- **Sales Management:** Began as a Consultant with this company and then became part-owner and Sales Manager. Managed entire sales cycle from initial client identification and account development through presentations, contract and price negotiations, and final sales closings. Brought an established group of clients to company as a result of being a Consultant/Broker for direct mail services prior to this.

Marketing Director & Controller
NATIONAL REAL ESTATE COMPANY, Raleigh, North Carolina - 1976 to 1981

- **Sales & Marketing:** Managed entire sales cycle from research and client identification, core prospect marketing, account development, presentations, and contract negotiations.

Relationship Builders, Creative Think Tanks, and Team Builders.

Lauren Alexandra Price
776 Ruby Road
Thomasville, Rhode Island 88772
(456) 338-0098

Professional Objective & Profile

High-caliber **Telemarketing Manager** with over 11 years of experience building and leading integrated operations for a major Telephone Call Center and all direct sales locations for Gaylord Entertainment. Consistently successful in positioning Customer Service as a critical business partner, supportive of and responsive to the needs of a large clientele base.

Strong general management qualifications in strategic planning, organizational reengineering, and process/productivity/quality improvement. Excellent experience in personnel training, development and leadership. Skilled public speaker and executive liaison with companywide committees and departments.

Seeking a career opportunity that will provide a challenging avenue to significantly contribute to a company's efficiency, organization, growth, and profitability.

Education   *Bachelor of Science in Business Administration*
RHODE ISLAND UNIVERSITY, Springfield, Rhode Island

Summary of Qualifications

Track Record of Success:
Background exemplifies a successful track record of career accomplishments and includes 11 years of progressive experience at Gaylord Entertainment. Consistently advanced throughout career to positions of higher levels of responsibility and authority.

Customer Service:
In-depth background in managing Guest/Customer Services. Proven methods in providing superior service to customers by utilizing creative problem-solving techniques to resolve any issues of concern.

Management - Sales & Marketing:
Conduct ongoing analyses to evaluate the efficiency, quality and productivity of sales operations within the Telephone Call Center and direct sales locations for Gaylord Entertainment. On an ongoing basis, implement a series of aggressive customer service/sales programs to increase overall revenue and profitability.

Leadership:
Strong motivator and leader of others with ability to inspire employees to achieve their maximum potential.

Employee Relations:
Support and encourage a synergistic environment among all departments at Gaylord Entertainment. This creates a teamlike work environment, which increases employee efficiency and productivity. Empower employees to work independently or as team members.

Public Speaking - Seminars:
Facilitate numerous seminars on various topics that focus on *Human Services, Customer Service,* and *Changes within the Workplace.* Serve as Spokesperson for the *Reservations & Ticketing Division.*

Professional Experience

Senior Manager of Consumer Sales
WALT DISNEY ENTERTAINMENT
Reservations & Ticketing
Springfield, Delaware - 11 Years - 1985 to Present

- *Company Track Record of Success:* Began as a *Customer Service Representative* in 1985, and consistently advanced throughout career to positions of higher levels of responsibility and authority. Promoted to *Senior Manager* in 1993. A brief synopsis of positions and responsibilities is highlighted below.
- *Management:* Hold full decision-making responsibilities for the overall operations and administration of the Reservations & Ticketing Division.
- *Administration:* Develop and implement company policies and procedures into everyday operations in order to ensure customer satisfaction.
- *Sales:* Direct and supervise all telephone sales of the Telephone Center, and all direct sales locations.
- *Personnel & Supervision:* Interview, hire, train and supervise 350 staff members. Delegate work responsibilities and monitor overall job performances to ensure accuracy and adherence to company policies and procedures.
- *Guest/Customer Services:* Committed to providing superior service to customers by responding to their requests, inquiries, suggestions, and/or concerns. Utilize creative problem-solving techniques to resolve issues and ensure guest/customer satisfaction, which results in return business and referrals.
- *Guest/Customer Relations:* Continuously establish and maintain an exemplary network of guest/customer relations by providing superior service.
- *Marketing & Advertising:* Create, develop and implement innovative marketing and advertising strategies to increase sales and profitability.
- *Employee Relations - Seminars:* Facilitate various seminars that focus on increasing Human Services and handling change within the workplace. Empower employees to work independently or in a team environment, and encourage and support synergism with all other departments.
- *Spokesperson:* Represent the Division on numerous companywide committees and serve as a Spokesperson regarding issues in Reservations & Ticketing.
- *Budget Management:* Analyze budget variances and initiate appropriate recommendations to more aggressively control annual expenditures. Design budget forecasting and analysis plans, and prepare future years' budgets based on previous expenditures and changes in organizational operations.

Park Operations Supervisor, 1991 to 1993
- *Supervision:* Directed and supervised overall operations for Walt Disney Theme Park.
- *Personnel:* Interviewed, hired, trained, scheduled, and supervised employees.
- *Budget Management:* Designed and prepared budgets based on previous operating expenditures and changes in operations.

Assistant Customer Service Manager, 1990 to 1991
- *Management:* Assisted in the management of Customer Service. This included preparing budgets, scheduling employees, and communication between all departments.
- *Computer Operations:* Utilized CTR System to input daily information regarding sales.

Senior Reservationist Coordinator, 1987 to 1990
- *Leader:* Guided and motivated Sales Representatives in the Telephone Center. Scheduled and delegated work responsibilities for up to 50 employees.

Lauren Alexandra Price
776 Ruby Road
Thomasville, Rhode Island 88772
(456) 338-0098

Date

Jim Robertson
Executive Sales Manager
Trifold Communications & Entertainment
2983 Moppet Street
Thomasville, Rhode Island 88772

Dear Mr. Robertson:

Are you looking for a highly motivated, goal-oriented **Telemarketing Manager** to become a leader in your organization? I believe that I can significantly contribute to your company's efficiency, organization, growth, and profitability. For your review, I have enclosed a personal resume which will provide you with details concerning my background and qualifications.

As you will note, I am not a beginner, but rather a well-seasoned professional with 11 years of experience building and leading integrated operations for a major Telephone Call Center and all direct sales locations for Walt Disney Entertainment. My success is due to my ability to build and lead sales and customer service departments, and to design and implement innovative marketing strategies that yield company growth and profitability. In addition, I am an effective Manager and Supervisor, with the ability to guide and motivate employees to achieve their maximum potential. With my experience and career goals, I am confident that I would be an asset to your organization.

I would like to request a personal interview at your earliest convenience so we can discuss ways that I can significantly contribute to your team of professionals. Please feel free to contact me at my home telephone number or address if you have any additional questions.

Thank you in advance for your time and consideration. I look forward to speaking with you soon.

Sincerely,

Lauren Alexandra Price

Resume Enclosed

Emma Dalmaty
3664 Kingston Lane
Nashville, Tennessee 37997
(615) 786-0091

Relationship Builders and
Team Builders

Professional Experience

Supervisor of Telemarketing Department
GAYLORD ENTERTAINMENT
Nashville, Tennessee - 1/96 to Present

- Supervise 5 telemarketing representatives. Delegate work responsibilities and monitor overall job performances to ensure adherence to company standards, policies, and procedures.
- Interview, hire, and train telemarketing representatives in all areas of sales and customer service.

Sales Assistant
JC BRADFORD COMPANY
Memphis, Tennessee - 8/93 to 12/95

- Developed and maintained customer relationships.
- Assisted multiple sales professionals in facilitation order entry for securities transactions.
- Observed and reacted to stock market trends.
- Organized and updated all internal documentation and company reports.
- Analyzed client accounts.
- Utilized Brokers Notebook computer software.
- Posted trades of securities.
- Served as liaison between client and broker.

Internship
MARRIOTT HOTEL
San Francisco, California - 6/92 to 8/92

- Made outside calls to various businesses.
- Developed business within the Bay area, contacting an average of 350 prospects per week.
- Researched various company travel from Europe to Japan.
- Planned catering events for hotel.

Education
MIDDLE TENNESSEE STATE UNIVERSITY, Murfreesboro, Tennessee
Area of Concentration: Prerequisites for Masters in Speech Pathology

UNIVERSITY OF MISSISSIPPI, Oxford, Mississippi, 1993
Bachelor of Science in Hospitality Management

Honors
The Statler Foundation Academic Scholarship Recipient
Chancellor's Honor Roll
Pike County, Mississippi "Miss Hospitality"
Tennis Matchmate for the Ole Miss Men's Tennis Team

Affiliations
Communication Disorder Club
Member of NSSLHA
Vanderbilt Volunteer Department of Speech Pathology
Student Programming Board
Student Alumni Council
Humane Society Volunteer

Closers, Relationship
Builders, and Team Builders.

Sunny Adams
2424 Franklin Pike
Nashville, Tennessee 37090
(615) 787-0000

PROFESSIONAL OBJECTIVE

High-caliber **Territory Manager** with over 18 years of experience building and leading integrated sales operations for major companies. Consistently successful in reengineering sales operations and increasing sales profitability. Self-directed and self-motivated with excellent experience in client relations, business development and leadership.

Seeking a position that will fully utilize an extensive background in Territory Management and Sales, and that will provide a challenging opportunity to significantly contribute to a company's efficiency, organization, growth, and profitability.

SUMMARY OF QUALIFICATIONS

TRACK RECORD OF SUCCESS:
Dynamic, results-oriented sales professional with a successful track record of career accomplishments. Consistently advanced to positions of higher levels of authority and responsibility.

HONORS & ACCOMPLISHMENTS:
- **One out of 12 Sales Representatives** in the nation recognized in the *Institutional Distributor Magazine* as the *Salesperson of the Month.*
- **First Salesperson** ever to achieve *$3 million in sales annually,* and the next year, *$4 million in sales* annually for Baird Foods Company.
- **Increased** a $15,000 weekly sales territory to $90,000 after taking over management.
- Launched aggressive marketing campaigns and tripled sales in one territory and doubled sales in another while working for Johnson's Dairy Distributor.

SALES & MARKETING:
Talented in creating, developing, and implementing innovative sales and marketing strategies to promote sales. Very skilled in reorganizing undeveloped sales territories and in expanding sales.

BUSINESS NETWORKING:
Extensive distribution network experience. Established and maintained a solid network of business relationships with clients as a result of strong communication skills.

TROUBLESHOOTER:
Adept at researching and identifying problems within sales programs or within customer service, and very creative in resolving problems.

COMMUNICATIONS:
Excellent interpersonal and communication skills. Effectively build client relations through comprehensive presentations. Ability to communicate with all levels of personnel and management.

EDUCATION

VIRGINIA TECHNICAL INSTITUTE, Richmond, Virginia
Advanced Training & Seminars in Sales & Management

PROFESSIONAL EXPERIENCE

Territory Manager
BAIRD FOODS COMPANY
Nashville, Tennessee - 1986 to Present

- **Sales & Business Management:** Responsible for directing and managing overall sales of food products to independently owned restaurants throughout south central Tennessee. Solicit and obtain new clients as well as maintain existing accounts. Conduct ongoing analyses to evaluate the efficiency, quality and productivity of sales and business operations.
- **Profitability:** Territory was achieving only *$15,000 weekly* in sales, and after taking over management of this territory, reengineering and streamlining operations, have increased sales to *$90,000 weekly*, which has significantly increased profitability for company. *First Sales Representative* to ever achieve *$3 million annually*, and then became the first Sales Representative ever to achieve *$4 million in sales annually*.
- **Budget Analysis:** Review and analyze budget variances and initiate appropriate recommendations to more aggressively control annual expenditures. Consistently achieve all budget objectives.
- **Account Management:** Responsible for managing new business development and strategic planning to maximize growth and profitability. Develop business opportunities, establish growth plans for individual accounts and personally manage account calls, presentations, and negotiations.
- **Inventory & Purchasing:** Monitor inventory levels of food products in warehouse, and purchase as needed regarding customers' orders. Work closely with accounts and warehouse personnel to facilitate distribution of food products.
- **Client Relations & Services:** Establish and maintain an excellent network of business associations with clients as a result of strong communication skills, and by providing excellent service, attention and follow-up to accounts.
- **Advertising & Marketing:** Create, develop, and implement innovative advertising and marketing strategies to promote products and increase sales.
- **Promotions:** Responsible for introducing new products into marketplace, and for coordinating promotional campaigns within store to increase consumer awareness.

Sales Representative
JOHNSON'S DAIRY DISTRIBUTOR
Nashville, Tennessee - 1978 to 1986

- **Sales & Marketing:** Responsible for soliciting and obtaining new clients for this dairy distributor. Built and expanded sales territory by calling on individual stores and restaurants. Launched aggressive marketing campaigns in 2 territories which *tripled sales in first route*, and *doubled sales* in the second route. Personally managed account calls, presentations, and negotiations.
- **Client Relations - Customer Service:** Provided excellent service to customers/clients through attention to detail, and by effectively responding to requests, inquiries, suggestions, and/or concerns. Established and maintained an excellent network of business associations as a result of strong communication skills and extensive interaction.

ROBERT JENSON
4545 West Highway 95
Columbia, South Carolina
(794) 570-2999

Closers, Relationship Builders, and Team Builders.

Professional Objective & Profile

A success- and profit-oriented, experienced sales professional is seeking a position with a progressive organization that will fully utilize my skills and abilities in sales, public speaking and business management.

Education

Bachelor of Arts Degree in English
UNIVERSITY OF SOUTH CAROLINA
Columbia, South Carolina, 1992
Pi Kappa Phi Fraternity

Summary of Qualifications

- *Sales:*
  Background exemplifies a successful track record in sales which includes experience as a *Territory Sales Manager* for Zytecerdin, Inc. Graduated *#1 in Sales Training Class.*

- *Public Speaking:*
  Experienced in public speaking, with 2 years experience as a *Professional Public Speaker* who traveled throughout the Southeastern United States, facilitating seminars for up to 400 participants. Spoke publicly on personal safety and crime awareness, and sold safety products.

- *Communications:*
  Excellent oral and written communication skills used to deliver seminars to large groups and communicate with all levels of management and personnel.

- *Time Management:*
  Exceptional organizational and coordination abilities used to manage strategic sales planning. Self-directed and self-motivated with a high degree of initiative. Successful in prioritizing responsibilities and accomplishing sales objectives.

- *Leadership:*
  Strong leader and motivator of others, with ability to guide and direct associates to achieve maximum results.

Professional Experience

Territory Sales Manager
ZYTECERDIN, INC.
VETERINARY DERMATOLOGY PHARMACEUTICAL DIVISION OF
VIRBAC CORPORATION
Columbia, South Carolina (Home Office - Fort Worth, Texas) - 1995 to Present

- Increased *YTD sales 21%* through establishment of new accounts and the expansion of existing accounts throughout Tennessee and Kentucky.
- Responsible for the management and promotion of Zytecerdin Virbac products for sales through distributors.
- Provide, coordinate and conduct educational in-service presentations/demonstrations for physicians, medical personnel, and veterinary school students, regarding the use of dermatological products.
- Responsible for the development of professional relationships with veterinarians and veterinary dermatologists via direct sales and trade meetings.
- Coordinate regional continuing education meetings for physicians and staff.
- Maintain a commitment of excellence with a strong work ethic, product knowledge, organization and interpersonal skills.
- Achieved the highest monthly sales in company during February 1996 out of 49. Have finished in the *top 10* every month since then, and constantly lead the Southeast in sales.
- Over 80% of client base requires travel; approximately 70% requires extensive overnight travel.

Professional Public Speaker
CITIZENS ADVOCATING PERSONAL SAFETY, INC., Columbia, South Carolina
CITIZENS AGAINST CRIME, INC., Spartanburg, South Carolina
1993 to 1995

- Began as a *Public Speaker for Citizens Against Crime, Inc.,* and then began speaking independently for self-developed company, *Citizens Advocating Personal Safety, Inc.*
- Responsible for producing and conducting personal safety and crime awareness training seminars for up to 400 participants.
- Developed and implemented innovative marketing strategies to sell new safety products. Solicited and obtained new accounts by calling on businesses and organizations.
- Traveled throughout the southeastern United States and conducted 6-8 seminars per week on personal safety and crime awareness.

Transition Coordinator
FRANK JOHNSON REAL ESTATE, INC.
Alexandria, Virginia - 1992 to 1993

- Coordinated and assisted the transition process resulting from a corporate merger.

Index

Please take a moment to let us know who you are!

We love to hear from our readers. Please let us know who you are and how you came to your current position. If you have any heart-warming, interesting, or funny stories regarding your career, we would love for you to share them with us! Contact us in the most convenient way.

WEB SITE   www.mindspring.com/heartsoul

E-MAIL   heartsoul@mindspring.com

FAX   (615) 329-3569

MAIL   Heart & Soul Career Center/ResumePLUS, Inc.
               1808 West End Suite 1012
               Nashville, TN 37203
               (615) 329-0300

We will be glad to send you free information on any of the following!

❑ ***Heart & Soul Sales & Marketing Resume Tool Kit***—Save time writing your own resume by utilizing our resume styles and formats already on disk. Choose from hundreds of *Heart & Soul* resume and cover letter samples (different from those in the book) to help you generate ideas for your own. Listen to our audio cassette tapes and hear the authors explain in detail the important steps in successful *Heart & Soul* resume preparation. The audio tapes work in conjunction with this book. Manual, Computer Disk, & Audio Cassette Tape included in Tool Kit.

❑ ***Heart & Soul Sales & Marketing Job Search Tool Kit***—Build and track a comprehensive proactive job search plan with our in-depth *Heart & Soul Job Search Manual*. Find the fastest-growing, future-oriented, and highest ranking "heart & soul" companies to work for. Track your networking calls, job opportunities, and contacts with our practical and insightful *Heart & Soul Job Search Calendar*. Listen to our audio cassette tapes and hear the authors illustrate the important tools necessary for a quick, easy, and meaningful job search. Manual, Heart & Soul Job Search Calendar, Computer Disk, & Audio Cassette Tape included in Tool Kit.

❑ ***Heart & Soul Interviewing Tool Kit***—This Kit provides you with today's hottest interviewing questions, ideas, and common problems that job candidates face today, and serves as a *Heart & Soul* resource to use with the audio tapes. Listen to real life interviews that illustrate the "do's" and "don'ts" in an interview. Use the many encouraging *Heart & Soul* tips and motivating thoughts to help you succeed in your most challenging interviews. Manual & Audio Cassette Tape included in Tool Kit.

❑ ***Starting a Home-Based Business Tool Kit***—Use this step-by-step manual to guide you through the process of starting and growing your own home-based business. Learn which of the most profitable home-based businesses would be best for you. Hear how the Founder of the Heart & Soul Career Center got started in his own home, and how he has helped others do the same! Manual & Audio Cassette Tapes included in Tool Kit.

❑ ***The Insider's "Tell All" Guide to Getting a Job in Pharmaceutical & Medical Sales***—101 Top Pharmaceutical and Medical Companies. Over 200 Pages of Insider Tips and Job Winning Advice. High Profile Drugs & Surgical Equipment "In the Pipeline" Expected to Be Approved by the FDA. Decision-Makers & Contacts at Headquarters and Around the Country. Important Phone Numbers, Addresses, and Fax Numbers to Help You Make the Connection. Job Winning Insider Tips from Within Each Company. How People "Really" Get Hired.

❑ ***The Insider's "Tell All" Guide Job Search Series***—Complete series of books that put you in touch with the key decision makers that will make a difference in your career.

❑ ***Career, Writing, and Success Seminars and Workshops***

❑ ***Heart & Soul Professional Resume Writing, Career Consulting, & Job Search Assistance***

About the Authors

Chuck Cochran is the Co-Founder and President of the Heart & Soul Career Center, and Founder and President of the ResumePLUS, Inc., a full-service career development center specializing in resumes, recruiting, job search assistance, and training. **Donna Peerce** is Co-Founder and Vice President of the Heart & Soul Career Center and Vice President of ResumePLUS, Inc.

Chuck and Donna are also coauthors of the critically acclaimed "Heart & Soul" Career Series, including *Heart & Soul Resumes* and *Heart & Soul Internet Job Search* from Davies-Black Publishing, Palo Alto, CA. Both are Certified Professional Resume Writers and members of the PARW. Each conducts Writing, Career, and Success Seminars throughout the United States.